DATE DUE

DEC 2 0 1998	

PRINTED IN U.S.A.

Raymond C. O'Brien
Michael T. Flannery

Long-Term Care
Federal, State, and Private
Options for the Future

Pre-publication
REVIEWS,
COMMENTARIES,
EVALUATIONS . . .

"*L*ong-Term Care: Federal, State, and Private Options for the Future is well researched and annotated and is a mandatory desktop reference for attorneys, clinicians, health care consumers, and others having a stake in the long-term care industry. The authors effectively summarize and analyze the most recent state and federal legal developments and initiatives in this rapidly developing area. The text provides insightful analysis of the societal and systemic factors influencing the financing and provision of long-term care services, and fosters an understanding of the current long-term care environment. Particularly forceful is the authors' explanation of personal circumstances and incentives to humanize the challenges of long-term care. This is an excellent presentation and synthesis of widely disparate federal and state approaches to long-term care law and financing."

Christopher L. White
Partner, Health Law Group,
Gardner, Carton & Douglas,
Washington, DC

More pre-publication
REVIEWS, COMMENTARIES, EVALUATIONS . . .

"**W**ith the transfer of responsibility for many fiscal programs to the states from the federal government, the local counties will have to bear the burden of qualifying for fewer dollars and entitlements under competing programs. The entire entitlement program is changing. This book offers a state-by-state description of government programs and what works and what has not worked. This is invaluable for busy officials seeking to assist the present and plan for the future. I have a firmer grasp on both because of this book on long-term care."

Daniel G. Birmingham, JD
Deputy County Executive,
Putnam County,
Carmel, NY

"**A** powerful work that interweaves issues ranging from the graying of America to immigration patterns, as well as gender and longevity, so as to paint a vivid picture of the current state of long-term care across our nation. The authors have performed a tour de force analysis of the effects of state health care reform initiatives on long-term care and conclude with insightful proposals for the future of long-term care."

Joe Zumpano-Canto, JD, MPH
Attorney, McDermott, Will & Emery,
Miami, FL

"**G**eneral practice of law in a small New England city is a composite of injury, property, and death. This book on long-term care offers me a readable source of information that I can use to advise my clients regarding care of family, protection of wealth, and planning for the inevitability of death. It is a valuable tool in a rapidly developing area of law."

James J. Tenn, Jr.
Partner, Tenn and Tenn,
Manchester, NH

Long-Term Care
Federal, State, and Private Options for the Future

HAWORTH Health and Social Policy
Marvin D. Feit, PhD
Senior Editor

Long-Term Care
Federal, State, and Private Options for the Future

Raymond C. O'Brien
Michael T. Flannery

The Haworth Press
New York • London

The Haworth Press, Inc., 10 Alice Street, Binghamton, NY 13904-1580

Cover design by Monica L. Seifert.

Library of Congress Cataloging-in-Publication Data

O'Brien, Raymond C.
    Long-term care : federal, state, and private options for the future / Raymond C. O'Brien, Michael T. Flannery.
        p. cm.
    Includes bibliographical references and index.
    ISBN 0-7890-0173-X (alk. paper).
    1. Long-term care of the sick–Government policy–United States. 2. Long-term care of the sick–United States. 4. Medicaid. I. Flannery, Michael. II. Title.
RA644.6.O37 1997
362.1'6'0973–dc21   97-1573
                                                                                        CIP

For

Alba Cecelia O'Brien,
the inspiration for this book
and much more;

and

Francis and Dorothea Flannery,
the foundation of all long-term care: family;

and

The Little Sisters of The Poor;
the mystery within long-term care: fidelity.

ABOUT THE AUTHORS

Raymond C. O'Brien, AB, MChA, DMin, JD, is Professor of Law at the Catholic University of America School of Law in Washington, DC. He also holds a joint appointment at the Georgetown University Law Center. A professor of law for more than 25 years, he has taught primarily in the areas of decedents' estates and family law. He has taught at schools in Texas and California. Professor O'Brien is the co-author of a leading casebook on family law and has written many book chapters and articles ranging from wealth transfers to AIDS to child abuse issues. He is also a Roman Catholic priest of the Archdiocese of Washington.

Michael T. Flannery, JD, is a Legal Writing Instructor at Villanova University School of Law in Villanova, Pennsylvania, where he teaches research and writing. He is a former associate of the law firm of Wolf, Block, Schorr and Solis-Cohen in Philadelphia. Mr. Flannery now maintains a private family law practice in the Philadelphia area. A former Assistant City Solicitor with the City of Philadelphia, he has prosecuted hundreds of cases of child abuse and mental health commitments. He has written extensively on children's issues, including the medical aspects of child abuse, and in the area of domestic relations.

CONTENTS

Foreword

As the average life span increases in the United States, the number of persons who will need long-term care grows correspondingly. More and more families already find themselves the key characters in poignant scenarios involving the progressively more expensive and unrelenting needs of their parents, siblings, spouses, or even children for such care. Often it is only when the need for long-term care is imminent or immediate that relatives and family first learn that alternatives for receiving governmental assistance are very limited and, for many, virtually nonexistent. For others, a diagnosis of Alzheimer's disease or some other condition that will cause long-term disability or incompetence at some undefined point in the future serves as the trigger for hurried financial planning (or, more to the point in most instances, financial divestiture) in the hope of qualifying the afflicted person for assistance under a program such as Medicaid.

The increase in numbers of persons who anticipate and will ultimately face difficulties funding long-term care for themselves or a family member is helping to increase popular awareness of the fragmentation of our health care and welfare systems. Such fragmentation will almost inevitably remain after the latest round of welfare-system tinkering and the tremendous mutation now taking place in health care delivery.

The timeliness of *Long-Term Care* is unquestionable. But what is special about it is the combination of sensitivity to individual needs and thought-provoking analysis of how we might address the burgeoning problem of long-term care on a macro basis. While it details the approach that each state is taking and explains the intricacies of "estate" planning for long-term care, it also reveals the tensions that are increasing within existing social programs and between age groups in our society. Solutions will require a global approach, but this is likely to occur only when there is much wider understanding and appreciation of the problems, and popular pressure sufficient to motivate workable political responses. This book's explication of our present plight should further enlighten and activate any reader and provoke serious interest in how the dilemma of providing long-term care can be addressed effectively.

Walter Wadlington
James Madison Professor of Law
University of Virginia

Preface

Each of the long-term care options discussed within this book could and has qualified as a topic for a book in and of itself. Indeed, many books have been written about these topics. Long-term care is a part of the health care network—the two overlap; the two are integral to each other. Yet, while America, especially following the health care initiatives of the first Clinton administration, has discussed and rejected many aspects of health care, little attention has been paid to long-term care in America. Options such as Medicare, managed care, insurance, affordability, and the level of expectation American citizens have concerning their health and the role of government have been discussed, defined, and, for the most part, disputed by politicians and the public alike. But while Americans may recover their health, they will not recover their youth. The necessity of and thus the options for long-term care have become a priority to be addressed now.

The options are confusing; too little education has been done within the general public. Try to recall the last time you witnessed a scene involving a nursing home or home care, or even the medical dilemma of family or elder parent on television or movie screen. What did you gleen from the spunky and forever-driving *Grumpy Old Men*, of the institutionalized yet wise old lady in *Fried Green Tomatoes*? Such images mask the reality of declining health; jolting catastrophic stroke or Alzheimer's; horrific medical bills; tenacious, technological life support; and the recently born behemoth, managed care. Mainstream America avoids the consequences of getting older; this is a fact of life. But if we look beneath the surface we can easily find a person, a family, an association of elderlaw attorneys, the political rhetoric regarding Medicare and Medicaid, and increasing numbers of newly built or expanding nursing homes. What is happening? What options do the elderly face? What options do their families have? What options do we as a society face when confronting the reality of the aging of America? It is confusing to consider all the possible options, but the alternative to thought is acceptance of a status quo that invites Medicaid spend-down disparity, generational competition, and factious litigation over assisted suicide.

The United States has a number of options in providing long-term care for its elderly. The states are experimenting with reform of the entire health care delivery system. Tennessee, Hawaii, Oregon, and New York are among those offering models that address how society might contain costs, offer fair and competent treatment to the poor as well as the wealthy, and balance a system inherited from a time when government thought it could afford to do *everything* for *everybody*. Every state is doing something. But no matter how the states experiment, the bottom line is that every person will need to plan for a time when he or she is no longer able to take care of him or herself and the government just will not step in and do it. This personal responsibility demands education of all, exploration of insurance plans which are voluntary or mandated (as is Social Security), and development of care options that would defer institutionalized care for as long as possible. The governmental responsibility demands fairness, honesty, and an incremental approach that would create a vision of what long-term care could be; leadership is absolutely crucial.

As always, the enemy is ourselves. In researching any book on long-term care, any author would discover hundreds of stories of women and men who thought they would never grow old, never need to go into a nursing home, never believe they would not die in their beds surrounded by memorabilia of proms and weddings and parties, with their children and grandchildren gently stroking their hands. Such scenes occur in fiction—*Brideshead Revisited*—not modern American life. Something has changed. Americans used to die in their beds; now they die in hospitals, hooked up to machines and often as a conclusion to years of technological care. Medicare, the federal government program which begins at 65, finances this; newly developed technologies, thwarted only by managed care, eagerly anticipate this. How to integrate Medicare, technology, and managed care invites human, ethical, moral, and extremely practical considerations and this can be accomplished by no one other than ourselves.

If this book offers any solution in the understanding of long-term care, it is this: Integration of all of the options into an incremental plan that Americans will accept and to which Americans will contribute is the only viable option. Sadly enough, the battle among managed care institutions across the country may one day result in the winner prescribing the manner and method of integration for everyone. This would be a victory for free-market competition, but perhaps so devoid of public policy integration as to omit many of the care and support prerogatives for which America is so justly proud. Thus, integration of the options should not be left solely to the battle over managed care. The government, private business, and public policy groups must make a contribution, and they must begin now.

It is impossible to build a political platform, an economic policy, a theology, or a long-term health care plan without developing the options, the ingredients, and the results of experiments in change. This is a book describing all three: options, ingredients, and results. Its goal is to spark the human initiative to take seriously the challenge of long-term care.

Chapter 1

Introduction to Competing Interests

CHANGING TIMES: AN HONEST NEED FOR LONG-TERM CARE

American health care is a captive of posturing. Initiatives at the state, federal, and private levels affect the bedrocks of health care planning: Medicaid, Medicare, insurance, nursing homes, and public versus personal responsibility. Everyone is posturing. In 1965, when Medicaid began, health care for all seemed attainable. Wealthier Americans would have insurance coverage, usually through fee-for-service insurance, and the poor would have a safety net—Medicaid. The elderly, having worked all of their lives for a comfortable retirement, would have Medicare. But as the years passed, affordable health care for the poor and the not-so-poor has been overshadowed by the growth of the human population, particularly the elderly. There has been extensive developments in expensive technology, and governments, quite frankly, have gone broke. Within the next decade, Medicaid as we know it could end, and Medicare, sustained by a cohesive group of elderly voters, will change drastically.

An erratic collision is occurring between reality and expectations—the collective politics of state and federal governments versus individual expectations—and it offers both opportunity and concern, but the status quo is not an alternative. Health care reform is no longer a viable federal option, the states are experimenting with—and suffering from—block grants and reduced funding, family budgets are shrinking due to insurance and medical expenses, and the looming presence of health maintenance organizations is uncertain, but expanding rapidly. This is a unique time for American health care. The only solution is for each of America's bedrocks of care to be integrated into a comprehensive plan of health care that includes the most foreseeable concern of all—long-term care for the growing numbers of elderly.

The health care problem in America is very confusing. Ask yourself the following questions. If I or someone I love were to develop a serious illness, how would I meet the rising costs of care? And what if that illness demanded a long-term care solution? Would I be willing to spend all of my assets, including even those monies or properties I have reserved for retirement? To whom would I turn? I have a vague understanding of Medicaid and Medicare, and the language of my health care insurance policy is stupefying at best. What should I do? Add to this dilemma the fact that some people are able to retain elderlaw attorneys, and with legal expertise, gradually spend-down some assets so they can qualify for medical assistance, which should be reserved for the poor. Thus, compounding the confusing laws and policies, there is an inequality and an unfairness that aggravates the stultifying predicament.

Government efforts to alleviate the confusion felt by so many Americans is often frustrated by differing definitions and expectations. For instance, for some the focus is only upon the persons without health insurance in America. So too, for some the concern is with persons with too little insurance or those whose health insurance is paid for by the employer or by the state; thus different proposals have been made. These proposals are still insoluble because they are complicated by poverty and its status, which is too often void of choices. Then too, government must address the insatiable individual expectations of so many Americans. Is government to be a caretaker for all, or a safety net for a few?

Perhaps long-term care, as compared to health care in general, is more capable of comprehension. It is possible to predict the numbers needing long-term care in the future only if the statistics regarding growth of the elderly population are collated. The point is that at least with long-term health care, it is possible for the federal and state governments and for private individuals to plan ahead. The states are currently experimenting with medical savings accounts, there are suggestions of mandatory withholding for long-term care insurance, and prioritization of health care services in states such as Oregon offers insight into questions of values and litigation questions regarding assisted suicide.[1] The point is that it is time to determine the options and develop a comprehensive plan for the future of millions of Americans.[2] Medicaid should not become—and can not remain—the safety net for long-term care, a safety net that is often necessary because no one knew he or she would need long-term care.

How did Medicaid become the entitlement program of choice for millions of Americans needing long-term care? The Medicaid program is only part of America's health care system.[3] It is different from Medicare in that the latter program is primarily directed toward the elderly, those 65 years of age and older, providing them with a hospital insurance program and a supplemental medical insurance program.[4] Both programs have taken on increased importance among the poor and the elderly. Furthermore, among persons needing long-term care who qualify for assistance under Medicaid and Medicare,[5] the numbers needing these entitlement programs expand more rapidly than anticipated or than can be accommodated. It is these numbers that precipitate the reality of posturing for alternatives.

In 1975, Medicaid provided nursing home care to approximately 1.31 million persons.[6] By 1981, Medicaid assisted 1.39 million persons; in 1989, 1.45 million persons; in 1990, 1.46 million persons.[7] By 1991 the number had expanded more rapidly—1.5 million persons were assisted, or a 40,000 increase in recipients. By 1992, there was a one-year growth of 80,000 to 1.58 million persons.[8] During 1992, state Medicaid programs spent over $21 billion providing nursing home—or long-term care—assistance to nearly 1.6 million persons. This amount was more than one-quarter of all Medicaid expenditures.[9] As nursing home residents live longer, costs escalate with the aging of America and a paucity of alternatives to provide for long-term care.[10]

Perhaps because of the posturing that exists in America in regard to health care, "[m]iddle class interest in Medicaid has grown because long-term care insurance is not provided effectively anywhere else."[11] Medicaid has become a safety net for long-term care simply because there are no incentives for planning, and the expectations that government will provide makes reliance on tax entitlement programs acceptable. In other words, Medicaid has become a safety net because citizens expect government to take care of them whenever there is a medical catastrophe.

For instance, if a family has been able to accumulate a middle-class lifestyle with assets of about $500,000, there will be too many assets to qualify for public assisted care, but too few assets to absorb the costs well. Thus, the only alternative is to seek advice on Medicaid spend-down policies. In fact, "thousands of middle-income elderly people . . . have transferred their assets . . . to qualify for Medicaid."[12] An example is illustrative.

> In February 1992, an elderly man came into the local Medicaid eligibility office to make a Medicaid application on behalf of his female cousin, who was the beneficiary of an irrevocable family trust with a principal value of approximately $1.5 million. Although she was the trust beneficiary, the income generated by the trust was placed in a joint bank account, which she and her cousin jointly held. The balance in the account was approximately $279,000. A few days before coming to the Medicaid eligibility office, the man had made a withdrawal of $184,000, leaving $95,000 in the account. Seeing this fund balance, the eligibility worker informed the man that his cousin was not eligible for Medicaid. At that point, the man wrote himself another check on the account for $93,000, leaving a balance of $2,000. "Is she eligible now?" he asked. "Yes, she is," the eligibility worker replied.[13]

Despite the painfully obvious need for immediate and drastic alternatives to affordable long-term care, policy decisions on welfare reform are proceeding at a snail's pace through congressional debate due to interpartisan posturing regarding the punitive nature of reform.[14] GOP leaders assert that there is little partisan division and that the difficulty is simply in the magnitude of the need for reform.[15] In the middle of the partisan attack on welfare is former Senator Bob Dole, who maintains a middle-ground position on the issue (of long-term care), which fuels the fire for other presidential hopefuls. Yet, much of the dilemma faced by Senator Dole can be traced to the political backlashing all politicians would face in proposing any long-term health care reforms in Medicare and Medicaid, even though all believe reform is necessary for the survival of these programs.

Both Medicaid and Medicare are catastrophically on the brink of failure and both are fueled by the "politics" of politics. Each is its own self-fulfilling prophecy: Americans want and need a more affordable plan but are not likely to accept, and therefore, vote for the full-scale reformations necessary to achieve the ends that are demanded. Instead, the American people want a promise of change, but nothing so drastic that they have to pay for it. Consequently, bankruptcy for the Medicare and Medicaid systems approaches at a rate much faster than that of the proposed changes, and the systems will inevitably fail.

In 1996, Medicare expenses alone will exceed income from taxation revenues for the first time.[16] To compensate for these expenses, Republicans propose raising $60 billion by increasing Part B premiums, which help pay doctor's fees and other costs.[17] Currently, beneficiaries pay $46.10 or 31.5 percent of Part B costs.[18] President Clinton's proposal would reduce this percentage to 25 percent, thereby saving $16 billion. Thus, by 2002, the partisan difference in beneficiary Part B payments will be $97.50 per month under Republican rule, and $77.40 if Clinton's plans are adopted.[19] Republicans defend their increases with analogies to status quo reasoning. After all, the monthly premium started at $3 in 1966 and covered 50 percent of the respective costs.[20] In 1994, the $41.10 monthly premium covered 33 percent of the costs of doctor's fees and other out-of-hospital expenses.[21]

The GOP proposed that increases would begin on January 1, 1996, and would jump to $55.10, $60.40 in 1997, and $66.30 in 1988, until eventually reaching $97.50 in 2002. Without Republican modifications, the status quo 1996 premium would be $43.70, $47.90 in 1997, and $52.60 in 1998—representing only 25 percent of the costs.[22] A consistent personal 25 percent contribution, as proposed by the Democratic administration, would stabilize 2002 monthly premiums at $77.40. Currently, premium increases are restricted to the rise in inflation; however, since historically medical costs rise faster than inflation, beneficiary contributions would be 19.4 percent by 2002, which means little, if any, savings for the Medicare system.[23]

Thus, bipartisan debate will have significant consequences for the financial health of Medicare. Republicans focus on the failure of the past while Democrats highlight the empty rhetoric of drastic change and rest secure in complacency of the status quo.[24] This is posturing. Unfortunately, neither side possesses the stamina for implementing a solution. Failure to do so will be catastrophic. Said one former Ronald Reagan aide, now head of the Family Research Council, who supports an entire overhaul of the welfare system, "This is about the survival of the republic, and if we don't succeed, all of us will have to answer to history."[25] This is a correct assessment and there are significant factors affecting any future course taken.

Population Growth

The American government has lost hold of the reigns that once contained the costs of long-term care. As the population needing health care continues to grow, and grow older, costs slip further and further away from any semblance of control due to the seemingly exponential growth of the human population. By the year 2040, when the working-age population and the paucity of the youthful population will have remained stationary, the number of elderly over age 85 will have quadrupled.[26] The percentage increase in population growth between 1989 and 2040 grows consistently and dramatically with the increase in age. By 2040, the 20 to 64 age group population may increase by as little as 15 percent; the 65 to 74 age group population may increase by as much as 84 percent; the 75 to 84 age group is expected to increase by as much as 196 percent; and, incredibly, the population of the elderly, age 85 and older, is expected to increase by as much as 375 percent.[27]

Because the elderly clearly require more medical services and resources—as much as four times as that of a younger adult and eight times as much as a child—and the rate of health care use increases with each increasing age bracket, there is an added effect to this imbalance.[28] Additionally, as the elderly population grows, the greatest growth occurs in the minority sectors, which rely even more heavily on public assistance.[29] The American Association for retired Persons (AARP) states that in 1990, 7.5 percent of the "over-65" population—more than 4.2 million elderly—were non-white: 2.5 million were African American, 1.2 million were Hispanic,

455,000 were Asian, and 114,000 were Native American.[30] By 2025, the percentage of minority elderly will increase from 7.5 percent to 25 percent and by 2035, the increase will be 35 percent.[31] Thus, should socio-economic conditions continue to affect nonwhites more harshly than whites, with every increase in the elderly population, the need for expenditures on long-term care increases even more drastically.

Immigration is responsible for approximately one-half of the population growth in the United States.[32] Frankly, immigration is the wild card in the projections for the future. The expanding immigration base of the United States, which has increased since 1965 after a 40-year closed-door policy in effect, may add relief to the drastic imbalance in the outlays (monetary expenditures) of Medicare and Medicaid for the expanding population. The majority of the influx will be young females, who will rely heavily on Medicaid and less on Medicare.[33] In 1993, there were an estimated 900,000 legal immigrants introduced to the United States.[34] Including illegal immigration, the annual total may average 1.3 million new arrivals.[35] More than 25 million have crossed the American border in the past 20 years.[36] For example, Mexico's population is expected to reach 130 million by the year 2010; thus, Mexico's growth far exceeds its economy. The resulting immigration presents a potential increase of 40 million unemployed youth in America.[37] This forecast has spurred even further political posturing as debate flourishes as to how to respond to the effect of immigration on America and its economy.[38]

Proposals have included both immigrant population ceilings, such as that proposed by Wyoming Senator Alan Simpson, and restrictions on the services afforded to new immigrants. Texas Senator Phil Gramm called for broader restrictions on the distribution of welfare benefits to legal immigrants.[39] Bob Dole, a former presidential candidate, positioned himself just left of Gramm and was more generous with America's contributions to noncitizens. Yet, California Governor Pete Wilson proposes a constitutional amendment to deny citizenship to the children of illegal immigrants.[40] Pat Buchanan proposed to moot the issue by initiating a comprehensive plan to reduce both legal and illegal immigration,[41] yet House majority leader Dick Armey opposes Buchanan's plan and supports the expansion of legal immigration.[42]

Most of the 1996 presidential candidates cautiously maneuvered themselves closer toward alliance with Armey than with Buchanan, at least on the issue of legal immigration.[43] However, many politicians think the real problem is the increase of illegal immigrants, yet statistics from the Urban Institute, a Washington, DC think tank, reveal that approximately 6.6 percent of all foreign-born U.S. residents rely on welfare benefits, while for native-born residents, the percentage is much lower—only 4.9 percent.[44] Most of these are comprised of elderly immigrants who retire on social security shortly after entering the United States.[45]

The balance is between illegal immigrants entering the country and requiring publicly funded services, and the ability of all immigrants to generate sufficient tax revenues to support a ballooning elderly population demanding services to which they have been told they would one day become entitled. Wherever the posturing rests, there will be an inevitable and noticeable burden placed on the already devastated health care system when the demand for Medicaid expenditures increases, but the ability of the influx of young immigrants to subsidize it decreases. It is possible that GOP reform to eliminate federal benefits to immigrants could be even more costly than to provide the benefits and services since the demand for service will remain the same and will simply be absorbed by local service providers instead of the federal government.

Because of the inequities to the states in federal reimbursements, taxation through employment is unlikely to stabilize any imbalance. Estimates from 1992 show that immigrants incurred $42.5 billion more in services than they paid in taxes.[46] Therefore, taxation through sales is more apt to contribute to the subsidization of increased long-term care expenses, which is greatly stressed by the growing immigrant population. However America positions itself politically, it is unlikely that the country will be able to integrate the increased expenses of long-term care brought by the annual wave of immigration in light of the limited financial alternatives to neutralize this increase.

Thus, the issue of population, both in terms of the growing number of elderly persons in America and the number of immigrants arriving each day, is a factor that must be addressed in planning for the future. True, each state shall be affected differently, but the posturing needed to adjust can be adapted accordingly.

Technological Advances

Americans are beginning to live too short and die too long. We are expending our health long before expending our life. Modern technology in health care for the elderly has been compared to "a triumph of knowledge over wisdom . . . [l]ike the man who knew seven languages but had nothing to say in any of them."[47] Medical technology is a noble effort that serves no stated valued purpose. In 1965, when Medicaid was inaugurated, it was impossible to predict the changes that would occur in medical technology.[48] People are living longer, thus requiring care for a longer period of time, with new technology that is often expensive.[49] For instance, persons with chronic kidney disease, often termed end-stage renal disease, exemplify this growth through technology pattern. "In the past, most of these people would not have entered dialysis treatment because of their age and severity of illness . . . ."[50] Nonetheless, through dialysis treatment and the fact that physician practice has shifted to this area of elder care, these patients are receiving treatment and surviving longer.[51] One nursing home administrator said the following:

> We are caring for a much more acute patient than we used to. . . . Ten years ago, when we talked about a feeding tube, that was a major issue. . . . Fifteen years ago, you would never have done an IV in a nursing home. You would have called an ambulance, and [the patient] would have been in the hospital for six days. Now we do it all the time.
> To put it very simply. . . the people we're seeing today are of a level where ten years ago they would have been in an intensive care unit. [Or because medicine was not nearly as effective then as it is now,] they would have been dead.[52]

It is clear that the older, more sickly nursing home resident requires longer, more effective, more expensive care.[53] "Americans are living longer, and when they finally succumb to illness, lingering longer, either in great pain or in a stuporous semi-comatose condition that results from the infusion of vast amounts of pain-killing medications."[54] Indeed, most Americans used to die at home, but this no longer is true.

> In 1939, only 37 percent of Americans died in hospitals or nursing homes. . . . Today, by contrast, between 80 and 85 percent of Americans die in institutions . . . About 70 percent of those who die in institutions do so after a decision to hasten their death by withholding or withdrawing medical treatment or technology."[55]

Confronted with the increasing risk of malpractice for failing to use advanced technology, doctors are more likely to provide sustaining care.[56] Perhaps this is why many doctors believe that setting limits on tort malpractice awards would contribute to savings in the health care system.[57] For instance, in California, there is a ceiling of $250,000 on malpractice awards for pain and suffering; New York has no ceiling. As a result, New York doctors have higher insurance premiums and this results in higher costs for consumers.[58] Placing caps upon tort awards in malpractice suits is one of the means states seek to control costs for both long-term care and health care in general.

Increased technology undeniably prolongs life,[59] but it does not necessarily ensure a quality life. Thus, the technology that affords the sustaining care also magnifies the problem.[60] Consequently, advancements in technology have brought increased litigation—not only concerning malpractice and sustaining care, but regarding the right to die or the right to deprive one's self of care; this is the issue of personal autonomy.[61] Only recently the Ninth Circuit Court of Appeals in San Francisco decided an issue that is the first of its kind to date. The issue is "whether a person who is terminally ill has a constitutionally protected liberty interest in hastening what might otherwise be a protracted, undignified, and extremely painful death."[62] The court found that there is "a constitutionally protected liberty interest in determining the time and manner of one's own death . . . [and as] . . . the Washington statute prohibits physicians from prescribing life-ending medication for use by terminally ill, competent adults who wish to hasten their own deaths; it violates the Due Process Clause of the Fourteenth Amendment."[63]

The Ninth Circuit's decision will face rigorous scrutiny from those unwilling to accommodate any right to assisted suicide[64] and any right whatever to commit suicide,[65] and those who also reject any court's role in providing or denying such a right.[66] In New York, the Second Circuit Court of Appeals has also decided that state statutes prohibiting assisted suicides in specific situations are a denial of equal protection.[67] The American Medical Association (AMA) has joined other legal groups in asking the Supreme Court to resolve the issue of assisted suicide and withdraw from the physician the burden of assisting in death, and instead allowing the physician to promote the patient's health. The future litigation concerning assisted suicide for terminally ill patients will continue, no doubt fueled in part by the expense and promise of technology. The Ninth Circuit's recognition of a right "to refuse or terminate treatment and the emergent right to receive medical assistance in hastening one's death are inevitable consequences of changes in the causes of death, advances in medical science, and the development of new technologies."[68]

The problem is that the costs of sustaining or depriving care, and consequently, of promoting rights, are not a concern for a science that is continually on the brink of discovery or for a patient on the brink of death.[69] And yet, perhaps, the cost of dying does have a voice in the all of the turmoil surrounding a long-term care patient. Again, the Ninth Circuit offered this assessment:

> Faced with the prospect of astronomical medical bills, terminally ill patients might decide it is better for them to die before their health care expenses consume the life savings they planned to leave for their families, or, worse yet, burden their families with debts they may never be able to satisfy.

Money is thus a factor to consider and anyone who has been in the situation of working with a dying person knows that money is a concern in a majority of cases. But here lies the emptiness of the present situation, a situation in which few manage to amass sufficient wealth to pay for anything, few manage to spend down to qualify for government-assisted care, and a majority of people simply worry about money. The absence of values lies in our refusal as a society to take charge of the situation and provide for integrated planning. There must be some stated values decided upon and brought about through integrated planning. To date, the only stated values seem to be the need for added discovery, a right ensconced in reason, and the need for unbridled individual license. The two are mutually incompatible in a devolution of material goods in a responsible society.

America refuses to acknowledge that it cannot afford all it invents in the name of technological advancement. "As the costs of each use of a new technology drops, the number of potential people who will benefit from the technology increases.[70] Consequently, our inventiveness is outpacing our ability to pay."[71] Instead, America blindly surges forward in technology without considering the real effects of the advancement. Some think that modern medicine makes it possible "to continue or discontinue life-sustaining technology for ideal timing of organ transplantation, to allow family to be present for a loved one's death, or to delay death for the convenience of court deliberations."[72] In reality, instead of providing "a new lease on life," most patients just receive an expensive death. As a result, death becomes "a starkly unnatural event."[73] The question, then, becomes not how far or how much medical technology should advance, but at what point does the technological advancement become a medical digression?[74]

Many physicians continue to recommend using advanced medical technology on the hopelessly ill, who are often elderly patients, because "it is better to do something than to do nothing, even if that action is known to have no benefit."[75] If balanced in terms of the greatest amount of health care for the greatest number, many of the life-sustaining technologies now available would not be justified. For instance, why is it that Medicare will pay for end-stage renal failure but does not pay for flu shots? Why will it pay for heart transplants but not gynecological exams? There must be a balance,[76] a stated value. Now, many in the health care field interpret what has been termed "the medicalization of death"[77] as a "pernicious trend" that "is intuitively a wasteful use of the limited resources that we are willing to spend on medical care."[78]

> [I]n classic fee-for-service medical plans, the incentive of money and the professional imperative to intervene in nature's

processes are perfectly aligned. This built a health care system that reliably promotes invasive care over conservative management, heroic measures over compassionate ones, and pursuit of futile intervention over peaceful and painless death. Enlisting technology to keep terminally ill people alive serves an ethical mandate, and it also pays.[79]

The argument does not focus on abandoning the ill and the poor to lack of care, but rather the argument suggests a need to identify and promote a sense of value that takes into consideration the person and the society in a context of a presumption in favor of life,[80] but tempered with the reality of the circumstances. Perhaps the real issues are fear of death, the materialism of our age surfacing now as medical technology rather than audio-visual technology, and the inestimable horror of saying goodbye to one who is loved.

In 1975, about half of all nursing home residents needed assistance using the bathroom; today, 75 percent require aid for the same purpose. The number of residents requiring someone else to feed them has increased from 30 percent to 60 percent in the same time. As America ages, these figures will increase. In the next 20 years, the number of people over age 85 who require nursing home care—the most expensive and intensive care—will increase by 900,000, bringing America's total number of nursing home residents to two million.[81] However, science will continue to pour billions of dollars into technologies that will benefit few, and Medicare and Medicaid will continue to pay.

The dichotomous imbalance between the advantages and disadvantages of technology and the "value" of it are sharply contrasted and vividly demonstrated in Oregon and California—states that pioneered the current posturing for alternative means of financing today's health care.[82] Most states ration their health care simply by disqualifying members as did, for example, Oregon, by previously eliminating from its Medicaid system any family of four earning more than $7,800 a year. Then, state lawmakers in Oregon proposed coverage for all people and eliminated certain high-tech procedures, such as transplants, from its Medicaid provisions, opting instead to use that money for basic health care of noninsured persons. In effect, it "prioritized" its procedures and placed the poor at the top of the list. Now, the question in Oregon is not who is covered, but what is covered? California, on the other hand, took the opposite approach. It opted to provide Medicaid coverage for transplants by eliminating 270,000 people from its Medi-Cal system. Studies now show that the decision was significantly devastating to the overall health of low-income families.[83]

Cost containment by California and Oregon is mirrored in the managed care revolution in all parts of America. Remember, the single most important goal of managed care is the reduction of costs. Health care providers are implementing health care plans in order to provide health care services to a designated pool of covered enrollees.[84] The essence of managed care is to harness market forces to improve cost and efficiency. And, of course, it was this market-force mentality that most conflicted with President Clinton's American Health Security Act of 1993; Americans were too concerned with big government in general and the establishment of a National Health Board, specifically, to adopt the President's proposal. How to provide for competition and yet protect those most vulnerable to discrimination and exclusion is the issue that must be faced.[85]

This issue must be faced because managed health care is growing rapidly; managed care is projected for Medicare recipients and states are shifting Medicaid recipients into such plans. Professor Marc Rodwin describes some of the advantages of managed care:

> [It] frequently reduces financial barriers to care by cutting copayments and deductibles, thereby minimizing the out-of-pocket costs to subscribers. Moreover, [managed care] potentially provides medical care superior to fee-for-service practices financed through indemnity insurance. They can assemble teams of doctors with different specialties; they can deploy modern information systems to monitor quality; and they can assess the performance of both the organizations and individuals within them. The fee structure of [managed care] also eliminates the incentive for overuse of services present in fee-for-service practice.[86]

Disadvantages include the fact that the patient is seldom the center of attention. This is reflected in the need to reduce cost by keeping the doctor at the gate to restrict patient access to specialty services. This often places the patient in a conflict with the physician's need to make a living. Another disadvantage is inherent in any large organization: bureaucratic mazes impede change. A third disadvantage is restricted consumer choice, which could result in lack of quality care.[87] But in all of these disadvantages, there is the need to recognize that the objective of managed care is cost containment, which requires an organized delivery system that will make fiscal accountability and coordination essential. This is why it is called managed care, be that managed care a HMO (health maintenance organization), a PPO (preferred provider organization), or a managed fee-for-service group.

Research on managed care has been a constant companion to its rapid growth. At this point in time, there is evidence that suggests the following:

1. Most forms of managed care are effective in reducing health care utilization, especially inpatient care.
2. Health maintenance organizations (HMOs) also appear to reduce utilization of tests, procedures, or treatments that are expensive or that have lower-cost alternatives.
3. There is no evidence of lower quality of care under managed care, but there is some evidence of lower patient satisfaction compared with fee-for-service plans. However, most HMO patients rate their care highly.
4. Evaluation of Medicare and Medicaid managed care programs suggest that publicly insured individuals in managed care enjoy access to care that is comparable to or better than access under traditional Medicare and Medicaid arrangements.
5. There is preliminary evidence of cost savings in Medicaid managed care programs in the range of 5 to 15 percent.[88]

Because managed care is nascent, it is both open to criticism and revision. Suggestions for reform include the establishment of consumer advocacy groups within managed care organizations. Of course, state and local governments can provide advocacy and consumer protection as a last resort.[89] There is evidence that suggests there will be fewer managed care plans, and these will be more economical. Also, "managed care firms will size their provider networks to achieve increased enrollee volume per provider, giving managed care organizations greater economic leverage over providers and leading to increased attention to the provider selection process."[90]

As technology advances, a new infrastructure of managed care has emerged, and be it health care or long-term care, this is the future. There will continue to be reductions in costs associated with care, and there is already concern that managed care may have an effect upon technology itself. For instance, *The Washington Post* reports that "HMOs and insurers are sharply reducing the fees they pay university hospitals and medical school doctors, which in turn shrinks the amount of 'discretionary' revenue available to support promising scientists."[91] Thus, managed care is affecting technology itself, the means by which persons are living longer and the protagonist in the debate concerning when life should cease.

The manner in which health care is delivered is pertinent to long-term care. Researchers project that, no matter how much medical technology advances, genetically, humans are and will always be incapable of living much longer that 115 years.[92] Thus, as technology continues to advance, the scope of its effect will be restricted to a constantly enlarging elderly population, who will continue to live longer—because technology is simply keeping them alive longer (one machine to breathe, one to pump blood, one to maintain vital signs, one to feed, etc.), but with less quality—because they are older and physically unable to function well, or at all. "Ironically, the very stuff that gives us life also slowly works against it."[93]

There are additional examples, but the point is simple: Changes in medical technology are expensive and yet able to prolong life. How to provide these changes as part of a health care plan in a fair manner and still contain costs is the issue. To date, positions have been developed and proposed mostly concerning the issue of health care, but if health care is successful, long-term care becomes the next and inevitable goal. The two are intertwined. Medicare is an excellent example.

Medicare's Success: Longer Life

The fountain of youth is Medicare, and the water flowing from it is money. The health status of the elderly has been improving constantly with a concomitant increase in the percentage of the population that is becoming elderly.[94] The present increase in the elderly population is small compared to that which is expected in 15 years. The newcomers to the elderly population now are those who were born during the depression, which accounted for the lowest birth rate in the country's history. But by 2010, the elderly population will be flooded with baby boomers reaching retirement age.[95]

For the first time since 1988, American births fell below four million, due to the daughters of baby boomers growing out of the child-bearing years combined with an ever-present concern about the economy.[96] At the same time, the number of deaths reached a record high because of the growing proportion of the elderly population.[97] "The number of deaths is rising, not because the U.S. is becoming more unhealthy, but because the number of elderly is rising,"[98] and those who comprise the elderly population are living longer. For example, in 1900, total life expectancy was approximately 37 years.[99] When social security was founded in 1935, life expectancy at age 65 was only 12.6 years.[100] In 1950, it was 13.9 years, and this figure increased to 17.2 years in 1989.[101] This figure will increase to as high as 21.3 years by middle of the twenty-first century, when it is estimated there will be 392 million people inhabiting the United States.[102] This rate of longevity has been greater for females than for males. Because of continuing advancements in medical technology and its ability to prolong life,[103] by the year 2000, there will be 10 million more Americans over age 65 than there were in 1980.[104]

"A recent study found that the 6 percent of Medicare beneficiaries who died in 1978 accounted for 28 percent of Medicare expenditures,"[105] but more money is being demanded of Medicare beneficiaries. "In 1975, about 4.3 percent of enrollees' per capita income went to cover their share of acute health care costs under Medicare. By 2000, enrollees will have to pay an estimated 8.6 percent of their per capita income to cover their share of costs under Medicare."[106]

Medicare sought to limit costs through a peer review organization that would "monitor inpatient cases for appropriateness of treatment and site of care."[107] There are also smaller payment rates, preadmission approval requirements, increased outpatient services and supervision of these in-home services as ways to reduce costs. Nonetheless, "expenditures for personal health care services for the elderly nearly quadrupled between 1977 and 1987, rising from $43 billion to an estimated $162 billion."[108] Perhaps this is why, in a recent poll, 63 percent of those surveyed who were under age 65 agreed that the Medicare system was in major financial trouble, while only 36 percent of those surveyed who are over age 65 agreed.[109]

Medicare pays for nearly half of the aged's health bill.[110] Yet Medicare may not be effectively contributing to the recipients it is designed to serve. The debate is whether Medicare should be a program only for the elderly poor. To date, only Medicaid is expressly for the poor; to qualify for Medicare, one only need to reach 65 years of age. Reports from the Concord Coalition provide that figures are often misleading, such as reports that between 75 and 83 percent of Medicare's outlays go to beneficiaries with incomes under $25,000 and that between 3 and 5 percent go to income earners of more than $50,000.[111] Some say such figures are representative of health care service "utilization" by reimbursed beneficiaries, and not actual insured income ratios.

Critics argue that when calculated using the actual insurance values of Medicare benefits, in 1990, more than one-half of Medicare benefits were afforded to households with incomes over $20,000, one-third to households with incomes over $30,000, and 15 percent to households with incomes over $50,000, which is up to five times that cited by opponents of Medicare cuts.[112] It might be said, then, that the system is not failing—it is just failing those whom it was designed to serve, namely, the poor. Since 75 percent of the electorate favor means-testing Medicare benefits as a source of distributive assessment, it is imperative that the figures tested are accurate if the system is to be effectively reformed.

Medicare has been highly successful and any attempts to modify the purpose of the ingredients of the program would likely be defeated. The 1996 presidential election provided numerous examples of rhetoric singling out Medicare and Social Security as sacred cows within the American pantheon. Americans rely upon the program and more importantly, these Americans vote. Since the 1980s, women have consistently voted more than men,[113] and in 1992, 62.3 percent of eligible voting women said they voted, compared to only 60.2 percent of men.[114] Many persons believe that women bring a different list of priorities to politics than do men. This is demonstrated in congressional votes, such as the Family and Medical Leave Act, which was supported by 87 percent of the female lawmakers and 57 percent of the male lawmakers. Different priorities are also demonstrated in the support of other legislation, such as legislation involving breast cancer research.[115] Thus, legislators must recognize the significant impact that women's issues will have on maintenance of Medicare and Medicaid.[116] Despite the many changes that have occurred in Medicare and Medicaid since these programs began, more changes will follow as the various issues influencing political lobbying for reform are addressed. Whatever their effect on political reform, changes make certain that alternatives must be found to offset the new and rising costs of long-term care for Americans who are living longer.

Needs: Death with Dignity/Finishing Well

In the last 20 years, every state has grappled with the issue of the rights of the dying. Needless to say, every person in America will die, but the issue upon which there is debate is whether or not each person is permitted the assistance of a physician to accelerate the inevitability of death without criminal sanction.[117] Today, it is axiomatic that every person should have a living will or a health care durable power of attorney. A living will is an effective way of avoiding the problem of undesired care when suffering from a terminal illness; however, interpretations of living wills are state specific and sometimes ignored. Thus, despite the creation of the Patient Self-Determination Act of 1990,[118] which requires federally funded hospitals to inquire and inform the patient of the right to advanced directives, for 75 percent of elderly patients admitted to the hospital, doctors are not even aware that the patient has expressed particular directives.[119] Therefore, a health care proxy who is deputized to remind and demand all pertinent parties of health care wishes is recommended.[120] If not, each person and each family may be confronted with the case of Cruzan, Karen Ann Quinlan, or Dr. Kevorkian—or the endless array of extraordinary means that technology maintains a "precarious and burdensome prolongation of life."[121]

The issue of prior directive seems to have been reduced to paper and, thus, is rendered manageable. Not true. The issue is far more complicated because the living will/health care proxy only allows for "extraordinary means" to be withdrawn, but what is extraordinary? Is it nutrition and hydration? And what is the level of life beyond which there will be no ordinary means to support life?[122] Do you need Dr. Kevorkian to pull the plug? Or is it safe to assume that a family physician will be there to prescribe the correct amount of sedatives—that hopefully you will not regurgitate? And how could you suffer such a loss of hope? Even though you tell everyone you would not want to live like that, are you willing to die as an alternative? To die?

The difference between death today and death even 50 years ago is that technology has advanced to a level that obscures what is extraordinary. "Two decades ago, those who were not and could not swallow and digest food, died . . . Today, various forms of artificial feeding have been developed that are able to keep people metabolically alive for years, even decades."[123] Indeed, "Medical technology has effectively created a twilight zone of suspended animation where death commences while life in some form, continues."[124] From such technological advances have come new terms, such as outcome assessment,[125] value purchasing,[126] quality of life assessment, and rationing health care.[127]

In the end—and that is meant nonfiguratively—dying will always be as Woody Allen said: "I don't mind dying; I just don't want to be there when it happens." Thus, the issue of choice and individual liberty focuses on the person dying; however, it also concerns the state's choice in paying for an expended life. Years ago, the governor of Colorado raised ire when he said that life support should be withdrawn from those who have lived long enough. The significance of the most recent federal court decisions regarding assisted suicide is that each of the decisions regards the issues to be decided not as suicide but as "decisions that are highly personal and intimate, as well as of great importance to the individual."[128] There is a shift from suicide and the senseless loss of life to the image of "a terminally ill adult who ends his life in the final stages of an incurable and painful degenerative disease, in order to avoid debilitating pain and a humiliating death."[129] Thus, the individual and the state are often in agreement that expensive technological efforts to prolong life are not worth the money or the pain.

This concept comes within the description of the Kevorkian ethic. "It is designed to restrain the limits of excruciating human suffering and is, thus, not only humane but compassionate."[130]

For others, the absolute sanctity of life prevails, no matter how fragile or debilitating.[131] This is the easiest position to advocate as it is the one with the fewest ethical dilemmas. For instance, what is an extraordinary means? Is the issue to be resolved at the private (individual) level or the public (state) level? Must money always be the deciding factor? Is it not true that whenever the state withdraws the public support it has given for medical assistance, the state then assists in bringing a life to an end? That is, is not the state assisting the person to die by withholding that which has been proven to be able to prolong life? Just recently, *The Washington Post* reported that the District of Columbia would stop accepting people with AIDS into a program that pays for their medication because the new therapies have produced a surge in demand for the drugs and left the program on the brink of bankruptcy.[132] This is the dilemma of managed care, of Medicaid, of the entire death with dignity debate. It is all so complicated because there are no proven paths to follow, there is so little direction, and the stakes are so high.

There are so many changes. Foreign countries have passed assisted suicide legislation and, based on the decisions of two recent courts of appeals[133] cases, it seems logical that American states will do the same in future decades. Issues of privacy, the American penchant for individual liberty, and voter collaboration are likely to bring this about. Perhaps the paucity of government funds and the demise of both Medicare and the fear of technology will hasten the arrival. Nonetheless, at issue will still be the human person confronting death, and this is the value issue that is needed, essential, often forgotten in the debate over long-term care. As difficult as it is, public policy must consider the human emotional confrontation with death.

HUMAN CONTENDERS

The Gender Factor: Women

Presently, women tend to live longer than men. Thus, regarding the issue of long-term care, it necessarily follows that a majority of the recipients will be women. Yet, with added employment stress and more women partaking injurious behaviors such as smoking and drinking, projections as to long-term survival of women and men may be more similar. This is an unknown. But it is arguable that women receive inferior medical treatment when compared to men, and this may be the primary means by which the life expectancies of the two genders will parallel.

Because of the gender disparity, issues arise as to equal protection and privacy, both within the federal constitutional cases as well as with the state's. These issues are implicit within any discussion of health care or long-term care. If legislators limit the benefits currently awarded under Medicaid—or Medicare—judicial litigation would be an issue. For example, as the debate regarding spending cut proposals intensifies, women's groups are becoming an increasingly loud voice in the fight for federal funding, particularly with regard to Medicaid funding for abortions for rape victims.[134] The controversial Appropriations Bill, which is touted by Republicans and denies Medicaid coverage to rape victims, is condemned by women's rights supporters as ":part of an ongoing Republican assault on low-income women and children, on minorities and on women's reproductive rights."[135] Children are especially vulnerable. Twenty-five percent of all children receive health care through Medicaid, which funds nearly one-half of all inpatient care at children's hospitals.[136]

Restrictive proposals were successfully defeated by women's groups who rallied against Pennsylvania's abortion-control law, which was initiated nearly a decade ago. President Clinton's federal regulations mandate that Medicaid cover the costs of abortions for pregnancies resulting from rape or incest, or for those pregnancies wherein the mother's life is endangered. Proposals to restrict Medicaid funding for abortions were temporarily stifled when a federal appeals court ruled that a state's regulations for Medicaid eligibility can be no more restrictive than federal regulations,[137] but Congress will have the final say. The August 5, 1995, the 50 to 44 Senate vote to deny funding for abortions for federal workers except in cases of rape or incest was described by Senator Arlen Specter as "a meltdown on women's rights" and "an assault against a woman's right to choose."[138]

The final House bill, which was approved by a 219 to 208 vote, overturned the Clinton administration's requirement for Medicaid funding for abortions for rape and incest pregnancies.[139] Under the Clinton administration, tax dollars pay about 72 percent of the costs for abortions under federal employee health plans.[140] The House bill also prohibits the government from withholding funds from medical schools that do not provide abortion training.[141] Where the House and Senate will compromise is yet to be seen and is a key factor for a large chunk of Medicaid "change." Whatever the result, Medicaid spending and savings hinge not only on medical technology and the elderly demographic, but on every development affecting women and issues pertaining to their health and welfare. Long-term care is decidedly a women's issue.

In an effort to restore $193 million in federal funding for family planning services to low-income women, Republican Senator James Greenwood sponsored a proposal to become part of the Labor/Health and Human Services Appropriations Bill.[142] The program is primarily funded by federal Title X funds, which were implemented by the Nixon administration to support family planning clinics for low-income women, but which were recently eliminated. Senator Greenwood opposes a block grant distribution of Title X funds because the newly allowed state control will allow for greater restrictions on family planning, which will result in more abortions and larger expenditures for welfare.[143]

Insurance companies have also taken part in the debate over federal funding involving women's issues, most recently in Pennsylvania, regarding the legislative debate over a woman's maternity stay, which is developing a trend of one-day limits.[144] Independence Blue Cross and Pennsylvania Blue Shield, however, has implemented new guidelines for 48-hour maternity stays.[145]

Opposition to certain proposals involving women's rights or services to low-income families is in line with President Clinton's assertion that sharp cuts in areas of education, training, welfare reform, and health or child care provisions are tantamount to an attack on family values.[146] As funds for the elderly diminish and services dependent on those funds are depleted, the scope of the "family" that is "valued" may broaden to include elderly parents in need of long-term nursing home care. Accordingly, support for extensions of the Family and Medical Leave Act to include broader categories of elderly needs may be an integral part of legislative compromise.

Clearly then, women and family issues have a significant impact on how states posture for eligibility for federal funds and how those limited funds will be administered internally. As the female voting population increases and as women's health/women's rights issues become enmeshed in entitlement debate, legislative changes regarding women's issues will play a major role in the state's ability to provide for an expanding elderly population. This is even more important as the federal government moves toward block grants and the states must debate every dollar they spend. To overlook this point is to overlook the massive differences women have made in the judicial, legislative, and public policy debate in America.

The Geriatric Factor: Voting

A difference between Medicaid and Medicare is that Medicare benefits a portion of the population that consistently votes and can be organized to do so. This is not true with Medicaid. Each day, the American Association of Retired Persons (AARP) lobbies for retention of current benefits under Medicare and strenuously argues for more. For older people, the issue is one of fairness: "I counted upon this and worked hard to get where I am; I deserve the protection that Medicare offers."

In 1988, the 18-to-24 year-old age group accounted for 14 percent of the voting-age population, but accounted for only 9 percent of all voters, while voters over age 65 made up just 16 percent of the voting-age population but accounted for 19 percent of the voters.[147]

In 1990, 41.8 percent of the voting-age population was at least 45 years old.[148] By 1994, this class grew to 43.6 percent—an increase of 7.2 million people, bringing the total voting-age population over age 45 to 84.4 million.[149] The total voting population increased from 184.8 million in 1990 to 193.7 million in 1994.[150] In 1994, persons over age 65 accounted for 17.3 percent of the voting-age population—33.4 million people, which was an increase from 16.8 percent in 1990.[151] Comparatively, the percentage of 18-to-44-year-old voters diminished between 1990 and 1994 by 1.8 percent.[152] By the year 2000, it is expected that there will be 95.2 million voting-age people over age 45, while the total number of voting-age 18-to-44-year-olds is expected to stagnate at about 109 million through the year 2000.[153]

An equally disproportionate percentage of elderly Americans registered to vote in 1994—60 percent—while only 35 percent of those aged 25 to 34 registered.[154] For political candidates in states such as Florida, Pennsylvania, and Iowa, which are the top three ranked states for percentage of population over age 65,[155] these statistics are not ineffectual.[156] Elections tend to have a greater effect on "older" issues, such as long-term health care or taxes, than on "younger" issues, such as a mandatory draft, domestic partnership legislation, or when marriage is considered legal. Plus, more often than not, the elderly retiree simply has more time to get involved and to stay interested in politics. These factors are important for legislators. For example, every year, the Older Iowa Legislature gathers for a two-day session to address issues affecting solely old Iowans.[157] In 1994, the legislature voted to increase nursing home reimbursements under the state's Medicaid program.[158] Typically, the Older Iowa Legislature approves an annual measure to set aside up to 1 percent of the state's gambling revenues for the elderly.[159] Continued backing of such measures, and even the $13,000 needed to fund the two-day session, is critical for the legislators since a much larger percentage of voters in Iowa are elderly.[160]

Other aging states have followed similar patterns of voting percentages. In Massachusetts, elderly residents vote at rates 50 to 130 percent higher than residents in their twenties and thirties.[161] No state is unique in this regard. As each state and each state legislator comes to experience the reality of these statistics, Americans will quickly find that health care reform can be a weapon in the hands of those able to elicit votes from this voting elderly population. During the 1996 presidential election, the issue of age and certainly sound bites on Medicare and Social Security were like sparks in a dry forest. Politicians understand very quickly the implications of angering a segment of the population that votes and is organized.

The Unknown Factor: The Future

For Americans in their forties, fifties, and even sixties, long-term care is a concept that is often thought of as "a bridge I hope I don't have to cross." Middle-aged Americans are confronted with two approaches to the health care bridge, financially constructed with a concerted effort of personal assets and Medicaid funding. Middle-aged Americans will cross the bridge for either their own long-term care in the future, or the present long-term care needs of a parent (or parents).[162] Unfortunately, the former consideration is often set aside because "I'm healthy; it's not something I need to worry about for another twenty or thirty years." The hope is to stay healthy long enough so as not to require long-term hospice care or long-term catastrophic care. The latter consideration, involving elderly parents, is often not confronted until it is too late, as often occurs with diseases such as Alzheimer's.[163] Other Americans stay healthy, but are afflicted by the danger of living longer than their money lasts.[164] Thus, most Americans are only concerned with where they are on the bridge and completely ignore the fact that the bridge is insufficiently constructed (financed) on both sides. This is the human factor.

Many Americans find themselves halfway across an unfinanced bridge before they experience the need for long-term care. "[A]s long as money is the bottom line in health care and as long as everything is based on an inconsistent interpretation of the law, consumers will never know what they are entitled to until they learn they need it."[165] However, this unexpected need for long-term care is unaffordable for most middle-aged, middle-class Americans. In scrambling for resources to finance their long-term care, many Americans find that they have burned their bridge behind them by failing to prepare themselves for long-term care. Thus, they look ahead for the government to take care of them, for Medicaid assistance. However, because Medicaid is collapsing, most Americans find themselves trapped in the middle of a shaky health care bridge and in need of care they cannot afford and will not be provided.

At present, long-term care has become possible for many Americans through spend-down planning allowed by Medicaid. Much of the people utilizing spend-down procedures are older; indeed, greater than one-fourth of all Medicaid expenditures go toward long-term care of the elderly. But some recipients are younger. This is because Medicaid does not restrict benefits to older persons, but instead requires states to protect persons who are "categorically needy."[166] Persons here could be families receiving Aid to Families with Dependent Children (AFDC) benefits, and most aged or disabled persons receiving assistance through the Supplemental Security Income (SSI) program.[167]

A second protected category is the "optional categorically eligible," which permits states to extend Medicaid coverage to needy individuals from designated groups.[168] The groups include the following: individuals receiving optional state SSI supplements but not federal SSI payments,[169] residents of nursing homes or other specified institutions who would be eligible for cash assistance,[170] persons receiving home- or community-based services,[171] and institutionalized individuals whose income does not exceed 300 percent of the federal SSI payment level.[172] The states make the decisions about beneficiaries of these optional categories, but once the state chooses to extend benefits, it must do so for all persons[173] meeting the description and it must provide the same level of benefits given to the categorically needy persons.[174]

Finally, states may elect to extend benefits to the "medically needy,"[175] those persons with incomes greater than the categorically needy, yet effectively reduced by catastrophic medical expenses; thus, their income is no larger than the categorically needy.[176] The eligibility requirements must be "reasonable"[177] and both paid and unpaid medical bills may be proof of eligibility for spending down to meet the medical requirements of the category "medically needy."[178]

The availability of Medicaid and the spend-down method of eligibility for long-term care, thus, is not restricted to the elderly, but to those persons meeting the available categories.[179] Infants such as the famous Baby K, born in Fairfax Hospital, or thousands of persons with AIDS could equally qualify under existing guidelines.[180] Of course the individual states, the rules the states establish,[181] and the planning expertise of participants will make a considerable difference.

There are difficulties, however. For example, AIDS is the leading cause of death in the 25- to 44-year-old age group. The Centers for Disease Control reports that New Jersey had a total of 26,606 reported cases of AIDS as of June 1995. Of those, 9,826 have died since the mid-1980s. Between January and March 1995, 796 new cases of AIDS were reported; between April and June, 1,135 new cases were documented.[182] Unfortunately, most infected people are too young to qualify for Medicare and not poor enough to qualify for Medicaid. The Ryan White Care Act was designed to protect those who fall through the cracks. So too, the Ricky Ray Hemophilia Relief Fund Act was recently introduced to Congress. This act proposed to grant $125,000 to each of the more than 10,000 hemophiliacs infected with HIV in the 1970s and 1980s, prior to the availability of blood-clotting medicines now heat-treated to kill viruses.[183] Prior versions of the bill have been warmly received by bipartisan members. Reports point to a failure of federal regulation, which led to thousands of deaths due to tainted blood-treating products. At least 17 other nations have implemented similar government funding programs.[184] In this way, AIDS is unique, in that Congress has appropriated funds to provide specific remedies to AIDS' effects.

AIDS research receives significant amounts of federal monies research. For example, for the first time, the federal government's Food and Drug Administration has given a green light to experimental injections of baboon bone marrow, which is impervious to the AIDS virus, into the cells of a person with AIDS.[185] Approval was granted despite a grim prognosis and unknowns regarding the spread of other diseases carried by baboons. Nevertheless, this year, the National Institutes of Health will finance $310 million each on Alzheimer's and diabetes research, $817 million on heart disease research, $2.2 billion on cancer research, and $1.3 billion on AIDS research.[186] Yet heart disease accounts for some 721,000 deaths annually, and cancer claims 538,000 deaths; AIDS deaths, however, total 35,351.[187] These mismatched figures are what stimulate debate over appropriate federal spending, especially on the dawn of such dramatic and seemingly unreasoned federal spending cuts in Medicaid.[188] It is logical to assume that there will be competition for dollars spent for health care and this competition will encroach upon—out of necessity—those dollars spent on long-term care for the elderly.

When viewed from the perspective of years of life lost, AIDS surpasses all others in terms of need. But does this lessen the blow to the elderly and disabled? Does it make federal Medicaid reductions any more palatable? Is federal assistance in the form of block grants on its way to becoming a state-managed limited resource to be monopolized by the young? By the elderly? By women? By lobbyists? Statistics show that America is posturing itself for such a future debate, whether it likes it or not. As with value decisions regarding the use of technology, assisted suicide, and Medicare's success, fewer dollars will account for a debate on the expenditure and appropriateness of long-term health care.

The Specific Factor: Alzheimer's

Most of the people left stranded in the middle of the bridge are Americans with elderly parents suffering with some form of dementia or mental illness—usually Alzheimer's disease.[189] Notwithstanding its physically and emotionally draining effects on the victim, the disease financially devastates family members who must care for the Alzheimer's sufferer.[190] Because the disease is progressively degenerative, hospitalization is unlikely and the type of care required is most often custodial in nature.[191] However, two of the most common forms of provisional health care programs, Medicare and Medicaid, are not readily available for the care of Alzheimer's patients. Medicare does not cover "custodial care" except for hospitalization, and Medicaid is not available until the family has exhausted its own financial resources.[192] Consequently, "since people 85 or older make up the fastest-growing segment of the population, Alzheimer's could have devastating consequences for the country's already strained health-care system."[193] For families with little or no financial support of their own, options are limited. One commentator noted the following:

> My doctor told me that the only way to get assured of financial assistance for my mother would be to break her arm, and have her put into a hospital. When her arm heals, he said, break it again, and keep breaking it if you . . . want to assure financial assistance. Of course, my doctor was not serious about going to such lengths, but the point was well made: because the essential elements of treating Alzheimer's disease patients can be provided in the home and do not require hospitalization, financial assistance is negligible.[194]

Thus, when confronted with the failure to plan ahead and the lack of posturing for long-term care, forcing hospitalization may seem like the only available option short of ending a loved one's life.[195]

In an effort to address the increasing health care costs of families faced with Alzheimer's disease and other catastrophic health care crises[196] and the difficulty of obtaining services, the government has advanced legislation on both the federal[197] and state levels.[198] However, as is evidenced by the increasing number of families reaching the poverty level because of escalating health care costs,[199] most attempts to advance a comprehensive health care agenda have failed because they do not protect those most in need.[200]

Increasingly, of the elderly population, the group most in need but least protected in terms of coverage are those suffering with some form of dementia—usually Alzheimer's disease. Because Alzheimer's disease is the most common cause of dementia,[201] families with Alzheimer's sufferers are quickly becoming one of the nation's neediest groups. Still, there is no known cure.[202] Because it is a progressively debilitating disorder, the victim gradually becomes less capable of independent existence. Eventually, the affected individual requires 24-hour-a-day care for the rest of his or her life.[203] For many Alzheimer's victims, there are no family members to care for or financially provide for them. Alone, they are forced to confront a disease that renders them incapable of functioning on their own.[204] Without a cure, the only hope for Alzheimer's victims is effective and affordable care.[205] Presently, America is not postured to provide Medicaid as a source for that care.

Federal contributions to research on dementia have increased from $3.9 million in 1976 to $67 million in 1987.[206] In the past, Congress has enacted legislation to increase research on diseases of the aging.[207] Under this legislation, the National Institute on Aging increased its 1990 fiscal-year funding by $85.3 million, bringing its 1991 total to $325 million.[208] Much of this increase goes toward drug-therapy research.[209] Should this research prove successful, up to $1 billion a year in diagnostic costs could be saved by Medicare alone.[210] This type of legislation suggests that a direct relationship exists between the effectiveness of the American health care system and successful research for long-term care.[211] However, some feel the opposite is true. Some newly established Republican representatives believe that high taxes and restrictive regulations are "strangling innovation." Therefore, many propose to cut nearly $6 billion from science and technology research by the year 2002 in an effort to help eliminate the federal deficit.[212] Twenty-eight percent of these cuts will be in the area of health research.[213] Supporters of research technology call the proposals "neanderthal" and "cannibalistic," given that the United States ranks twenty-eighth in the world with respect to the proportion of wealth invested in science.[214]

"Long-term care refers to medical, mental health, and personal services rendered to those with diminished capacity for self-care due to illness."[215] The largest population of people who require long-term care are those suffering from some form of dementia.[216] Alzheimer's patients often require long-term care from the time symptoms are first recognized.[217] Eventually, all Alzheimer's patients will require long-term care until death.[218] Some receive long-term care at home[219] while others are more properly cared for in nursing homes,[220] care facilities,[221] hospitals,[222] state mental hospitals,[223] hospices,[224] or other nonresidential facilities, including adult day care centers,[225] community mental health services,[226] outpatient facilities, clinics,[227] and senior centers.[228]

Theoretically, where one receives long-term care will depend on how one theorizes the point at which care is most critically needed during the course of the disease. For example, a continuum theory would hold that the need for long-term care intensifies until death as the deteriorative effects of the disease progress.[229] On the other hand, because caregiving is most burdensome during heightened changes in the patient's behavior, and because behavioral problems such as mobility, aggression, and depression diminish after a certain point of deteriorative progression during the disease, care would be most critical during the apogee of behavioral changes.[230] This apogee theory, therefore, would decree that long-term care would be most needed midway through the disease and would diminish in necessity at some point thereafter. Adoption of the apogee theory would intimate that proper services provided to the family during the critical stage of the disease would help to alleviate the decision to institutionalize.[231] Regardless of the theory adopted, however, the final stages of Alzheimer's disease are usually spent in the hospital since the culmination of the disease is often accompanied by another serious disease, such as heart disease, cancer, or stroke, which results in death.[232] These final stages are often spent with a focus on easing pain rather than prolonging life.[233]

Proper services provided to Alzheimer's families may alleviate both the physical and the psychological burdens of caring for an Alzheimer's victim.[234] However, adequate services are limited; those that are available in any given locality are usually very expensive, understaffed with trained service providers, and of poor or insufficient quality.[235] Furthermore, services that are affordable are often overlooked or ignored by many families because of the difficulty in accessing and utilizing organized support methods.[236] Too often, families rely on inadequate services or no services at all.[237]

"Although Medicaid will cover nursing home costs, no government program will pay for long-term care at home. Medicare usually does not pay for either nursing home or in-home care."[238] Thus, family members caring for Alzheimer's victims must rely on private insurance. Presently, although 165 million Americans have health insurance,[239] more than 30 million Americans have no health insurance.[240] Some estimate that this figure may be as high as 37 million—more than the entire population of Canada.[241] At some point during any given year, this figure reaches 65 million.[242] These millions of Americans will most likely be able to afford only one-half of their medical bills.[243] The other half will be recorded as a loss.[244] Nevertheless, former President Bush, in a State of the Union speech, said that "[g]ood health care is every American's right."[245] However, the status of the American health care system would suggest otherwise. Presently, there is no national health insurance plan, and the Bush administration remained firmly committed to a privately supported system.[246] Despite President Bush's statement, his 1992 budget proposal offered no indication of reconsideration for a movement toward national health care coverage.[247] The failure of President Clinton's plan leaves all in the mediocrity of status quo.

Some studies show that for those that are uninsured under the current system, proper treatment may not only be unaffordable, but inaccessible.[248] Researchers suggest that when faced with uninsured patients, physicians often provide inadequate care at a much cheaper cost to increase the likelihood of payment and to minimize hospital losses.[249]

Indeed, the uninsured population is significant. Between February 1990 and September 1992, 60 million Americans, or 25 percent of the population, were uninsured for at least one month. As much as 85 percent of the uninsured Americans are employed or are dependents of working Americans.[250]

At least 24 states have established high-risk pools for people who are not eligible for conventional insurance.[251] California, which patterned its plan after Minnesota, developed the Major Medical Risk Insurance Program, which will protect as many as 10,000 residents of the state.[252] Before leaving office, New York's Mario Cuomo proposed similar legislation in order to protect those who cannot afford insurance because of preexisting conditions such as AIDS or cancer. Portability, contained within the federal Health Insurance Portability and Accountability Act of 1996, would be an assist here, too. This legislation also allows dying persons, including those with AIDS, to draw on their life insurance while still living. These are recent initiatives and are prompted by state experimentation.

Most insurance plans, however, will not cover Alzheimer's disease. One very rare legal case that perfectly demonstrates the eligibility dilemma faced by Alzheimer's victims is *Brock v. Guaranty Trust Life Insurance Co.*[253] This case involved a long-term care insurance policy that attempted to disqualify persons suffering from Alzheimer's disease. In *Brock* the insurer attempted to disallow the Alzheimer's claim by claiming that it was a preexisting illness and therefore exempt from the protection of the policy, which stated that preexisting illnesses would only be covered after a two-year waiting period. Although the insurer failed under this theory, the plaintiff was denied protection under the policy because of a prior hospitalization requirement contained in the agreement. Such a requirement is found in most long-term policies. In *Brock*, as with most Alzheimer's victims, the patient had not been hospitalized for Alzheimer's disease before entering the nursing home and was therefore denied coverage.

For Alzheimer's victims, innovative policy plans that avoid this dilemma by including no preexisting condition limitations and no prior hospitalization requirements are critical.[254] Newer and broader policies now cover Alzheimer's disease, specifically, and have narrowed preexisting-condition waiting periods to six months.[255] But such plans are not always helpful even though they are otherwise applicable. Most dementia victims, because of their old age, suffer some other form of illness that requires medical attention. Because of their inability to function independently within the home, Alzheimer's patients are more likely to suffer from medication overdoses, falls, and other household accidents.[256] But these may not qualify as hospitalizations for Alzheimer's disease specifically, so as to warrant coverage under the prior hospitalization requirement.

Notwithstanding the devastating physical and psychological demands of Alzheimer's disease, an overwhelming financial impact is inevitable. "Although there is 'more money for aging services than ever before, there is less per capita' from governmental agencies because medical advances have resulted in a large increase in the elderly population."[257] Unlike the physical effects of the disease, however, the financial impact is immediately intense. Within three months of nursing home care, two-thirds of elderly patients are reduced to poverty.[258] For patients over the age of 65, medical costs will amount to 20 percent of their annual income; for patients over 85 years of age, 40 percent.[259] Long-term care in the home or in a nursing home could cost anywhere between $25,000 and over $1 million per year for a single Alzheimer's victim and family.[260] In 1987, of the more than one million Americans who were forced into destitution because of long-term health care costs, two out of three were elderly.[261]

Health care costs have risen dramatically, particularly over the past seven years due to larger catastrophic claims, increased mental health and substance abuse claims, larger claims due to advanced medical technology, and increased reliance on medical care during the recession.[262] Medicaid payments for long-term care of people with dementia may constitute up to 10 percent of some state budgets.[263] American corporations now spend one fourth of their net earnings on employee health care.[264] To alleviate some costs, companies have charged employees more for the opportunity to choose their own doctor. However, at the current rate, despite efforts by major companies to offer new long-term care insurance plans,[265] many companies are beginning to simply cut back on coverage altogether.[266] Recent studies show that although the cost of corporate medical plans is increasing, it is increasing at a slower rate than expected, due to the success of managed-care health insurance plans in absorbing rising medical costs. In 1994, the average cost of a comprehensive corporate plan in the Philadelphia area was expected to increase by 16 percent. In 1995, the projection dropped to 14.25 percent.[267]

Generally, there are four ways in which an individual or a family caring for an individual will pay for the long-term care necessary for Alzheimer's victims. These are the following: (1) Medicare, (2) Medicaid, (3) social security or other insurance, and (4) personal savings. Personal savings as a means of paying for the costs of long-term care are limited and almost always unavailable.

When Medicare was created 30 years ago, it was designed "to cover acute but not chronic care—the heart attack patient in the hospital, for example, not the [Alzheimer's] patient in a nursing home."[268] As of 1988, Medicare extended its services to include catastrophic illnesses.[269] Nevertheless, protection against the increasing costs of catastrophic and long-term health care under Medicare is minimal.[270] In fact, since 1986, "[o]lder persons [have paid] a larger portion of their income for health care than they did before Medicare was enacted."[271]

Medicare has four policy goals. They are as follows: to "provide access for Medicare patients; increase access for patients requiring resource-intensive care; contain growth in program costs; and assure the delivery of high quality care."[272] However, at a time when medical costs increase at a rate twice that of general inflation,[273] cutbacks have proven inevitable.[274] Since the Bush administration, proposed budgets have continually sought reductions in reimbursements to service providers.[275] Medicare has "hardly been a showcase for cost containment."[276]

Medicare's hospital insurance is available at no cost to everyone who is entitled to Social Security.[277] Still, in 1987, Medicare costs were approximately $67 billion.[278] By the year 2040, this figure could reach as high as $200 billion.[279] Under the catastrophic health insurance plans of this country, however, less than 3 percent of Medicare's 31 million beneficiaries receive help with the care they need.[280] In 1985, Medicare paid only 1.7 percent of all nursing home bills, and private insurance covered even less—0.8 percent, while 51.4 percent was paid out-of-pocket by consumers.[281] Recent reports by the Social Security Advisory Council suggest that because of figures like these, the Medicare Hospital Trust Fund, which pays hospital bills for approximately 34 million elderly who receive social security benefits, will be bankrupt in 15 years.[282] "[I]t is a very sick future for Medicare unless policymakers take the window of opportunity afforded to them before the baby boom starts to retire in ten short years."[283]

The reason for the dismal outlook is that the costs of the benefits are now rising above the 2.9 percent fixed tax-rate for the program. The trust fund for Supplemental Medical Insurance, which covers doctor bills, will probably survive bankruptcy because of more stable resources. However, costs will still increase; consequently, so, too, will premiums.[284] The problem for Alzheimer's victims is that they are only eligible for funds under the potentially bankrupt hospital fund.[285] These figures and resulting dilemmas demonstrate the need for supplemental insurance programs that offer comprehensive long-term plans with effective and affordable service provisions.

Medicaid provides 93 percent of the nursing home costs produced by elderly nursing home residents.[286] Most long-term care insurance policies that offer comprehensive care, such as those now offered by many major companies, however, have premiums that are beyond affordability for most elderly persons. Consequently, those policies with lower premiums that are affordable contain restrictions on certain types of care. The restrictions in many of these policies include restrictions for Alzheimer's disease.[287] However, some commentators suggest that it is possible to maintain affordable premiums and still provide adequate comprehensive care. Armond Budish suggests that "[b]y limiting the benefit period to 30 months, or as close to 30 months as possible, the maximum exposure of the insurance company will be limited, permitting the insurer to reduce premiums even on a high-quality coverage plan.[288]

Combining this 30-month premium plan with Medicaid planning strategies, the nursing home resident will be afforded adequate care at an affordable premium. However, the way to effectively combine the two strategies is to effectively divest oneself of sufficient assets to fall under the Medicaid qualification threshold. To do this, one may take advantage of two techniques provided by law: transferring assets to other individuals, or use of a Medicaid qualifying trust.[289] Qualifying for these techniques was restricted by the spousal impoverishment rules, which were instituted with the Medicare Catastrophic Coverage Act of 1988, but were not repealed with the act.[290]

Using the transference-of-property technique, a nursing home resident will not qualify for Medicaid until approximately 36 months after the transfer. As a result, the resident must use the principal of his or her assets to pay for costs for the initial 36 months. Also, if assets are transferred to children, the assets may be subject to the childrens' creditors, or upon divorce or death, subject to the rights of the childrens' spouses. Therefore, the Medicaid trust may be the better alternative in some situations.

Unless an elderly individual is one of only 5.6 percent of the elderly with incomes over $50,000, he or she would most likely fall into poverty without Social Security or other private insurance.[291] Thus, to alleviate the surge into disparity, there has been a recent push for private insurance for long-term coverage.

In the last four years, employer-sponsored group long-term care programs have rapidly increased in popularity. Since 1993 and the introduction of the Health Security Act of 1993 (HSA), employer-mandated health insurance has gained prominence. While the federal legislation pertains to health insurance in general, it should be noted that the employer-mandated program, whereby the employer pays 80 percent of the universal health insurance coverage, has been criticized for sheltering hidden costs. For instance

> Employer mandates would continue to foster indirect and hidden costs and result in serious misallocations of national economic resources; employer mandates should therefore be rejected as a financing vehicle for reform.[292]

Such caution could equally apply to employer-mandated long-term health protection.

The first state to initiate such a long-term plan was Alaska, in 1987. The Alaska plan is very restrictive, however, and would not, as a single-option plan, be instituted today in light of the more flexible option plans now available. In the past several years, the number of people covered by employer insurance has increased by 300 percent.[293] However, only a handful of major companies participate in such programs. While only 153 companies were committed to a long-term care plan as of June, 1990, 79,500 employees were participants in the same companies.[294] An additional 32,000 employees enrolled in a plan at IBM, alone. Despite these seemingly promisingly high figures, only 5 percent of all eligible workers participate in the programs.[295]

Maryland has proven to be the most receptive state to the employer plans. It began its participation in 1988 and has recently introduced a "second generation" plan, which supplements many of the older plans. Such supplemental features include respite care coverage and nonforfeiture clauses, which would only reduce coverage, not abrogate it, upon nonpayment of premiums. Another appealing feature is a death benefit, which would return premium payments to the estate of the participant should the employee die before obtaining any benefits from the program.

Most employer long-term care plans include coverage for custodial nursing home care and home health care, which begin 90 days after the cause of the need for long-term care. Eligibility is usually based on objective criteria based on inability to participate in daily activities. Most plans specifically cover impairments caused by Alzheimer's disease, set premiums based on the age of the participant and the care required, and continue after discontinuation of employment, subject to continual premium payments. Employer plans introduced through major corporations have spurred similar option plans. For example, The University of Michigan was the first institution to initiate similar coverage when it began its program on January 1, 1991.[296]

Despite the continuing growth of employer plans for long-term care, they are not available to everyone and for those for whom they are available, they are often not enough. Inevitably, families confronting long-term care needs—whether they be for Alzheimer's or AIDS, disabled children or elderly parents—are reduced to and must rely on "spend-down" practices.

The Family Factor: Heirs

Few of the elderly actually elect to enter into long-term care or the Medicaid spend-down that may pay for it. Few were perspicacious enough to purchase long-term health insurance when they were healthy. Choosing spend-down is usually caused by the advent of a medical emergency and the election is that of the applicant's children or family. And the nature of family in America is changing. There is an increase in the number of multigenerational families, due partly to advances in prolonging life and partly to the families' ability—through private means or government programs—to afford long-term hospice care or nursing home care. Thus, there are "sandwichers" who are breadwinning adults with both elderly parents and children for whom they must provide; then there are "club-sandwichers" who have an even larger responsibility: for children, parents, and grandparents.[297]

These are the people who are suddenly faced with stroke, heart disease, or Alzheimer's, who scurry to find adult day care and sit in silent shock as physicians and hospital social workers explain that care will cost upward of $150 day. Faced with this horror, families scramble for information about Medicare and Medicaid and consider anything that will allow for a little dignity and for life to go on. Knowledge is essential.[298] Some will discover self-help information through groups like the United Seniors Health Cooperative. The provide a phone number (202-393-6222) and a pamphlet titled: *Long-Term Care: A Dollar & Sense Guide.* The Family Caregiver Alliance can direct you to local long term care resources if you call 415-434-3388, and the ElderCare Locator sponsored by the National Association of Area Agencies on Aging, offers free health insurance counseling and information. Call 800-677-1116. Best of all, Virginia Morris has written a marvelous book titled *How to Care for Aging Parents.*

Medicaid spend-down is often the object of attention because of greater amounts of information available to the younger family member, but it is not necessarily true that the younger persons are anxious to trick or defraud the government and take from the taxpayer. Medicaid spend-down is simply an available method to achieve an end sponsored by the government, and it fits quite comfortably within the public perception that some things should be free. The possibility of the average young family member being able to decipher the sources and opportunities within the health care system is very slight. Emotion and lack of preparation often predominate.

Consider the following: Your mother is in Nursing Home X and you are paying about $4,000 a month in fees and services. At last you can sleep at night, no one calls to tell you to come and take your mother home because she has wet the bed or screams all day; for the first time in a long time you go out to dinner, dress up, and even catch yourself laughing the kind of laugh you had *before* your mother had the stroke or reached that stage in Alzheimer's. For a second you feel guilty, but then you realize that your mother is clean and safe and has a routine in the nursing home that you could never provide if she were home with you. Then someone you respect finally says the magic words: "You did the right thing." Suddenly, the $4,000 a month is worth it; it is worth every penny.

Gradually, you begin to take control of your life again, your visits to the home become a routine, and you even try to be there at meal times so that you can help feed the woman that fed you long ago. It is a kind of communication and it is a kind of intimacy. You begin to tell yourself over and over that you did do the right thing. You believe it because it is true. Then you begin to meet the families of other people at the nursing home and you share stories and the feelings that seem so understandable and mutual now, even though a year ago the situation conjured up terror, confusion, and complete powerlessness. One of the people you meet at the home tells you that her mother has been at Nursing Home X for five years and you respond that it certainly costs a fortune, but it is certainly worth it. "Oh no," she responds, "Medicaid pays for it all and the state even gives mother $70 a month for spending money." "You pay nothing?" you ask incredulously. "No, not since we spent down mother's assets and thus qualified for Medicaid," she responds.

As soon as you return home, you call a lawyer friend who gives you the name of an elderlaw attorney, or you find one through the National Academy of Elder Law Attorneys at 1604 N. Country Club Road, Tucson, Arizona 85716. For $25 you will receive a list of member attorneys in your area. You call and then meet with the attorney, and she or he tells you what you must do to enable your mother to qualify for Medicaid. The attorney's fee is $2,500 for doing all of the paperwork, but eventually your mother will receive exactly the same care, in the same Nursing Home X, and you will no longer have to pay the $4,000 a month. You are incredulous. But soon someone you respect tells you that you are doing the right thing and very quickly you pass the financial responsibility for your mother to the state and federal Medicaid program. This program will cover all costs until your mother dies.

Families and heirs are often the ones to decide on Medicaid spend-down, but there may well be a shift in initiative in the future. The elderly are frequently provided with seminars that explain the intricacies of spend-down. There are also attorneys who specialize in this area of the law who offer complete guides and procedures, which include books you can buy in pharmacies and shopping centers. There are advertisements in magazines in doctors' waiting rooms. There are many case studies documented with personalized involvement with friends and relatives.[299] Books, journals, and newspapers offer guidance and incentives.[300] And yet, one of the most grievous discrepancies among families and heirs is between those who know of Medicaid spend-down and those who do not. Just as with Nursing Home X, there is one patient on Medicaid and one with a family working two jobs to pay the bills. Each nursing home resident receives the same care but one has a family member who knows how the system works and one does not.

IMMEDIATE NEED

Cost of Long-Term Care

Most people would think that Medicare would pay for nursing home care. Especially with the elderly—those for whom Medicare was designed—hospital and thus Medicare payment seems a certainty. But no, Medicare was not intended for long-term care. Medicare is limited. It does provide some nursing home payment, but only in conjunction with treatment of an immediate illness. It is not associated with long-term care.

For instance, Part A for Hospital Insurance will cover all nursing home costs for the first 20 days if admission to the nursing home occurs within 30 days of the individual's discharge from a hospital stay of three days or more.[301] Medicare will pay a portion of days 21 through 100, but nothing after 100 days.[302] This is certainly not long-term care.[303] The daily cost for one day's stay in a nursing home for a resident with private health insurance, which 30 percent of patients have, may average $146. This cost is rapidly escalating. Medicare pays for a small percentage (roughly 5 percent) of nursing home residents at $189 per day. Medicaid, on the other hand, which covers 65 percent of nursing home residents, reimburses much less than the costs of daily care, usually around $105. Thus, nursing home providers must make up the difference.[304]

Without Medicare payments, a person privately paying for nursing home long-term care is confronted with an average cost of $40,000 yearly or $3,333 each month.[305] Some of the nursing home facilities require "founders' fees" of a specified amount—$100,000, for example—and then a lesser charge each month for rent on a unit—$1,400, for example. Taken in conjunction with Medicare availability and private insurance to cover the amount approved by Medicare and costs, a person could afford long-term care if he or she had saved sufficient assets to meet the monthly payments and the incidentals that arise. Part of the problem today is that few persons are given an incentive to provide for long-term care and, thus, to privately meet the costs.

Therefore, any plan for posturing to meet the needs of long-term care recipients must include incentives.[306] These will be the focus of posturing by state and federal officials—and by all persons who realize the inherently fraudulent system that allows spend-down so as to qualify as needy when need has become voluntary. Few can disagree with the fact that the Medicaid program was not designed to allow for persons with assets to isolate those assets, even though there is a government-sponsored plan that allows this to occur. Incentives allow for those most likely to have assets to utilize alternative payment procedures, such as insurance and Social Security-like payments; politically, however, this is no easy task.

For example, in 1980, when Wilma Lelak was 67 years old, she was diagnosed with Alzheimer's disease. Her husband cared for her until he died in 1990, at which time her daughter sold Wilma's home and cared for her in her own home. As Wilma's condition worsened, she could no longer be cared for at her daughter's home and was forced to enter a nursing home. With her savings long depleted, Medicaid paid for the costs.

Technically, the state could claim a portion of the proceeds from the sale of Wilma's home to cover some of her nursing home costs borne by Medicaid, but it does not because it is "politically unpalatable."[307] More important, Wilma's scenario is not unique. Most residents enter the nursing home as modest-income, middle-class disabled persons or financially depleted elderly who have already spent their life savings on the initial stages of illness. Thus, even if the state were willing to take on the political backlashing and try to recoup more of the elderly's assets to cover costs, there are usually no assets to claim.

Often when there are heirs with advanced knowledge of Medicaid availability, the elderly person never has a chance to deplete assets, but instead, with the help of an elderlaw attorney, immediately begins the process of Medicaid spend-down, thus saving the assets for inheritance or gifts to the heirs. Partly because of the increase in this practice, the states and the federal government are scrambling to close the loopholes and bar those who are not truly needy from Medicaid entitlement. As can easily be imagined, the process is filled not only with emotion, but with political posturing. The costs are high, both for the recipient of long-term care and for the governments seeking to provide a safety net for the poor.

Fear and Envy

Emphasis upon the costs of long-term care is only part of the story. There is also a fear of death and the desire to postpone it as long as possible. Death is a source of great fear among the elderly and those witnessing the years pass quickly. Perhaps it is incorrect to say the fear is of death; rather, the fear is of dying. In 1949, half of all people who died in New York City died at home in bed. By 1989, this number had reduced to 16 percent.[308] Thus, dying in the hospital has become routine, but the implication of this is that before I die I shall be probed, perforated and pillaged, and worst of all, I shall die away from the people and things that have been the fabric of my life. This is the gist of the fear of dying.

Perhaps to make the dying more palatable, the "old-old" spend 20 times as much on nursing home care than do "young-old".[309] And the government is quick to assist in spending money to make dying more palatable. For instance, although the elderly comprise only one-eighth of the population, they receive about 75 percent of the federal health benefits.[310]

Often, the health care benefits received by the elderly have little effect. In fact, 30 percent of expenditures for hospitalization of Medicare patients is for those patients who will die within one year—most within six months.[311] Nonetheless, 70 percent of people surveyed who had survived intensive-care hospitalization said they would endure it again, even if it meant only one extra month of life.[312] Perhaps the reason is that with one more month to live, it may be possible to maneuver yourself into a position in which you could die with dignity, with friends, with family, with those things that mean something to you. It is like landing a plane on the deck of an aircraft carrier; you keep trying no matter what the cost so that you can get it right and end the journey with dignity.

It is not surprising that the assisted suicide movement in America is attracting increased attention. Amidst the national attempt to create alternatives to financing health care, there exist similar local posturing—namely, the right to die. This too seems like a simple dollars-and-cents issue, but at its core is a fear of dying. There, too, reside morality and ethics.[313] Recently, a jury in Michigan acquitted Dr. Jack Kevorkian of charges that he assisted in the suicides of terminally ill persons. This is not the first time he has been acquitted. Indeed, the state of Michigan has not been able to convict him to date.

While it is impossible to read the minds of the jurors, it is possible to listen as Dr. Kevorkian and his attorney tell of the suffering, the costs, and the rights of those dying to put an end to the process of death—a process many fear will become their fate in the future. There is an attitude that enough is enough.

Additionally, the United States Court of Appeals for the Ninth Circuit, in San Francisco, recently held that a Washington statute which made assisted suicide a felony was unconstitutional because it interferes with an individual's right to decide "how and when to die."[314] Over a strong dissent, the court allied itself with reasoning from the abortion cases[315] and decided that there is "persuasive evidence that the Constitution encompasses a due process liberty interest in controlling the time and manner of one's death—that there is, in short, a constitutionally recognized 'right to die.'"[316] This right is subject to state interest regulation,[317] but as to competent, terminally ill adults who wish to hasten their deaths by obtaining medication prescribed by their doctors,[318] there is now the possibility to do so.

On the other side of the nation, the United States Court of Appeals for the Second Circuit, in New York, decided that a New York statute making it a crime to aid a person in committing a suicide or attempting suicide is unconstitutional.[319] The basis of the unconstitutionality is different from that recognized in the Ninth Circuit. Here, in the Second Circuit:

> it seems clear that New York does not treat similarly circumstanced persons alike: those in the final stages of terminal illness who are on life-support systems are allowed to hasten their deaths by directing the removal of such systems; but those who are similarly situated, except for the previous attachment of life-sustaining equipment, are not allowed to hasten death by self-administered prescribed drugs.[320]

The court found that such inequality was irrational:

> The New York statutes criminalizing assisted suicide violate the Equal Protection Clause because, to the extent that they prohibit a physician from prescribing medications to be self administered by a mentally competent, terminally-ill person in the final stages of his terminal illness, they are not rationally related to any legitimate state interest.[21]

These two cases have caused heated debate within an already factious public, afraid of death, increasingly sensitized to its cost, and susceptible to the advances of technology offering longer and longer life. The Ninth Circuit majority opinion recognizes these conflicting issues. At the conclusion of its opinion was written the following: "We recognize that this decision is a most difficult and controversial one, and that it leaves unresolved a large number of equally troublesome issues that will require resolution in the years ahead."[322]

Both opinions, in California and New York, will have decided effects upon the rights of individuals to have assistance during competent periods should death be desired. The decisions will be debated in terms of personal autonomy and individual liberty, equal protection and due process rights, and the right of the courts to fashion liberty interests irrespective of legislatures and history. Both decisions also have something to say about the fear of dying and the costs, technologies, and prioritization associated with the process. This is the message coming from the middle of the country, Michigan, where prosecutors try unsuccessfully to convict Dr. Jack Kevorkian of assisted suicide. That is, the process of dying has become too frightful, too attenuated, too complicated, too real. In short, the process of dying has become like tar baby, you get stuck to it and it forces you to be there through the long and bitter process.

Health care is a business—a growing business. Therefore, death and how it is brought about have serious business implications. And these business implications can be complicated by an appeal to the fear of dying in each of us. For example, Oregon's Death With Dignity Act, or Measure 16, has caused even more posturing on this particular issue of health care and its financial effects.[323] Prolonged life equals greater fees for the health care institution, accelerated death means less health care spending and increased financial savings for the elderly, with a greater inheritance for their children,[324] along with, many argue, the dignity of a peaceful and painless death. Does being in charge of the end lessen the fear of the process? While the idea that death and dying really boils down to a dollars-and-cents issue may seem cold and insensitive, it is certainly acknowledged. And implicit within the acknowledgment is perhaps a mask to hide the fear of dying.

Litigation is a good signal of what is happening in America regarding death and technology. In a lawsuit filed to defeat the implementation of Oregon's Death With Dignity Act, doctors Gary Lee and William Perry claimed that if any of their patients, in reliance on the Act, enhanced their own death, the doctors would suffer a loss of service fees.[325] Their claim was denied. Meanwhile, the health care institution's consumption of lifelong savings while lifelong savers linger in prolonged but quality-free life has been likened to theft.[326] Such legal posturing seems to rest upon financial underpinnings, but there is a deeper sense of fear of dying at its source. In the posturing for solutions to long-term care, this fear must be addressed.

One form of managed care which aspires to avoid the inclination to provide excessive and wasteful therapy and treatment on the elderly and dying is "capitation." But the bottom line is the same. Under a capitation managed-care system, doctors secure a predetermined fee each month for each patient, notwithstanding the amount of care that is provided. Naturally, then, the inclination is to recommend less care, thereby spending less money; the health care provider has no incentive to order more and more services. Ideally, the inherently altruistic qualities of the health care profession and professionals are far too conscientiously ingrained in the institution of medicine for such suggestions to become a problem. Such altruistic measures only add to the "medicalization of dying"[327] and wasteful health care expenditures. Perhaps, the incentive within a capitation system to more carefully consider the merits of a long-term, lifesaving treatment plan—even if only a financial incentive—is the stabilizing factor in a system so quick to extend life beyond its resources. As Barbara Coombs Lee, who led in the successful posturing of Oregon's Measure 16, writes:

> If the coming of capitation payment means that financial incentives are no longer in perfect alignment with medicine's cultural imperative, it should be viewed with relief, as the injection of some modicum of balance in the determination of rational treatment plans.[328]

The thought often arises that with the advent of health maintenance organizations (HMOs), technology, costs, and patient health will be better controlled. But costs of HMOs, which experienced an initial one-time savings compared to unmanaged care, have since risen at about the same rate as unmanaged-care costs.[329] In 1988, 40 percent of all HMOs lost money, the largest of which—Maxicare—went bankrupt.[330] Nonetheless, managed health care has become the fastest growing portion of the health care workforce,[331] and bankruptcies only signal the vitality of a quickly evolving infrastructure.

The HMOs will continue to be players in the efforts on the part of the federal and state governments to control costs. So will capitation, so will fear of dying, and of course, so will spiraling costs. With this posturing may also come a sense of envy—envy of those with better resources to provide relief of fear of dying, envy of those who can legally have death with dignity, and even an envy of those who manage to find that dignity in the last moments of dying. Whatever the human predicament, fear and envy must be addressed within the equation.

Chapter 2

Medicaid's Provisions: Federal, State, and Future

FEDERAL INITIATIVE

The competing interests grappling for a hold on long-term care have as a major factor Medicaid spend-down and its ability to provide money for expensive nursing home daily care at government, rather than private, expense. How does Medicaid spend-down work? How does a person with millions of dollars of assets become poor so as to utilize a state and federal program designed to provide nursing home care for the poor? The answer is a complicated one in part because the program is political.

The Social Security Act of 1965 included the Medicaid program. In describing this program and what has developed since, the United States Supreme Court wrote that it is "among the most intricate ever drafted by Congress."[1] Earlier, a federal judge described the regulations developed under the Medicaid legislation as "labyrinthine"[2] and almost unintelligible to the uninitiated.[3] It is said that on Capitol Hill, only Congressman Waxman understands the complexity of the issue and he guards his knowledge well.

The issue that most concerns long-term care is the method by which Congress and the states allow for spend-down and consequent entitlement to the benefits allowed. The federal control has come from progressive Omnibus Budget Reconciliation Acts (OBRA) providing, among other things, changes in the months required to demonstrate need and other remedial devices that test need. The changes affect the manner that the elderly and the disabled confront only three options pertaining to long-term care needs. The first option is whether to purchase long-term care insurance, but this is usually cost-prohibitive and considered only when care is imminent.[4] Second, an individual needing care may spend-down almost all of his or her assets on bonafide medical care so as to become "medically needy" enough to qualify for Medicaid. But most people with assets also have health insurance; thus, this is not a logical option for them. The third option is to purposely divest yourself of all of your assets—usually in gifts to the children—so as to qualify for Medicaid on paper.[5] In this way, "the elderly . . . [are] forced to rely on basic welfare mechanisms to assure protection against the catastrophic costs of nursing home services."[6]

New Jersey has recently added another alternative as a means of qualifying for Medicaid benefits, but one to which few couples would resort. Few, that is, unless they are an elderly couple faced with a similarly "cruel dilemma" as that of "L.M." and his wife of 63 years.[7] L.M. and his wife were married in 1929. In 1992, L.M. suffered a stroke, which made it necessary that he receive long-term nursing home care. L.M. and his wife could not afford continued nursing home care—at least not as a married couple. L.M. and his wife had a monthly pension and social security income of $1,441.17, which is $175.17 above the monthly limit for Medicaid eligibility, thereby placing L.M. within the "Medicaid Gap."[8] L.M.'s income would sufficiently decrease so that he would qualify for Medicaid to pay for his nursing home care only if he were single. And so after 63 years of marriage, L.M. and his wife reluctantly divorced. But the County Board of Social Services still denied L.M. his Medicaid benefits, claiming that he improperly diverted his income by using a property settlement agreement to transfer his $657.37 per month pension income to his wife, thereby qualifying himself for Medicaid.[9]

The newly divorced couple appealed to the New Jersey Appellate Court, which upheld the denial of benefits for public policy considerations as a promotion of divorce as a means of obtaining Medicaid. The New Jersey Supreme Court held on June 7, 1995 that once L.M.'s pension was transferred to his wife through the settlement agreement, the pension could not be considered as part of his income for Medicaid eligibility and, therefore, he was legitimately entitled to Medicaid benefits. New Jersey state officials reeled after the decision, suggesting that the ruling effectively takes the eligibility determination out of the hands of the state and puts it in the courts, and will now open a floodgate of divorces manufactured as yet another Medicaid loophole.

The court, with confidence in a new state proposal to assist "Medicap Gap" members[10] and with obvious insight into the ominous federal changes in Medicaid policies which lie ahead,[11] determined that the public-policy concerns expressed by state officials and the lower court are premature and unfounded. Nevertheless, this Pandora's box is now open and it allows for an additional means of Medicaid eligibility through the divestment of available income in the distribution of marital property upon divorce. In addition, the decision is another example of how with every proposal that tightens the reigns on rules for Medicaid eligibility, there is a loophole through which millions of Americans achieve eligibility. Some enter satisfactorily, and some, like the divorcing couple, with great reluctance but with few alternatives.

Rules

In 1980, through passage of the Boren Long Amendments,[12] which were included in the Omnibus Budget Reconciliation Act of 1980 (OBRA '80),[13] Congress allowed states to withhold Medicaid eligibility from persons who transferred "countable"[14] assets for less than fair market value within the previous 24 months. Congress had always allowed for some assets to be excluded from consideration. These included a fixed amount of personal property, life insurance up to a certain face value, an automobile below a certain value, burial space, funds for burial, and a personal residence as long as it was the primary place of residence.[15]

The important change was the 24-month rule; this prompted much debate. The distinction between countable and excluded assets remained a part of Congressional changes in the Tax Equity and Fiscal Responsibility Act of 1982 (TEFRA '82). Restrictions became more imposing. Congress, for instance, allowed states to impose liens on the homes of institutionalized individuals as a means of eventually recovering Medicaid expenditures made on their behalf.[16] The statute allowed the home to be taken into consideration because:

> The amendment intends to assure that all of the resources available to an institutionalized individual, including equity in

a home, which are not needed for the spouse or dependent children, will be used to defray the costs of supporting the individual in the institution. In doing so, it seeks to balance the government's legitimate desire to recover its Medicaid costs against the individual's need to have the home available in the event discharge from the institution becomes feasible.[17]

By 1988, asset transfer was further affected by the Medicare Catastrophic Coverage Act of 1988 (MECCA '88).[18] This made the restrictions on transfers mandatory and it extended the transfer period from 24 months to 30 months.[19] Now, any transfer made within 30 months preceding application for eligibility would be considered as resources. Finally, it allowed assets owned by an applicant and his or her spouse to be totaled and divided equally between them for the purposes of determining resources. This was true even though the applicant may have owned all of the assets individually. Thus, transfers between spouses in this manner were allowed.

Spouses and transfers made to them will always be of concern. This was true in 1989, when Congress passed the Omnibus Budget Reconciliation Act of 1989 (OBRA '89),[20] modifying the provisions of MECCA '88 which had allowed an applicant to transfer assets to a spouse and then have the spouse transfer assets to a third party without the assets being considered as resources.[21]

By 1993, Congress passed the Omnibus Budget Reconciliation Act of 1993 (OBRA '93),[22] providing, among other things, for the expansion of the definition of assets,[23] and extended the look-back period for asset transfers to 36 months.[24] In addition, the new act exempted certain transfers of assets,[25] formulated new rules for the treatment of trusts,[26] increased the penalty for asset sheltering,[27] and expanded the right of the government to recover assets from a decedent's estate.[28] With OBRA '93, it appeared that Congress was getting tough with entry into Medicaid through spend-down. One elder law attorney, Armond Budish, admitted that ten loopholes in eligibility were closed with OBRA '93.[29]

Interpretations

When Congress enacted Medicaid, it did so because of a demonstrated need among the poor for long-term care. If the wealthy were able to afford this care through assets or insurance, fairness dictated that the nation and the states should provide similar services to those unable to pay for it because of poverty or disability. The motives were good; the motives still are good. Indeed, if it were not for the economic strains placed upon the nation and the states, there would be fewer calls for reform of a system that has merit, because it does provide needed long-term care for the elderly and disabled, but also because it responds to a belief among Americans that such long-term care is so catastrophically expensive that it should not be borne by any private citizen. This belief seems to override the ethical concern over "whether people with money should benefit from a medical program intended for the poor."[30]

When the 1980 Omnibus Budget Reduction Act was enacted and economic restraints began a reform of spend-down, Congress still sought to balance the "truly needy" and the "system abusers." But most of all, Congress sought to question the notion that government should pay for these services at all. Congress was really seeking to limit the role of government and exclude that which it could no longer afford, but had become a "given" in the American culture. This is the real issue, not whether the rules are just, or how a home or a savings account is considered for eligibility. There has been a shift in attitude whereby Congress and certainly the states are seeking to transfer responsibility for care and support to the private realm where, as far as Congress is concerned, there are more effective checks and balances. Undoubtedly, this is the reason for the sudden rediscovery of federalism.

This shift from public control to private enterprise is illustrated in opposition to President Clinton's health care reform. Polls and editorials were preoccupied with the notion that a health care system administered by a combination of federal and state bureaucracy could be both lethargic and expensive. Perhaps it is correct to say that this aspect of the President's plan, more than any other, brought a needed reform in America to a halt. Despite the admittance that excessive government is the culprit, nothing has been done for health care reform. Thus, nothing has been done as a complete response to Medicaid spend-down abuse. Both of these issues, health care and spend-down, are intertwined and each is part of a common public perception. Any reform of spend-down can only come about with a reform of health care in America. This is the point of the debate over federalism, cost containment, and the role of government.

Posturing for a better solution for long-term care or for health care in America will not find an adequate solution by creating more laws or enforcing existing regulations better. Rather, posturing will be most effective in its approach toward a combination of privatization and public supervision. A shared approach—perhaps through a combination of private insurance, perhaps a bit of employer-mandated payment, government subsidy, and Medicaid/Medicare—is the approach that seems most warranted.[31] As with health care costs in general, many argue that any "system should require individuals or households to visibly and directly bear the largest part of the cost."[32] Still, private involvement must be brought about through incentive: incentive to obtain insurance, incentive to contain cost and effectiveness, and incentive for private responsibility. Recent efforts on the part of Congress to provide tax incentives for long-term insurance coverage is a good start.

STATES' RESPONSES

After Congress enacted tougher regulations in 1993, all states were required to have some form of estate recovery system. Under such a system, the state places a lien on a recipient's home or other property, which is "cashed in" before the decedent's estate passes to his or her heirs. Most recovery systems, however, are not effective; some are. In fiscal year 1992/93, a total of $63 million from 26 states was recouped.[33]

California now recovers approximately $21 million yearly at a cost of $2.5 million using 35 employees and a mandatory estate recovery system.[34] Comparatively, Wisconsin recovered $3.3 million from 443 estates in fiscal year 1993, with a staff of one part-time and four full-time persons, and at a cost of only $162,400.[35] Massachusetts organized an effective program in 1992, which requires administrators of all probated estates to file the probate petition and the decedent's death certificate with the state Medicaid bureau.[36] Illinois passed legislation to slow the growth of Medicaid,[37] as did Tennessee.[38] Arizona was granted a demonstration waiver in 1982 and has since operated a federally assisted medical assistance program that was designed by the state.

States must meet basic federal guidelines, but in an effort to contain costs, some have sought to charter their own course. For example, some states are termed 209(b) states because they are allowed to utilize SSI standards that were in effect on January 1, 1972 to determine Medicaid eligibility.[39] Some states have their own set of rules concerning transfers of assets between joint owners.[40]

The Supreme Court of Oklahoma, in determining eligibility, recently held that when assets are transferred to an applicant from a trust that would be exempt in determining the applicant's eligibility, that applicant has received income in any case,[41] and the income must be counted. And Connecticut and Ohio have each explored the possibility of extending the look-back period, presently at 36 months under OBRA '93.[42]

Prior to OBRA '93, some states had established programs whereby persons who had purchased long-term care insurance would be granted asset protection and Medicaid benefits after their policy benefits had been exhausted.[43] After OBRA '93, such plans may be in jeopardy,[44] but for those states with existing programs, OBRA '93 provides an exception.[45] Indeed, in New York, long-term insurance has become popular, with the state requiring policies to provide for at least a $100-daily nursing home benefit with a three-year coverage period and a $50-a-day home care plan with a six-year coverage period. Furthermore, the plan must have an inflationary clause at 5 percent annually for premiums until the beneficiary reaches the age of 80. Additionally, all approved policies have a special stamp guaranteeing that it has been approved under the New York State Long-Term Security Program.[46] The insurance would save the state Medicaid money and allow the insured to keep his or her assets intact.[47] Such plans are certain to become prototypical. Some states, such as Connecticut, Indiana, and New York, allow estate recovery exceptions with the purchase of long-term care insurance.[48]

Some states have explored the possibility of revoking the licenses of attorneys who advise clients how to transfer assets to qualify for Medicaid,[49] implying fraud on the part of attorneys. These efforts are futile; the attorneys simply explain existing government programs in the same way that tax attorneys explain tax provisions.[50]

But what do all these reforms mean? And how do they fulfill the original purpose of Medicaid and Medicare to provide adequate health care to *all* those who need it but, honestly, cannot afford it? It is clear that the GOP proposal now hotly debated between the House and the Senate to "reform" the health care system has a bottom line of cutting costs—at all costs. So the proposal is not really a reform at all, but rather an overhaul, implemented by literally weeding out the dead (or dying) wood. Undeniably, the federal reorganization plan has as its sole purpose the cutting of costs. Unfortunately, no matter how delicately or politically palatable legislators explain it to their constituents, as most states become besieged with the tidal wave of costs for long-term care for the elderly and disabled, there are few options for cutting Medicaid costs: reducing services, raising taxes, and limiting the number of Medicaid participants.

Until now, cost cutting has been done federally through the continuing increases in look-back periods and greater restrictions on eligibility. Some states have approached the problem from the other end as well. For example, Pennsylvania has attempted to limit the growing nursing home Medicaid population by not reimbursing nursing home operators for depreciation or interest on any new nursing home construction for Medicaid recipients. The only result has been a shortage of over 10,000 beds in the Pittsburgh and Philadelphia areas alone.[51] Thus, new proposals are necessary as the state can no longer balance the increasing Medicaid population with the increasing costs of their care.

Clearly, however, reducing costs solely cannot be the solution. Were that the case, the ideal health care plan would likely be one in which all demographics, rich and poor, disabled and elderly, person with AIDS, and mothers of dependent children alike fend for themselves. The goal of reducing health care costs would be achieved, but there would also be the elimination of health care services, and only those who can afford to be healthy will remain so. Health care would be, in a sense, a survival of the financially fittest. Conceivably, the federal proposals to seal loopholes and equitably distribute funds through state administration is not far from this extreme.

No, merely reducing costs is not the priority. In posturing, the purpose of the American health care system is a comprehensive and affordable health care plan that covers *all* demographics in need. To date, the system has failed. New federal proposals suggest that cutting costs by cutting membership is the solution, but the numbers simply do not add up. For example, under the pending block grant proposals, the Senate plan holds annual increases to 5 percent; however, annual cost increases for Medicaid have averaged 10 percent.[52] In other words, the American people are aging and becoming needier faster than the federal government is reforming. As a result, states are beginning to scramble to position themselves in a way not just to cut costs—that has failed—but to cut costs and still promote the purpose of affordable and effective health care for those truly in need.

A constant reminder must be made that block grants simply shift cost and responsibility to the states; block grants are not secret treasure troves. If the states now have the responsibility to provide the same level of services as did the federal government, how will they find the dollars? Furthermore, the states will not have the ability to take from many and give to the few as did the federal government. A state with large numbers of retired persons will face catastrophic costs. What will the state do? What will the local communities within the state do?

Part of the problem is that the states have inherited a system that many think is inflated. Said one analyst at the Cato Institute in Washington, DC: "The current Medicaid system inflates costs. The Federal government has interfered with the states' ability to experiment."[53] Thus, the states must take on the inflated sense of public perception. This is an obstacle to the provision of what Supreme Court Justice Louis Brandeis described as "workshops of democracy which can conduct experiments with novel social and economic concepts without jeopardizing the security of the rest of the country."[54] Also, there is the obstacle created by multistate programs, inhibiting national business interests that thrive on uniformity among the states. Corporations such as IBM, UPS, DuPont, and Eastman Kodak wish to avoid the administrative nightmare of state experimentation, and they argue, any "ERISA amendments [allowing states to experiment] will enable the states to tax employer benefit plans which, in turn, will lead to higher state taxes and employee layoffs."[55]

For instance, at its inception in 1965, the Medicaid system established no standard rates for nursing homes. As a result, providers were shortchanged in Medicaid reimbursements compared to the minimum rates they received from the mandates of the Medicare system. Consequently, in 1968, language was added to the Medicaid statute to equate payment rates with the "reasonable charges" of the Medicare program.[56] Then, in 1972, the statute was amended to provide minimum standards for payments to providers, on a "reasonable cost-related basis."[57] Congress still found, however, that state flexibility was restricted and that the Medicare rates were ineffective. Thus, the 1972 amendment was replaced in 1980 with the Boren Amendment, which determined state rate-setting in accordance with the standard of care for efficient and effective nursing facilities.[58] In this way, states could develop their own payment methods for long-term care service providers, yet still remain regulated.

This continued regulation was manifested through the Health Care Financing Administration (HCFA), which reviewed state methodologies for rate-setting. Conflict arising from this oversight led to a surge of litigation and resulted in specific procedural and substantive requirements for rate-setting.[59] Much of the litigation regarded the states' attempts to base rate changes on budgetary considerations.[60] These challenges to state plans by hospitals and nursing facilities were authorized by the Supreme Court in *Wilder v. Virginia Hospital Association*, in 1990.[61] Since then, states have been restricted to the requirements of the Boren Amendment in setting Medicaid payment rates.

Regulation of actual service provisions were enacted through the OBRA '87 and OBRA '90 amendments. OBRA '87 required nursing home facilities to meet minimum standards, which included minimum standards for staff requirements, assessments, care plans, and social service requirements. Additionally, states would have to submit amended plans to accommodate the increased rates resulting from the new OBRA '87 mandates. Thus, federal mandates took control of state budgets. Mandated disclosure to the public of data and methodologies for payment schedules also placed the states under greater federal regulation.

Surely, since its inception as a state-run program, Medicaid has gradually and increasingly become "federalized." The federalization of the Medicaid program began in 1972, when the federal government implemented regulation of state payment rates. The Boren Amendment attempted to give control of rate-setting back to the states. Afterward, the federal government enacted the Omnibus Budget Reconciliation Act of 1987 and 1990, which implemented operation requirements for nursing homes. Finally, states began to implement tax and donation programs to increase their own Medicaid contributions, thereby increasing the funds matched by the federal government.[62] By increasing its share of the Medicaid expenditures, which are federally matched by the federal government, each state would have increased funds to meet the growing demands of the elderly population in the Medicaid system. This was done by obtaining donations from health care providers, which would borrow money from private financiers, who would then be paid back with the increased federally matched funds. The same procedure was utilized using provider-specific taxes, which were then reimbursed with the added federal outlays. Thus, the struggle between the federal oversight of the Health Care Financing Committee and the state efforts to maintain flexibility and to increase federal funds, which OBRA '90 attempted to protect, resulted in more litigation and more federalization. The HCFA finally established regulations that authorized federal deduction of certain state monies obtained by provider-specific donations and taxes. The regulations also restricted the states' use of provider contributions until September 1995. These counterresponses have added to the federalization of the Medicaid system.

FURTHER FEDERAL AND STATE POSTURING

Most families are financially discouraged by the tax code from saving personal assets for future long-term care. It just seems too far in the future. For some families, this is not even an option if family savings have already been depleted by caring for elderly parents. For those able to save for future medical expenses, government policies are sporadic at best. For example, the House Republican's American Dream Restoration Act purports to assist in this effort by proposing a return of the IRA (Individual Retirement Account), which enables families to make an annual investment of $2,000 in a tax-free savings account. These savings could then be withdrawn without penalty for limited purposes such as the purchase of a new home, education, or medical necessity. Such an incentive for individuals to plan ahead would alleviate the tidal wave of need for Medicare and Medicaid, providing an option otherwise not available when confronting prohibitive costs of long-term care. Additional tax credits for families who choose to care for elderly parents in their own home add incentive for individuals to lighten the collective burden on Medicaid.

Another example of long-term care planning by the government is President Clinton's Social Security benefit tax. Senior citizens with incomes as low as $34,000 had to account for 85 percent of their earnings.[63] The earnings test for seniors between the age of 65 and 69 required one-third of every dollar earned over $11,160 by working senior citizens to be taxed.[64] The policy provides an incentive to stop working. This conflicts with the fact that many more American elderly are living longer, healthier, more active, and more productive lives and wish to contribute to the marketplace. The Department of Labor reports that of the 31 million Americans who are over age 65, nearly 3.68 million, or 12 percent, are still working.[65] Another 153,000 are actively seeking employment.[66] The Senior Citizens Fairness Act proposes to repeal Clinton's benefits tax by raising the earnings test in 1996 to $15,000 and to $30,000 by the year 2000.[67] The Act also proposes to offer additional tax incentives to younger Americans to purchase long-term insurance for their future medical needs.

The Green Book by the Committee on Ways and Means of the U.S. House of Representatives illustrates that, during 1992, state Medicaid programs spent over $21 billion providing nursing home care for nearly 1.6 million persons.[68] This compares with that spent in 1975, which was a little over $6 billion. In 1981, under $6 billion was spent, and in 1990, over $8 billion.[69] Under current law, total federal Medicaid expenditures are projected to reach $105.8 billion in fiscal year 1997, an 11 percent increase over the $94.9 billion projected for fiscal year 1996.[70] By the year 2002, the number of Medicaid patients is expected to increase by 25 percent.[71] Stark new proposals by the House and Senate Budget Committees propose to reduce the growing rate to about 4 percent by that time. Forty percent of the savings would be accredited to just six states—New York, California, Texas, Florida, North Carolina, and Ohio—and would not occur until the last two years of the seven-year reformation.[72]

Both President Clinton and the Republican majority in Congress have sponsored legislation recommending reduction in the cost of Medicare and Medicaid. Terms such as *block grants* to the states offer models of cost-cutting, in part, because they would end the open-ended entitlements that Medicare and Medicaid enjoy at present. Block grants are popular among lawmakers. Reports in April 1995 revealed that 57 percent of lawmakers favored a block-grant shift in welfare responsibility to the states.[73] Only 38 percent favor federal administration of welfare and block-grant proposals. The reason seems quite simple: the states would then have to make the hard decisions as to cost containment.

Block-grant posturing for Medicaid cost reductions has been inspired by the reduction plans recently implemented for the AFDC program (Aid to Families with Dependent Children). This program adopted entitlement restrictions in an effort to cut welfare spending. While many legislators are eager to implement similar caps for Medicaid expenditures in an effort to buttress welfare reform, the block-grant reformation may prove inapplicable to the Medicaid program;[74] states are ill-equipped to take on such a fiscal burden, especially one so poorly managed by the federal government.[75] And remember, when seeking to reduce any expenditures for a program favoring the elderly, politicians are confronted by a huge voting constituency.

Medicaid expenditures are needed for nearly 25 million poor women and children, and this may prompt suggestions of block grants. But, Medicaid expenditures are also needed for nine million elderly and disabled persons, who have consistently absorbed approximately 66 percent of all Medicaid resources since 1970.[76] These figures represent the national average. In some states, such as Pennsylvania, the percentages are even higher and more significant under a block-grant system.[77] Despite that the poor women and children may experience some success in terms of welfare reform and diminishing membership, the elderly group has grown in recent years, both in number and in need,[78] and will continue to grow at an alarming rate.[79]

This growing burden on the states seems almost unmanageable, even if Medicaid funding were stabilized. Mere stabilization is simply not enough to keep up with the exponential growth of the elderly population and the costs associated with their continued and long term care. It is estimated that block-grant distribution will result in the loss of 318,000 elderly, 448,000 disabled, and 2.1 million children as Medicaid members. Low-income, low-Medicaid benefit states, such as North Carolina, West Virginia, Florida, Montana, Texas, and Oregon, will lose the most members. What will happen to these people? What about the legion of others rising to take their places? And what is to prevent them from moving to another state to qualify there, or to spend-down in such a fashion as to requalify? Medicaid cuts through utilization of block grants continue to play a leading role in the various proposals for federal reform, but the rationale is faulty. It rests upon only one premise: the need to cut costs.

So too with Medicare. Congress recently pledged a $182 billion reduction in Medicare by block-granting available funds over the next seven years.[80] A reduction in spending does not manifest a reduction in need, however. Consequently, if implemented, the states will be forced to shift the resulting cost difference, which has a domino effect. First, in order to cover the cost difference, eligibility will be further restricted.[81] These restrictions will leave some four million otherwise eligible and needy recipients without health insurance. Thus, this loss will be shifted to the private sector and will target geographical locations where need is already at its highest level. Additionally, the reduction will be shouldered by existing Medicare providers, who will be forced to depreciate services to make up for the added costs. Many providers will opt not to do so and will withdraw as Medicare service providers altogether, thereby increasing the burden on those who remain in the program. But the buck does not stop there. It continues to work its way through the state. Once the reduction costs saturate the beneficiaries and service providers, it will reach other state-funded programs, focusing first on taxes.

Unfortunately, states may not necessarily assume as much control over the block-grant distribution as many legislators would have their constituents believe. The added control may allow the states to manipulate managed-care service costs, but service costs for long term care are already escalating. Therefore, block-grant reformation offers little opportunity for control in states with a disproportionately high percentage of elderly and disabled.

Pennsylvania, for example, spends 78 percent of its Medical Assistance (Medicaid) on long-term community and nursing home care for the disabled and the elderly.[82] This leaves little else for other needy groups, like the poor, who, once identified as ineligible in one state, will merely migrate to another state where funds might be more readily available. Thus, as the intrastate debate over how to distribute a limited amount of block-grant funds begins, inter-state debate will escalate as migrating groups of elderly and the poor search for the state that is willing and able to pay for the services they need. Any migration that occurs, of course, only adds to the existing problem of already limited resources as needy groups begin to grow in each state. The result is that each state will be forced to expend the necessary funds to cover the costs not covered by the limited block grant.

Supplemental funds will be obtained from one of two sources: increased state taxes or funds allocated from other state services. Thus, block grants may actually reduce service benefits as individual states resist becoming "welfare magnets" to the transient poor.[83] Another alternative, of course, is to decrease the growing need for long-term care by providing incentive for families to provide their own in-home services for family members in need, such as those with Alzheimer's or the mentally retarded. So too, local state and federal authorities could encourage, through education and tax incentives, insurance plans by which people may prepare to pay for long-term care.

Therefore, block-grant implementation, while somewhat successful in the AFDC program, offers only a divestment of federal responsibility for long-term care of the elderly and disabled and a cost shift within the hierarchy of state programs. Regardless of the reformation structure, however, need will continue to grow, eligible recipients will be withdrawn, and those remaining will suffer a reduction of adequate services. In this light, the ends hardly justify the means as legislators wash clean the federal budget while the dust settles on the states.

An additional state concern associated with implementing block grants in the Medicaid program is the disproportionate distribution of funds in relation to state needs.[84] States such as Rhode Island oppose implementing block grants because it entails a lack of distributional standards.[85] Presently, disproportionate federal spending on Medicaid is baffling. For example, Connecticut, which houses 0.7 percent of America's poor population, receives 1.4 percent of federal Medicaid funds. Yet Florida must service 6.4 percent of America's poor with only 3.7 percent of federal Medicaid resources. Virginia, like Florida, is disproportionately funded, while neighboring Maryland and the District of Columbia receive more than an equal share, in comparison.[86] And where there is smoke, there is fire: with disproportionate funding comes disproportionate spending. For example, New York spends $4,852 per year on each of its recipient poor, while Utah spends only $953.[87] The bottom line in support through federal entitlement is that the entitlement formula is designed to offer incentives to poorer states to spend more on health care; thus, they are awarded a higher percentage, per dollar, of contributed federal funds.[88]

On the other hand, supporters of a move away from an entitlement structure toward block-grant reform visualize the greater flexibility afforded to the states under a blocked capping structure. Ideally, greater state flexibility will result in controlled spending, as the federal government will no longer be responsible for furnishing services to all eligible recipients and each state will no longer be restricted in its appropriate distribution of funds to its respective needs. However, interstate disparities fuel intrastate distributional fires. States maintaining a greater percentage of poor demand a larger slice of the $17 billion budget, but so do the higher tax states, as well as the states with higher population growths, and more disabled who require special services. Block grants carry a host of concerns.

Chapter 3

Posturing for Medicaid's Human Needs:
The Practical Effects

SPEND-DOWN

By now it is plain to see that one of the ways in which spend-down may be brought about is by massive medical expenditures on medical care which will categorize a person as poor enough to qualify for Medicaid. This is certainly the more anticipated definition of spend-down. The individual state's definition of what qualifies as poor will be important, as well as accurate receipts for both present and past medical expenditures. Few would question the motives of persons arriving at impoverishment in this fashion, but many of those who are wealthy enough to hire competent elderlaw attorneys or advisors would scorn such an approach to Medicaid.

It is the second method, voluntary spend-down through transfers without consideration—usually to children and at their suggestion—that state and federal statutes seek to prohibit. Of course, this is the method most often employed by the wealthy seeking Medicaid assistance. Ignoring gift taxes associated with transfers to anyone over a specified amount and without full consideration, persons willingly transfer assets to relatives in order to qualify for payments that can far exceed $4,000 a month for as long as they live. This is a method of human posturing that compounds a Medicaid program designed for the truly poor.

To qualify for spend-down, persons must initiate a Medicaid estate plan, often with the aid of an attorney specializing in this area of elderlaw, but it could just as easily happen with a manual, seminar video, or advice from a friend.[1] Books describing the procedure are available even in such places as the local pharmacy.[2] With the increasing numbers of older persons, videos, seminars, and word-of-mouth suffice as opportunities of involvement in spend-down. Beneath it all is a human need to survive with as little financial damage as possible. In her book *How to Care for Aging Parents*, Virginia Morris describes the moral and money dilemma of spend-down for family members:

> For some people, protecting assets and then going on Medicaid raises troubling moral questions. Medicaid and other public programs certainly are not intended to protect anyone's inheritance or extra spending money; they are meant for those who are truly needy. What your parent saves, taxpayers pay.
>
> Your family has to be guided by its own moral and political code on this matter. Some people argue that whatever money an older person has should be spent on making his last years as comfortable as possible—it should not be protected for his children—and that receiving public assistance is demeaning. Others believe that using public monies when personal funds are available is criminal.
>
> A third group contends that taxpayers who believed they were sufficiently covered by Medicare and were not offered adequate long-term care insurance (because until recently, it didn't exist) are justified in protecting whatever assets they can. Affluent people set up trusts to protect their estates from taxes, so why shouldn't people with smaller estates protect themselves from nursing home bills?[3]

Elderlaw Attorneys and Seminar Training for the Wealthy

What exactly do you do when you are told that you will require extensive care for what could be a very long time? For instance, what if you were told that you have Alzheimer's disease, kidney disease, or any of the other debilitating illnesses that demand attention and long-term support? Certainly there is the option of home health care, and many persons have availed themselves of this option.[4] Present law permits states to provide home care to functionally disabled Medicaid beneficiaries aged 65 or over.[5] Also, Medicaid provides home health services to those entitled to nursing home care.[6] Many of the services are capped to limit total expenditures but, if available, regulations would allow a person facing long-term care to remain at home at a reduced cost to Medicaid.

Whatever your options, it is likely that you would be prompted by children, family, or friends to inquire about planning to shelter assets and shift the burden of cost to government programs. "You have an option," they would tell you. "You get the same care whether you pay for it from your hard-earned money, or the government pays for it and you keep your money for your kids. Now, which option shall it be?" In presenting the option, the attorney recommending any Medicaid estate plan would be concerned about your income and resources. After OBRA '93, the attorney would be more concerned about the term "assets," as it is more inclusive.[7] Nonetheless, the old rules concerning income and resources are an important base. From here, you and the attorney or planner would have to work out a plan by which you could transfer assets to others, hopefully at a reduced gift-tax rate, and then deliberately impoverish yourself so as to qualify for Medicaid assistance. Hopefully, you will then live long enough to utilize Medicaid, but even if you do not, by transferring assets intervivos, you have at least avoided the estate taxes that would have been levied upon your estate upon the date of your death if assets had still been there.

Whether you are a married person or single, the rules differ, but in considering resource limitations, the following list is illustrative of what it would take to become Medicaid eligible.[8] To be eligible, an individual may have no more than $4,000 in nonexempt resources. The following resources are exempt:

- a principal residence
- household goods and personal effects up to $2,000 in value
- a car valued up to $4,500 or any car if needed to commute to work, receive medical care, or for use by a handicapped person
- an engagement ring or a wedding ring
- equity up to $6,000 in property essential to the individual's support
- cash-surrender value of life insurance up to $1,500
- term life insurance with no cash-surrender value
- burial plots for the immediate family

- burial costs up to $1,500 per person
- court-ordered support payments for dependents

For a married couple, the strategy would be to transfer ownership of the house to a community spouse and convert nonexempt assets to exempt ones.[9] The rules are more lax and the limits more generous with married couples because the states and the federal government want to avoid unpalatable actions. For instance, the couple could purchase a home with nonexempt assets, pay off the existing mortgage, or make repairs or improvements. It is also necessary to change beneficiary designations and enhance the community spouse's resources to the maximum.

If an individual wanting to shelter assets in order to qualify for Medicaid seeks to transfer assets to a person other than a spouse, assets can be transferred to a family member. There are separate restrictions, but the transfer must be made more than 36 months before Medicaid benefits are applied for, and if the individual is already in a nursing home or about to go into one, sufficient assets can be retained to last the 36 months, the balance can be transferred, and then the person can apply for Medicaid at the end of the 36 months.[10]

Other consequences will result from any transfers or assets. For instance, gift tax will be imposed if the gift exceeds the amount of the donor's available unified credit; the transferred assets will lose the step-up in basis available to assets held until the donor's death; liability for income tax on the transferred assets will shift to the donee; and the donee's creditors may be able to access transferred assets.[11] There is also the possibility that the creditors would place the transferor into involuntary bankruptcy and trigger fraudulent conveyance rules.

Income

Federal regulations require that "income and resources are considered available both when actually available and when the applicant or recipient has a legal interest in a liquidated sum and has the legal ability to make that sum available for support and maintenance."[12] Of course, the issue is how much income is sufficient to qualify for eligibility and how can the sources of that income be spent-down so as to qualify. The easiest way to spend-down is to pay off unreimbursed health care costs.

A spouse's income is not considered if the Medicaid applicant is institutionalized and the spouse is residing in the community. The law seems to favor what is palatable in light of the circumstances of each couple. This equitable factor is also present in the deductions allowed from an applicant's income before being considered for Medicaid. Allowances include the following: (1) a personal-needs allowance, (2) a monthly maintenance-needs allowance for the community spouse, (3) a dependent family member allowance, (4) medical or remedial care costs for the community spouse, and (5) at the state's option, a home allowance deductible for a six-month period.[13]

Resources

The federal regulations provide for both excluded assets and counted assets. Those which are counted constitute the resources that will determine eligibility—stocks, bonds, money, etc. The excluded assets are similar to homestead items or amounts excluded from probate in estate administration, that is, property which has a uniquely personal nature or should be present in case the person recovers from the long-term illness. Such items would include the following: a reasonable amount of personal property, life insurance up to a certain face value, an automobile less than a certain value, burial space and money for burial, and one's own home if it remains the primary place of residence.[14]

The point is to identify income and resources and the rules that affect them. Then, there is the process of planning for Medicaid spend-down. There is an incentive to transfer these assets so as to be eligible for public assistance through Medicaid. How does the system work?

Present Qualifications for Medicaid Spend-Down

The qualifications for Medicaid spend-down have been recited previously, but examples from estate planners within Pennsylvania, New Jersey, and New York would be illustrative. Also, an attorney in Cleveland, Ohio, Armond Budish, has published both *Avoiding the Medicaid Trap* and most recently, *The All-New Avoiding the Medicaid Trap*. Because each state may devise its own rules within the federal guidelines, the ability to qualify for spend-down will vary among the states, but each will have a common approach that reduces the chance of error and encountering claims against the estate in the future.

Surely the method by which a person qualifies for Medicaid spend-down will work in tandem with health care in that state. Taken together, they will form elements in a plan of incremental planning. The point is to be able to identify the increments and how they will work together to allow for spend-down. Since the states are not likely to implement a broad range of health care reforms, Medicaid reformation will likely continue to be incremental.[15]

ISSUES OF INCREMENTAL PLANNING

OBRA and Look-Back Periods of the Past and Present

There has been a steady increase in the number of months which Medicaid can use to "look back" and identify income or resources. Remember that there will be a point in the past beyond which the government will not look to include assets that may have been transferred without consideration. How long is that period? From where does Medicaid identify income or resources? From past income tax returns? From interrogatories? Does the state simply wait until the death of the decedent and look to the probate record?

Furthermore, what do the comments say in the legislation as to why these months have been increasing? Is it because people are living longer and thus Medicaid is having to provide support for a longer period of time, or is it because Congress is simply being more realistic about the efforts of middle-class persons to take advantage of medicaid estate planning? How have the look-back periods affected the incentives for using Medicaid?

The point still remains that with a look-back period it is possible to have assets at one point in time toward which the state will not look when determining if you are poor, that is, whether you qualify for Medicaid funds. Issues such as illusory transfer, fraud, or hiding assets have only recently been introduced and their effect is not yet known. Thus, the OBRA monthly calculations still form a major factor in the utilization of Medicaid spend-down.

Assets: Availability

Transfers for Less Than Market Value

Transfers of property—however that is defined—are affected most by the changes in the look-back period. The most recent act, the Omnibus Budget Reconciliation Act of 1993 (OBRA '93),[16] requires a 36-month look-back period among its other changes.[17] The changes brought about because of the Act have been characterized as sweeping.[18] Some transfers of assets were exempted,[19] assets became the rule and not income and resources,[20] and it became more difficult to become eligible for Medicaid through transfer of income or resources. Commentators suggest that the proposed changes all came about because of the declining assets in Medicaid funding and resources.

Under the new rules, transfer of assets for less than fair market value could result in a period of Medicaid ineligibility.[21] The definition of assets also became more inclusive so as to include jointly held property.[22] Then, of course, there has been the extension of the time period in which look-back is permitted. It still is not clear as to the effect of these rule changes regarding assets transfers. Is the addition of a name to an account as a joint asset an asset transfer? Such an account would still be included within the probate estate. Will tracing of the source of the assets become important? And will there be differences between community property states and common-law jurisdiction?[23] Who will police the transfers, and for how long?

Intent seems to play a part; there are also specific exemptions due in part to what is "politically palatable." The present statutes provide exemption for assets transfer if it can be shown that the transfer was made without the purpose of seeking Medicaid eligibility.[24] For instance, if the transfer was made for beneficial tax consequences, it is exempt.[25] Because of its unique character, a personal residence has exempt status.[26] The home will not constitute a transfer of an asset if made to (1) a spouse;[27] (2) a child of the applicant who is blind, disabled, or under 21 years of age; (3) a child who has resided therein for at least the two years prior to the applicant's institutionalization and who provided care for the applicant; or (4) a sibling with an equity interest who had resided therein for at least one year prior to the applicant's institutionalization.

So too, a spouse has a unique status under the transfer rules.[28] This is due in part to the law that originated in MECCA '88, allowing an applicant to transfer assets to his or her spouse without affecting the applicant's Medicaid eligibility. It seems that a transfer to a spouse would also be able to take advantage of the "undue hardship" exemption allowed by the statute.[29] The spousal rules form a significant part of what is politically palatable.

Self-Owned Property

Regarding asset transfer, self-owned property seems the easiest to characterize: there is no existent trust which obscures title; it is not held jointly, in common, tenants by the entirety, or with right of survivorship with any other persons. Clearly, unless made to an exempt person, or there is "undue hardship," this is the asset that is most likely to become the subject of scrutiny when there is an asset transferred without adequate consideration. In considering this asset for Medicaid eligibility, tax transfer consequences and valuation seem to be the operative incentives.

Jointly Held Property

The distinctive element here seems to be the state statutes and how they have been interpreted in the past and how they will be interpreted after OBRA '93. Who owns a jointly held asset? Clearly, the purpose of Congress is to prohibit the avoidance of transfer rules through the establishment of joint accounts and reducing or eliminating the asset's worth through a transfer for less than fair market value. In other words, if transfer of a self-owned asset without fair consideration is void, then so should asset transfers through jointly held mechanisms be void. Perhaps the answer is tracing; elderlaw planners could borrow from income tax rules. Nonetheless, jointly held assets shall continue to be elusive.

Trusts

Trust transfers became more difficult after COBRA '85[30] and the demise of the Medicaid Qualifying Trust device by which an individual could, other than through a Last Will and Testament, transfer assets to a trust for the purpose of qualifying for Medicaid. COBRA '85 repealed the shelter device of the trust and allowed for any maximum amount available to be distributed to the applicant to be considered income or as a resource available for Medicaid eligibility. The point is that a trust created from an applicant's assets will be assessed as part of the resources of the applicant for purposes of determining his or her eligibility.[31] This is unfortunate for those planners who sought to shelter self-owned assets within the legal confines of a trust device.

The trust is still an effective tool for disposition of property in an effort to qualify for Medicaid;[32] it is just that the Medicaid trust must fulfill specific contractual requirements. For instance, it must be irrevocable and unalterable, neither the settlor nor his or her spouse may be the trustee, and the principal must be inaccessible to the settlor (and his or her spouse).[33] By retitling assets to the trust, the settlor retains a right to the income produced by the trust, which will be used to pay the nursing home costs. The trust res may be distributed upon death to remaindermen designated by the instrument. As with transfers to other individuals, transfers into a Medicaid trust will hold the settlor ineligible for Medicaid coverage for 36 months. After 36 months, however, Medicaid will cover the difference between the interest produced by the trust and the costs of the nursing home. Because the settlor does not have access to the principal, however, it remains protected.[34]

> The upshot of all this is twofold: For the first time, we have nationally established ground rules. It is no longer up to the states to decide whether or not they want to review transfers of assets; the rules will be the same, by and large, for all states. The second point is that the Congress seems to be no longer concerned about people in the community who are receiving Medicaid and who transfer their assets between spouses or outside parties, prior to nursing home care. The focus is solely on spouses already institutionalized and the problem of the

impoverished community-dwelling spouse who faces paying for that care.

As an indirect result of all that, if people can stay in the community as long as possible on home care, they can preserve their assets. Obviously home care becomes even more desirable under this—if home care services can be found.[35]

Despite its obvious benefits, "clients may be unwilling to transfer a major portion of their assets into a trust that is not merely irrevocable but whose trustee has no discretion to reach principal no matter how dire the grantor's need may be."[36] For some Alzheimer victims, however, it seems important that they can utilize policies that have home health care provisions so that they are able to afford the costs of in-home care, thereby avoiding institutionalization for as long as possible. Such concerns prompt a review of the different kinds of trusts.

Revocable. OBRA '93 goes further than COBRA '85 and distinguishes between revocable and irrevocable trusts.[37] Obviously, the corpus of a revocable trust shall be considered an asset of the person applying for Medicaid eligibility[38] because the Medicaid applicant has total incident of ownership over the corpus property. Note that this is different from only having control over the trust income. Thus, any payments made from the trust shall be considered income to the applicant.[39] While income is not subject to the 36-month look-back period, it is considered a qualifying element for SSI and private pension payments in determining an applicant's eligibility for Medicaid under a different route.[40]

If income from the trust is transferred to a third party, rather than the applicant, the look-back period for this type of trust is 60 months, rather than 36.[41] Of course the 60-month period may be avoided by the applicant accepting the money and then transferring it to the third party, thus becoming a transferred asset and qualifying under the 36-month period. This all results in the revocable trust being treated as if it were an asset, both in principal and in income.

Because an irrevocable trust is similar to a complete gift of corpus, the only concern is with the possibility of any portion of the corpus or income derived from the corpus becoming available to the Medicaid applicant. Whatever the amount, it is treated as if it were an available asset.[42] Any payments made from the trust that would benefit the applicant are treated as if they were income from that trust.[43] Should the applicant make additional payments into the irrevocable trust, then these payment shall be considered as transfer of assets[44] even though the look-back period is only 36 months rather than the 60 associated with trusts that are revocable.[45]

There are some inconsistencies associated with irrevocable and revocable trusts.[46] They probably result from the rush to tighten requirements and provide greater fiscal restraint. It is certain that more stringent requirements which are more consistent shall follow.

Trigger or Convertible. In an effort to circumvent the Medicaid Qualifying Trusts restrictions, practitioners commonly use a trigger trust by incorporating language that terminates both the trustee's discretion to make distributions to the applicant and the applicant's ability to revoke the trust whenever the applicant is accepted into the nursing home for extended care. If the trustee cannot make payment to the nursing home, or the patient cannot revoke the authority of the trustee, then the asset is no longer available to the Medicaid applicant. Thus, nursing home entry triggers withholding of income and principal of the trust. This is just one of the many devices invented by elderlaw practitioners seeking a way to shelter assets so as to qualify for Medicaid eligibility and yet retain control over distribution for as long as possible.[47]

Because trigger trusts seek to circumvent the purpose of Medicaid legislation, efforts are made to characterize them as void for public-policy reasons.[48] Nonetheless, they were still only part of a response to a growing percentage of Americans needing long-term care who hoped to manage or hold onto their property long enough to qualify for public money to pay for their care. The equation always comes down to the same question: How can you have your cake and eat it too?

Supplemental Needs. These trusts, like others, are used to circumvent the Medicaid eligibility rules by allowing assets to be placed in a trust by the settlor or by another with the stated purpose being that the trust should pay only supplemental needs, or nonessential support.[49] This eliminates medical necessity and thus provides for Medicaid eligibility. Of course, the Omnibus Budget Reconciliation Act of 1993 sought to eliminate these practices,[50] and as a result, litigation over the effects of such trusts has increased.[51]

The effectiveness of special needs trusts will depend on whether the trust assets are "available assets" in calculating the beneficiary's resources. Much of the litigation concerns whether the trust is a "support trust," in which case the trust assets are considered as available resources, or "discretionary trusts," in which case the assets are not deemed as available. Some states have attempted to alter this approach. In 1988, in the case of *Bohac v. Graham*,[52] the court determined that a particular special needs trust was a support trust, thereby reversing the lower court, which determined it to be a discretionary trust. In an effort to avoid discrepancies regarding the identification of trusts, the North Dakota Department of Human Services redefined its regulations to include both support and discretionary trusts as including available resources. Consequently, special needs trusts became effectively obsolete as a means of qualifying for Medicaid. The state had successfully created a more restrictive methodology for Medicaid eligibility.

It was not until 1994, in *Hecker v. Stark County Social Serv. Bd.*,[53] that the Supreme Court of North Dakota reexamined the regulation and held that the state was without statutory authority to create such a methodology and held the regulation unenforceable. In *Hecker*, a mother established a special needs trust for her 54-year-old disabled son. The language of the trust provided that the trustee could pay or apply for the beneficiary's special needs as determined to be necessary or advisable according to his needs. The Department of Human Services, in reliance on the equalizing regulation, determined this to be a support trust and therefore an available resource. The District Court agreed. The Supreme Court, however, reversed the decision, holding that the regulation was void and the assets were not available as a resource for purposes of Medicaid eligibility. In effect, the Supreme Court of North Carolina gave new life to the special needs trust. Now, America must await the next set of sweeping editions to OBRA to see if Congress will moot the issue with a national rule.

Some supplemental needs trusts are exempt under the current rules, perhaps because these trusts were supposed to supplement Medicaid coverage.[54] Thus, a trust for a disabled person under

65 years of age created by a parent, grandparent, legal guardian, or a court[55] is exempt from the definition of asset in determining eligibility. OBRA '93 does not use the term "supplemental needs trust," but the legislation endorses the use of such arrangements for the care of disabled persons under the age of 65.[56] This generosity comes with the price of requiring the trust to specifically provide that upon the death of the disabled person, the remainder of the trust shall be used to reimburse the state to the extent of Medicaid expenditures on his or her behalf.[57]

In *Coye v. Hope*,[58] the decedent executed a revocable inter vivos trust in 1976. Between 1987 and 1992, the decedent received almost $300,000 in Medicaid benefits from the state. Upon her death, the Department of Human Services attempted to reclaim the cost of her nursing home care from her estate. The Trial Court and the California Court of Appeals affirmed the Department's petition. The crux of the legal issue, once again, was the disparity in definitions between the federal and state statutes. In this case, the term "estate," was not federally defined. In resorting to the state statute, the definition of "estate" would be narrowly defined as "probate estate," thereby necessitating that the court find the woman's trust to be valid and enforceable. The court, however, rejected such a narrow interpretation and broadly interpreted the term "estate" so as to fulfill the purpose of the federal law that "assets are used for the cost of the care rather than given away."

The posturing of the courts for interpretive license of federal statutes regarding Medicaid eligibility, such as that clearly evidenced in North Dakota and California, leaves one unresolved question: If or when control over eligibility and administration of benefits and services is passed to the states, who will take interpretive license? Will it be the state courts? The service providers? The insurance companies? The federal judiciary or government? While there is no clear answer with so much active posturing taking place presently, one thing is certain: Interpretive license will be achieved by political clout.

Income-Only Trusts. If the applicant were to receive income only from a trust, the corpus of which had been contributed by the applicant, the transfer of the corpus asset would be treated as if it were a transfer of assets; and depending if the trust were revocable or irrevocable, it would come under the applicable look-back period. If the trust corpus were contributed by a settlor other than the beneficiary, the asset would not be available to the applicant but the income would. The issue that would arise concerns the amount of income available to the applicant. May this income be used to determine Medicaid eligibility?

As with supplemental income trusts, there are certain types of exempt income trusts.[59] Each of these exempt income trusts involves restrictions. For example, (1) trust income or corpus paid to the applicant will be considered income of the applicant, (2) corpus will be considered as available to the extent it may be distributed to the applicant, (3) the transfer penalties and look-back period will apply for any amounts that could be paid to the applicant but instead are paid to another person, and (4) to the extent that the corpus cannot be distributed to the applicant, it will be considered unavailable.[60] The point is that the more an asset or income is unavailable—and for whatever period time—the better it is to qualify for eligibility.

The specific language used in establishing these trusts will effectuate how the trust is identified and interpreted in terms of Medicaid eligibility. The purpose underlying the trust will be revealed by the specific language used. Consequently, the qualifying nature of the transfer will effectuate whether the income after the determined date is available for eligibility considerations. For example, take the case of Louis Rosenberg.

On November 10, 1972, Louis Rosenberg executed a will, which contained a testamentary trust, wherein he distributed $65,000 to the trustee, directing that the trustee pay income from this to his wife, Mary Rosenberg. Louis also gave the trustee discretion to distribute the principal of the trust for his wife's medical and surgical expenses and other "unusual" needs. Louis died on January 2, 1976, and was survived by Mary, two sons, and two grandchildren. After one son died, Louis' second son, John, was left as sole trustee.

On February 27, 1992, John filed for MA benefits (in Pennsylvania, Medicaid is referred to as MA, Medical Assistance), at which time the trust left by Louis contained a principal of $55,000. Mary was denied MA benefits because her available income exceeded the eligibility limit of $2,400. Mary appealed, but before her appeal could be resolved, she died. Her appeal was subsequently denied and John appealed the decision for Mary's estate, claiming that the trust principal was not an "available resource." John asserted that the settlor intended the trustee to have the discretion to preserve the principal of the trust for his surviving issue rather than to dissipate it for the benefit of the Department of Public Welfare. Accordingly, he claimed, Mary's estate should receive Mary's MA benefits to which she was entitled. The Commonwealth Court of Pennsylvania determined that Mary's eligibility depended on whether Louis intended the trust principal to be used as a resource.[61] It further determined that because Louis indicated that the trust principal *could* be used for Mary's medical bills and Louis did not specify an intention that she rely on public assistance for her health care before relying on the trust principal (Mary was not already receiving other public assistance benefits), then the trust income was "available" as a resource for calculating medical assistance eligibility. Thus, while John's interpretation of Louis' intention was feasible, it was not specifically expressed, and the trust failed as a successful asset transfer for purposes of Medicaid eligibility.

Another type of exempt income trust is a result of *Miller v. Ibarra*,[62] a decision that establishes "income gap" rules. Persons with income over the amount allowed for Medicaid eligibility may nonetheless qualify by proving they have reduced their assets on medical costs.[63] The court case established Medicaid eligibility for four mentally incompetent nursing home patients. Each person had a trust provision which provided that:

> In no event shall such amounts paid or applied each month from Beneficiary's basic living need, from her income, the corpus of this trust, or any other source combined therewith, exceed the sum computed by subtracting twenty dollars ($20.00) from the monthly income eligibility standard currently in use by the Medicaid program.[64]

To be an exempt-income-only trust, the problem of availability must be overcome. The trust must consist solely of pension, SSI, or other income of the individual.[65]

Medical Qualifying. When referred to in conjunction with trusts, medically qualifying parallels that which is found as one of the classifications for Medicaid entitlement under the statute. Here however, it allows individuals in "income gap" states to spend-down their assets on medical costs and still qualify for Medicaid assistance even though their income is still above that which is allowed.[66] Thus, even though income is high, assets were so reduced so as to allow for qualification. It is like a trade-off entitlement.

Some states, however, have taken affirmative legislative action to restrict this method. Arkansas, for example, has a "Medicaid qualifying trust" statute, which,[67] in 1995, was disputed in *Thomas v. Arkansas Dept. of Social Services*.[68] In *Thomas*, the plaintiff was injured at work and settled a claim with his employer's worker's compensation carrier. The settlement established a "special needs" trust corpus of $270,000, with the employer as settlor and the bank as trustee. The State Department of Social Service asserted that this was the type of trust prohibited by the Medicaid qualifying trust statute. Thomas claimed that the trust was not included within the statute because he was not the settlor. The court, however, determined that the employer was an agent of Thomas as settlor; therefore, the statute was applicable to include the asset as an available resource. Now, OBRA '93 specifically exempts assets of a disabled person under age 65. Upon the beneficiary's death, the remaining assets are recovered by the state up to the cost of benefits received.[69]

A restrictive interpretation of who is the settlor of a trust was the key issue in *In re Estate of Hickey*,[70] wherein a trust was established for John Hickey, who was born in 1977. The trust was established with the funds received from a medical malpractice claim involving his birth. The doctor's insurer was named as the settlor of the trust. The trust was disapproved by the probate court in 1992, however, and the decision was affirmed on appeal. The court held that the boy, John, created the trust himself by exchanging his damage claim against the doctor for the settlement, thereby furnishing the consideration for the trust. Again, the courts took interpretive license to qualify eligibility requirements for public benefits.

Undue Hardship. An exemption for rules accompanying availability of assets or asset transfer results if there is undue hardship.[71] The Secretary of the Department of Health and Human Services shall establish the criteria for determining whether the application of existing criteria would result in hardship for the applicant.[72]

Penalties for Not Qualifying. There are a number of penalties associated with Medicaid eligibility rules not the least of which is fraud or perjury. However, the manner in which eligibility is determined can serve as a penalty for improper transfer. For instance, if eligibility is counted from the date of the transfer,[73] a means of penalty for improper transfer would be to uncap the durational period; that is, remove the 36-month period in OBRA '93 and have no durational rule.[74] This is what OBRA '93 actually did and it also provided that all states are to utilize the "stacking" method[75] whereby all transfers made within the look-back period must be aggregated for the purpose of calculating the penalty period.[76] This penalty will apply to Medicaid eligibility for any long-term care, not just to nursing homes.[77] Additional penalties would include estate recovery programs,[78] Medicaid fraud offices, and criminal as opposed to civil perjury.

Surely the future will be ripe with increased penalties and more open-ended recovery periods. Nonetheless, if such policies are not policed by the elderlaw attorneys and planners and even the people themselves, it is doubtful that the states will be able to provide effective enforcement. This much is certain, federalism, block grants, and the end to open-ended entitlement provided by the federal government will result in greater efforts by the states to prevent fraud or to restrict the programs so that fraud is impossible.

Spouses: Special Considerations

As pertaining to Medicaid eligibility under medically needy or categorically need classifications, the historical role of the spouse is significant. The rules that Congress has established regarding transfer, expending, divesting, or conversion of income or resources—or more recently assets—defer to spouses. Spouses form a politically sensitive group. This is especially true when women form a majority of persons defined as spouses in these Medicaid eligibility cases.

MECCA '88 had established comprehensive rules through which an applicant could transfer resources to his or her spouse.[79] The point was to prevent spousal impoverishment and allow for the spouse to maintain a separate existence in spite of illness. The problem for Medicaid enforcement however, was that MECCA '88 was broad enough to allow an "applicant" to "launder" transfers through a spouse. Hence, the Omnibus Budget Reconciliation Act of 1989 ensued.[80] OBRA '89 prohibited a spouse from transferring assets once received from the Medicaid applicant. Thus, the spouse could still forego impoverishment, but could not launder assets received.

Even though OBRA '93 closed many of the subtle ways of achieving Medicaid eligibility, it retained asset transfers involving a spouse.[81] Any transfers to or from the applicant's spouse are not considered transfers without fair consideration as long as they are for the full benefit of the spouse alone.[82] There is every reason to think that hardship rules promulgated by the Secretary of Health and Human Services would benefit the spouse as well.[83] Thus, spousal rules and the policy considerations concerning them form a vast resource when seeking to qualify for Medicaid eligibility.

Lessons for Asset Transfer

After 1993, Medicaid eligibility rules apply to any inter vivos transfer, either by outright gift or trust, involving (1) the applicant, (2) the applicant's spouse, (3) any person, including a court or administrative body with the legal authority to act on behalf of the applicant, or (4) a person, again including a court or administrative body, acting at the direction or request of the applicant or spouse. These rules apply irrespective of the purpose behind the gift or the trust, the trustees discretion over the principal or the income, any restrictions over distributions, and any restrictions on the use of such distributions.[84]

The lessons learned regarding (1) resources, (2) income, or (3) partial return of transferred assets, must come from practitioners, legislators, and editorials as to their success or present inability to establish fairness in the distribution of long-term care resources among those entitled under the congressional and state auspices to receive them.

Initial thoughts are that while the process of eligibility has become more restrictive and requirement oriented, persons able to afford expert advice, presumably those persons who would never be medically needy, will continue to have the advice necessary to become categorically needy. Also, as a practical matter, even though the state regulations, prompted in part by more stringent federal standards, have become more precise and more restrictive, they will have little effect if there is no one available to police or enforce the regulations. Since most enforcement comes from the vast army of social workers working within the institutions providing Medicaid, these social workers would likely be the enforcers. Inspections by the state would tally violations. Such enforcement is thus in the hands of laypersons, untrained in the lexicon of legal terms and interpretations rapidly being adopted. Discrepancies will result.

Such a discrepancy is evidenced by the various litigation involving different types of trusts. Confusion or uncertainty among the regulations allows for long-term care from public resources that might not otherwise be available. Creative lawyers can provide the loopholes by which the otherwise ineligible may qualify for public funds. In *Young v. Dep't of Public Welfare*,[85] procedural tactics meant the difference in the qualification of a discretionary trust as an unavailable resource. There, a trust was established for Janis Kokoska, which the Massachusetts Department of Public Welfare determined to be an available resource for purposes of Medicaid qualification. The trustee consequently sought declaratory relief from the Probate and Family Court, wherein the trustee requested an interpretation of the trust that would restrict the payments from the trust to supplements to Medicaid benefits. The court interpreted the trust as requested, and the Supreme Court of Massachusetts affirmed. Throughout this process, however, an administrative appeal of the Department's denial of benefits had been confirmed in favor of the Department. Thus, the trust, which was administratively disqualified, was validated by the court.

The most significant possibility for long-term care at Medicaid's expense is of course the 36-month period. For those simply aware of a long-term illness—and medical technology seems able to prolong life in ever-lengthening fashion—early transfer of assets to another provides complete fulfillment of the Medicaid eligibility regulations in just three years. For the middle class, the gift tax exclusion will eliminate any gift tax and the long-term expenditure can be limited to only those funds expended during the first 36 months of the illness.

Taken in abstract, Medicaid eligibility is like a game of chess. Yet, when the process becomes personalized, the legal gradations and exceptions awaken the ethical concern of those participating. Thus, perhaps the best lesson to be learned from asset transfer is that a cooperative stance among the person, private insurance, and government programs is the best recourse. It seems that the most recent rules and regulations are all posturing in this direction.

Chapter 4

Disincentives for Medicaid Spend-Down

ESTATE RECOVERY PROGRAMS

Definition

In an effort to monitor expenditures, states have long held the power to recover assets from the estates of persons who have received Medicaid funding but who have estate assets upon death.[1] Liens could be imposed and foreclosure could result after vacancy by the spouse, disabled child, or a sibling with an equity interest in the property.[2] Nonetheless, enforcement procedure was weak and less than half of the states even bothered to maintain an estate recovery program.[3] Also very few of the collection efforts were successful.[4]

Such programs were modeled on those enabling creditors to secure assets when property was held "as a matter of convenience" by a third party. Some states even have allowed augmented estates to provide election devices for spouses when the estate assets are held jointly with another and the third party seeks to deprive the spouse of his or her rightful share. As with estate recovery programs, the bulk of enforcement comes from the self-policing of the participants during life.

Present Practice

As Congress did with child support enforcement regulations, states had to meet certain requirements before the federal government would continue to provide payments. States are now required to recover the costs of Medicaid payments for nursing home or other long-term care from the estate of any recipient over the age of 55.[5] The point is that if the process of probate, to include both the intestate and testate, as well as will substitutes over which the Medicaid recipient had incidents of ownership, discovers funds in excess of Medicaid eligibility rules, then estate recovery is allowed.

It is noteworthy that estate recovery includes elements other than testate and intestate property. With so many assets held jointly or in trust so as to avoid probate, the additional inclusions of these assets is warranted if estate recovery is to have meaning,[6] yet in its effort to collect assets, Congress included long-term care insurance policies among the assets to be collected.[7] Persons receiving assets from these policies to offset the cost of long-term care would have them included in estate recovery and then Medicaid would be reimbursed.[8] If Medicaid recovery is great, it can act as a disincentive for seeking long-term care insurance. Such extreme measures are part of the dilemma of reduced funding and increasing participants.

Future Prospects

It is reasonable to assume that estate recovery programs will continue. California and Massachusetts have experienced success in recovery.[9]

OBRA: EXTENSION OF THE LOOK-BACK RULE

There has been a radical extension of the look-back rule from 1980, when Congress first sought to distinguish those who were needy from those who made themselves so just to achieve Medicaid eligibility. In 1980, when Congress passed the Omnibus Reconciliation Budget Act and required a 24-month period for look-back, it sent a signal. Now that same period has been extended to 36 months, as of 1993. A longer period shall certainly follow.

Yet, the elimination of the present 36-month period for what could be termed fraudulent transfers is very significant. Of course fraud will need to be proven and only significant amounts of property fraudulently transferred will be involved, but with OBRA '93 and the complicated method by which eligibility for fraudulent transfers will be counted, a clear line has been drawn in the sand. Such clarity will cause those with significant assets to seek to integrate personal, private, and government assets since the legal niceties will be unavailable.

ENFORCEMENT OF INDIGENT-PARENT SUPPORT LAWS

The moral and legal history of the duty of a child to support his or her parent(s) has its roots in the Hebrew scriptures.[10] The moral obligation of the child to support a parent was made a legal duty by the Roman common law.[11] There was no common law duty of a child to support a parent in England, but the duty was imposed by statute under the Elizabethan Poor Law.[12] This is the basis of many of the reciprocal support laws in the United States today.[13]

Any support law in the United States by which a child will have to support his or her parent must arise in the context of a statute that creates the duty, or a contract whereby the child guarantees the support in a civil sense for adequate consideration.[14] There is no common law duty of support.[15] The first statutes in the United States may be traced to the late nineteenth century and many states had reciprocal support statutes by the 1930s.

There are three statutory forms that require a child to support his or her parent: the criminal statutes, the reimbursement statutes, and the general duty-to-support statutes.[16] Indeed, many of the states have more than one type of "child obligation to support" statute in effect,[17] but the statutes are construed narrowly because they are in derogation of the common law.[18] Any defense of restriction on liability must be in the statute and only persons named are liable for support obligations; only those named are entitled to support.

The ability of the child to pay is the major obstacle in the statute,[19] and this hard-to-define ability causes confusion. The support itself is limited to necessities, defined as food, clothing, shelter, and, in a few states, medical care.[20] If a child is older, has been abandoned or abused by the parent, or has other conditions mitigating support obligations, the obligation to provide support is less.

If there are state statutes requiring support from children for indigent parents, why are these statutes not used to require private assistance rather than public funding? Why are the child support obligations not seen as assets subject to inclusion when eligibility is estimated under the Medicaid statutes? Perhaps one of the reasons is the fact that it may be too costly for the state to recover assets from the responsible relative.[21] Another reason may be that the states may be enforcing the duty so consistently that no cases are being contested and thus none are reported.[22] Then again, children may be supporting parents voluntarily; thus, the statutes are not needed. *The New York Times*, citing federal officials, reported that one in five families in America actually has an aging parent living in the home for whom care is given.[23] Indeed, 14 percent of those providing care to an elderly parent actually left a full-time job to do so.[24]

At present, the Health Care Financing Administration, an agency within the Department of Health and Human Services, allows states to require

> the adult children or other relative of adult Medicaid claimants to provide financial support for these claimants under state support statutes of general applicability. Such support can be counted for purposes of Medicaid eligibility and care only if it is required by the claimant. Medicaid's third-party liability and collection requirements do not apply to relatives under a state's support statute of general applicability.[25]

The initiative seems to lie with the states and the manner in which the states wish to respond to collection from adult children of persons applying for Medicaid eligibility.[26] Promulgation of additional state statutes, which would affect the common law rule of support from child to parent, would have an effect upon Medicaid support. It is part of the posturing for a solution to Medicaid funding.

Chapter 5

Posturing Alternatives: States As Laboratories

POLITICAL REALITY: CHANGE AND AMERICAN EXPECTATIONS

Clearly, as America's aging population continues to grow at an accelerating rate and as the baby boom generation reaches retirement eligibility, the ratio of working Americans to retired Americans will substantially decrease.[1] Consequently, more Americans will resort to federal entitlement programs, which will consist, mostly, of Medicare, Medicaid, Social Security, and federal employee retirement programs. These alone will monopolize all tax revenues collected by the government by the year 2030 if tax revenues continue at their present level.[2] Add to that the necessary payments for the interest on the growing $5 trillion national debt,[3] and in less than a decade, you have accounted for all federal revenues.[4] Is this the future?

Only 23 percent of all entitlement benefits, including Medicare and Medicaid, are provided based on need.[5] The other 77 percent, however, is distributed regardless of the recipient's income. In 1990, for example, almost $8 billion in Social Security benefits was paid to recipients with incomes over $100,000.[6] Comparatively, Medicare disbursed an average of $4,500 to 3.2 million families with incomes over $50,000.[7] Currently, more than $81 billion in entitlement benefits is provided to six million American families with incomes over $50,000.[8] These statistics are fraught with emotion, as persons on all sides of the issues are willing to debate with anger—if need be—the benefits and even morality of each expenditure. This was the case in the most recent federal election campaign.

A program such as Medicaid has survived too long to be changed easily. Exactly the form any change will take is the subject of posturing. Since far fewer Medicaid recipients vote than do those receiving Medicare, it is likely that future legislation will have more to do with reducing costs than maintaining benefits. In fact, 60 percent of the GOP proposal to achieve $983 billion in spending savings over the next seven years consists of changes and cuts in Medicare and Medicaid.[9] Certainly, the objective will be to reduce costs by reducing the number of beneficiaries.

Since its enactment in 1965, Medicaid has expanded to cover more and more people;[10] costs have escalated as well.[11] It is important to realize that the program's purpose—to furnish aid to families with dependent children, the aged, the blind, or the disabled who are being denied medical services because of lack of income or resources—remains concrete and valid. The program has always had problems. Certainly the discrepancies among the states as to benefits would be one of the reasons that California, with its inclusive regulations, attracted so many people. This is one of the issues of federalism, and it is not likely to be eliminated in the present political climate.[12] A person living in New Mexico would not have the same benefits as one living in another state.[13] "Historically there has been no pretense of uniformity in the treatment of similarly situated individuals across states in terms of eligibility as well as the type and level of benefits received."[14]

Another political problem with Medicaid is the fact that it is an open-ended entitlement program. Thus, it is difficult to estimate the costs,[15] and states have incentives to underestimate the projected Medicaid expenditures because this allows them to place more money into other state programs.[16] The federal government must reimburse the states for the actual expenses incurred, and there are very few penalties for low estimates.[17] Furthermore, the states, until recent legislation by the Clinton administration, could also obtain undeserved funds from the federal government through the disproportionate share program.[18]

The share programs allowed the states to accept large "donations" from hospitals with a large percentage of Medicaid patients and then, as those donations had become state funds, return the money to the hospitals as disproportionate share subsidies that would then be available for federal reimbursement.[19] Such implied fraud fuels the spend-down mentality of middle-class people.

It is estimated that 10 percent of total Medicaid expenditures is a result of fraud or abuse of the system.[20] Some of the fraud results from time constraints that make it difficult to examine each claim closely for abusive practice.[21] The lack of copayment, and thus higher levels of scrutiny, make the system vulnerable to fraud.[22] A recent national investigation of 130 hospitals revealed that more than $1 billion in experimental devices and equipment was fraudulently billed to Medicare over the past eight years by at least 21 major hospitals and research centers.[23] Nonetheless, the General Accounting Office has determined that sanctions against hospitals in noncompliance with Medicare participation conditions are often ignored or ineffective.[24]

Few could argue with the idea that a change in the provision of health care services in the United States would make a difference in the manner in which Medicaid money is spent. Health care and Medicaid go together. According to the United States General Accounting Office, "the United States is projected to spend 18 percent of its gross domestic product (GDP) on health care by the year 2000—far more than any other industrialized country."[25] The plan proposed by the Clinton administration after hearings throughout the country, provided for (1) a health security card for every American, (2) mandatory enrollment in an applicable health plan with required premiums, and (3) the ability to purchase additional coverage and services. The benefits package contained a minimum of 16 items and services that health plans must offer to eligible persons.[26]

The plan sparked wide debate, but there were unanswered questions, for instance, how would the services be rationed and what would be medically necessary? While health maintenance organizations are expanding rapidly in America—a growth rate of 13 percent since 1993[27]—many patients resent the limits that such organizations place upon them. Critics contend that there is no choice of providers once someone has chosen a plan because managed competition fails to preserve choice when it really matters most to someone who is ill.[28] There were other criticisms, and eventually health care reform drifted into oblivion. The effects of the lack of health care reform are very much a part of the Medicaid crisis and the posturing that will continue to address this issue. In fact, governors from 40 states gathered in Vermont to prepare for the congressional challenge of passing a social reform bill with bipartisan approval.[29] Their conclusion: states beware. While the numbers may differ between parties, the failure of the federal government to maintain control over the rising costs of care will put added pressure on the states. The pressure will materialize in the form of block grants to the states.

Just as the Clinton administration's Health Care Reform agenda of 1994 was cloaked in secrecy before its release to Congress, so too, the Republican proposal for the reorganization of Medicare is yet to be disclosed in detail.[30] With a fall 1995 deadline, Democrats and special interest groups had little time to mount a defense against the Republican proposals for the federal budget. Without the details, skeptics are hard pressed to see how $270 billion can be saved by 2002 without higher payments, less services, and fewer patrons. The skeptics always manage to delay when uninformed; delay can result in shutdown and the creation of even more proposals.

Republicans continue to insist that the system can fulfill its intended purpose of fiscal responsibility if Americans slow growth from the current rate of 10 percent to 6.4 percent.[31] Yet, changes in the Medicare and Medicaid systems are viewed by some to be "attacks on the elderly." President Clinton, on the thirtieth anniversary of Medicare's institution, stated that the Republican attempts to fix Medicare will "put elderly Americans in a fix."[32] Yet, something—anything—must change since maintaining the status quo is rapidly driving the systems to a grinding halt. The worst of all worlds could very well be that the same rhetoric gets passed back and forth with no substantive changes except the dwindling of funds.

It is interesting that six out of ten people surveyed said they favored a raise in monthly Medicare premiums for the elderly.[33] Roughly the same percentage encouraged HMO participation as a means of maintaining the Medicare system.[34] Some 58 percent opposed reduced payments to doctors if those reductions would result in less Medicare coverage and hospital closings.[35] Between the two options, House Republicans have relied more on the HMO participation, which they hope to be less controversial.

The Clinton administration's lack of receptiveness to the House Republican proposals in their "Contract with America"—the proposed changes of the first 100 days of Congress' new Republican majority—is indicative of this difference of perspective.[36] The Contract is a promise to balance the federal budget by the year 2002, and in it are drastic measures to revamp the Medicare and Medicaid systems, in conjunction with other federal cutbacks.[37] The problem is that federal funds are not growing as quickly as the American elderly population and its need for Medicare and Medicaid. There is also a need to provide national defense and deficit reduction. These are all conflicting interests. So, the only way to keep up with the need and keep the systems afloat is to create some common ground. That can only be achieved by increasing funds, i.e., taxes, or decreasing need, i.e., restricting membership. The question is, Which will work? Also which alternatives are the American people willing to accept?

On the one hand, there are ways in which federal funds can be better managed and put to good use in the Medicare and Medicaid programs, or to lower the national debt, which in turn frees federal tax dollars intended for Social Security or other entitlement programs. Far too few Americans, at least those who vote, do not recognize the integral connection between an individual's financing for long-term care and the government's spending on other failed or failing programs. For example, the AFDC program, which was as well-intentioned as any other federally created program, has become so corroded with regulations and abuse that it now causes more harm than good.[38] As special interest wells begin to run dry, it becomes clear that waste in one area must be redistributed for better use in other entitlement areas.

The political reality is that if any of the restructuring is to work, the programs must become understandable and manageable by human persons. Lisbeth B. Schorr, in her book *Within Our Reach: Breaking the Cycle of Disadvantage*, writes of the various programs administered by government agencies. She concludes that if a program is to be effective, "the biggest single need is for a far broader base of understanding among all Americans of what can be done, and what must be done."[39] If the states can better understand the programs and educate the population, greater utility could be achieved. The *New York Times* reported that activists for the poor say that on a wide range of social issues, states are much more responsive to their appeals than the federal government.[40] True, "a marvel of our pluralistic system in America is that everything can be tried, but the downside is that even when something works, it is very hard to make it work throughout the land."[41]

STATE PROGRAM INITIATIVES

General

States spend an average of 15 to 20 percent of their budgets on health care, which can consume up to 50 percent of new state revenues.[42] Consequently, states have much incentive not to await federal health care reform and instead, implement their own initiatives to try to reduce costs and provide universal care. However, Medicaid is the largest source of federal money for states.[43] In 1993, all but two state legislatures considered new proposals for health care reform.[44] While most legislative proposals address state-specific needs on a smaller scale, several states have implemented comprehensive reform and serve as a model of reform for other states. But just as with federal initiatives, state proposals are accompanied by controversy over who should pay and what should be paid for, as well as where the money will come from to pay for the care that is needed.

Federal law, particularly ERISA, has been a significant barrier to state flexibility in implementing new reform. ERISA preempts any state law involving a self-insured employee health plan and, therefore, bars the adoption of comprehensive reform.[45] Hawaii, for example, has been granted what is called a waiver from the prohibition on self-insured employer coverage mandates, but since 40 percent of employees are insured by self-insured employer plans, comprehensive reform is severely restricted.[46] After the Supreme Court's 1995 decision in *New York State Conference of Blue Cross/ Blue Shield Plans v. Travelers Insurance Company*,[47] the future is less certain as to what is the focus of ERISA and the preemption doctrine.[48] Nonetheless, ERISA, waivers, and federal involvement remain persistent partners.

Particularly since state Medicaid programs consume a large portion of state budgets, states have great interest in controlling Medicaid costs and access to the program for the uninsured. Federal Medicaid regulations, however, severely limit states' abilities to gain this control. Nevertheless, several states, e.g., Oregon and Tennessee, have taken advantage of federal waivers available under the Medicaid regulations and have initiated new and comprehensive reform.[49] Other waiver states, Arizona, Hawaii, Rhode Island, Kentucky, Florida and Ohio, and ten others presently waiting for waivers, are not so bold as Oregon and Tennessee. Reform is still restricted, however, whereas waivers are not exemptions, and states are still subject to federal discretion in obtaining them.

Medicare also has a restrictive role in terms of comprehensive health care reform. The Medicare program controls its own rates and pays for only 20 percent of all health care costs.[50] Thus, the outstanding cost of 80 percent of health care is shifted to other resources, which the individual states cannot control. Maryland, which sets its own Medicare rates, is the only exception to this rule.[51]

Despite these restrictions, every state has attempted to implement some type of reform to expand coverage and cut costs. Significant reform has taken place in the specific area of small business insurance.[52] Many states have focused on "guaranteed renewal" laws, which protect the continuation of coverage despite multiple claims or change of health status; "portability laws," protecting the continuation of coverage by limiting the exclusion period for preexisting conditions;[53] and "guaranteed availability laws," which mandate that insurers accept a minimum health plan for anyone who applies.[54] Many attempts have failed.[55] Expansion of indigent-care programs has been attempted in many states, including the subsidization of risk pools to insure otherwise uninsured individuals and expanding health care provisions for pregnant women and children.[56] Federal law recently accepted portability in the Health Insurance Portability and Accountability Act of 1996, thereby preventing insurance companies from denying coverage to Americans with preexisting conditions or because they lose their jobs.

Federal law also requires every state to provide payments to hospitals that service a disproportionate share of Medicaid or indigent patients.[57] Thus, state efforts to control access through legislative reform is available, but not often successful because of competing federal interests. Certainly the recently enacted federal Health Insurance Portability and Accountability Act of 1996 will further lessen the power of the states in health care, even as the federal government enhances state prerogatives through recently enacted welfare legislation.

In an effort to cut costs, most states utilize certificate of need requirements to control expanding services by health care facilities. Most states have begun a massive shift to managed-care programs to control Medicaid costs. Only a few states, however, have initiated comprehensive reform, the foremost of which are Hawaii,[58] Oregon,[59] Washington[60] and Tennessee.[61]

For example, Oregon implemented its own reform in 1991, which has created more controversy than any other state proposal. The plan proposed to prioritize a list of more than 650 services that would otherwise be covered by Medicaid and expand coverage to Oregon's 120,000 residents whose incomes fell below poverty level and who did not qualify for Medicaid. Ideally, the plan proposed that employers would then be subject to a play-or-pay option, wherein employers would be required either to pay what would otherwise be covered by Medicaid or to subsidize an insurance pool for alternative insurance,[62] but this aspect of the plan has been delayed. Because the plan denied some services to certain persons with specific disabilities, such as liver transplants for alcoholic cirrhosis or for extremely low-birth-weight babies, the Bush administration initially denied Oregon the Medicaid waiver necessary to implement its plan on the basis that the plan was subject to the requirements of the Americans with Disabilities Act. A subsequent and revised waiver request was granted by the Clinton administration in 1993, however, and the plan was approved through January 1, 1998.[63]

In 1993, Tennessee obtained authority to expand its Medicaid program to 500,000 uninsured residents by shifting to a regional managed-care system.[64] Kentucky has received a waiver to expand its Medicaid program, but has failed to secure sufficient funding for the expansion.[65] In 1982, Arizona received a federal waiver allowing it to operate its Medicaid program entirely under a managed-care system.[66]

Hawaii's 1974 Prepaid Health Care Act mandated employer coverage for 90 percent of the Hawaiian population, the cost of which was to be shared with employees.[67] Hawaii has since reduced its GDP expenditure to 8.1 percent, compared to the national average of 14 percent.[68] In 1991, Hawaii introduced the State Health Insurance Program of Hawaii (SHIP), which offered a basic health program of primary and preventive care that is state funded for persons with incomes below 300 percent of the poverty level.[69] In 1993, Hawaii received a federal waiver and created a purchasing pool from which Medicaid and SHIP participants could obtain services from bidding on other plans.

Massachusetts adopted a play-or-pay mandate in 1988.[70] Attempts to expand the Medicaid program and coverage for other uninsured groups were expected to result in universal coverage by 1992, but litigation involving ERISA has delayed a comprehensive reform package in Massachusetts.[71]

Florida has implemented the use of Community Health Purchasing Alliances in an effort to collaborate subsidies for the uninsured with a managed competition structure.[72] Minnesota has adopted a similar plan utilizing integrated service networks (ISNs) by offering standard yet competitive health packages.[73] The MinnesotaCare plan, which avoided ERISA restrictions, provides subsidized insurance for uninsured individuals with incomes 275 percent below poverty level.

Washington has effectively utilized a subsidized insurance plan—the basic Health Plan—for low-income residents.[74] Health care delivery by certified health plans was mandated in 1993.[75] It is hoped that by 1999, an employer mandate will become effective, requiring that all employees and their dependents be covered and that employers pay 50 percent of the cost of premiums.[76] All individuals will be required to be enrolled in a certified health plan by 1999.[77] Costs will be controlled by a phased-in premium cap.[78] Washington failed to obtain a federal waiver from ERISA in 1993, however, and the employer mandate is still an uncertainty.

Instead of opting for a managed competition system, as do most states, Maryland has opted to control costs and accessibility through regulating rates. Maryland insurers are required to offer standard insurance packages to employers with between 2 and 50 workers, and strict limits are enforced.[79] Provider rates are also regulated by considering specific factors based on the individual provider and the individual services rendered.[80] Every state is posturing.

Rather than wait for the federal government to "fix" long-term care regulations and Medicaid, states have begun to institute reforms of their own.[81] This practice results in part from the organization of Medicaid itself, a joint venture between the state and federal governments, but also because of the traditional role of the state in the protection of health and security. Surely, the most recent surge of federalism within the state judiciary and in the government fuels the individual efforts of states. Finally, the economic crisis at hand is always an impetus to seek less expensive and more effective means of providing health care and ensuring future election.

Between 1990 and 1993, 27 states utilized specialized task force commissions to develop unique health care initiatives in their respective jurisdictions.[82] While all states basically agree that universal health care coverage is ideally the ultimate goal, not all states—and not all state legislators—agree on how to finance or implement that goal. For example, New Hampshire gets $9,700 each year for each beneficiary while Mississippi gets only $2,381.[83] States with high growth rates, such as Florida, are demanding a different formula.[84] As with health care costs in technology, where spending in one area means cut backs in another, excessive grants to one state reduce grants to another. The Republican plan hopes to institute equalizing regulations to its block grant plan.

Health care reform packages address one of two problems, or some combination of both—(1) cutting costs, which entails administrative reforms, subsidization for the uninsured, and employer-mandate proposals for more comprehensive benefits; and (2) expanding access, which entails more effective and efficient delivery systems through affiliated services, and reorganization of insurance acquisition methods, such as group plans. However, there are drawbacks to each proposal and to each goal. Administrative reforms call for comprehensive overhauls; subsidization provides for few at the expense of many; employer mandates are confiscatory and difficult to administer, particularly for small businesses; collaboration of services is a reactive, not a proactive, activity; and insurance cooperatives only expand coverage for those who can afford it.

Despite these hurdles, however, state initiative is imperative. As evidenced in states such as Hawaii and Oregon, universal coverage is possible only through proposed action. Waiting for long-anticipated federal reform does nothing to provide greater access to coverage or increased savings in each of the states, and offers little to the collective information necessary to organize and initiate national reform. Nonetheless, looking at all the states and what each has been able to do with health care initiatives provides a synopsis of what works and what has failed. Utilizing the states in such a way recognizes the newly discovered federalism often seen as providing such localized results.

Specific

Alabama

In 1994, Alabama enacted Alabama Act 94-638, better known as Alabama's Willing Provider Law, which allows health care subscribers to assign benefits to the providers of their choice "even if that provider eschews membership in the plan's network."[85] The scope of the enforceability of the Act epitomizes the tug-of-war between managed-care providers and private providers who refuse to participate in the regulatory scheme of the managed-care system. Litigation has arisen involving Blue Cross, which is attempting to achieve exempt status from the Act, claiming that federal employee benefit statutes, like ERISA, preempt the state's Act and the requirement to pay benefits directly to a private provider.[86]

Many nonparticipating doctors feel the problem facing Alabama and the enforcement of Act 94-638 is typical of all states—insurance companies, e.g., Blue Cross, pay for the cheapest procedure available, for instance, the extraction of a tooth instead of a root canal. Many doctors, however, refuse to recommend or perform a procedure because it is cheaper if it is not necessarily the most appropriate. In the pending litigation involving Blue Cross, certain doctors opted out of the Blue Cross preferred provider system because of overregulation. Many subscribers, however, continued to patronize the doctors and, under the authority of Act 94-683, assigned the benefits to the nonparticipating providers. Blue Cross objected and, instead, paid the benefits directly to the subscriber, thereby generating litigation over the scope of the Act.

In its complaint, Blue Cross alleges that "[t]he Act will result in the erosion, and ultimately the collapse, of Blue Cross' provider networks . . . It fulfills no public interest but rather serves only the individual, private interests of health care providers . . . at the expense of cost-containment and health care reform."[87] The same argument was presented to the legislature before the bill passed, however, to no avail. Now, Blue Cross fears that if the Court determines the Act is not preempted by federal law, thousands of non-participating doctors will claim damages for lost revenues, which will all but tie Blue Cross to the courthouse steps.

Other Alabama initiatives are being implemented by small hospitals and service providers, who are pooling their resources through collaborative take-overs in an effort to posture themselves for the new wave of managed-care efficiency. "What's driving this is health-care reform—small players just can't survive."[88]

Alaska

Alaska was actively involved in health care posturing in 1994. Said one state worker representative: "states that pre-position themselves will have more flexibility in dealing with the federal plan. The feds will be more likely to grant exemptions when a state's health care plan is already in place."[89] With the added focus on welfare reform in 1995, however, Alaska welcomed a short reprieve and felt less pressured to initiate immediate health care reform. Instead, the legislature focused on limiting the growth of the uninsured populous as programs for the poor were eliminated through welfare reform.[90] Because doctors who treat Medicaid recipients are already reimbursed less than the cost of care, it was thought that every effort should be taken to limit further reductions for the poor.

Related legislation did reach the discussion table in Alaska in 1995. For instance, tort reform legislation, wherein limits on certain damages in medical malpractice lawsuits, and frivolous lawsuits, were proposed. Other proposals included House Joint Resolution 18, which encourages tax-free medical savings accounts; House Bill 214, which encourages computerization of medical records; House Bill 259, which requires hospitals to report discharge data to the state; and House Bill 266, which allows nonparticipating HMO providers to be used if they accept the HMO rate of service.[91] In 1994, Senate Bill 284 proposed to establish a single-payer system, which would monitor claims and costs, in an effort to establish universal coverage in the state.[92] Insurance companies oppose the single-payer system because it eliminates the large group-insurance providers in the market, which create higher administrative costs and premiums.

Overall, Alaska hopes to incrementally move to a single-payer health care system, which has an estimated projected savings for the state of $202 million per year.[93] State legislators do not anticipate such a system will be adopted under a Republican regime. While it waits, Alaska hopes to collect data on health care costs and create options on how those costs can be contained. Alaska has relied on private organizations and businesses to experiment with various managed, preventive, and homecare systems.[94] Privatization has proven successful in Alaska and on a national basis, limiting the growth of business health care costs to between 6 and 8 percent— about half of its expected increase in 1994.[95]

In Alaska, nearly 70 percent of private-sector employees obtain health insurance benefits through self-funding, wherein instead of paying premiums far above what the total cost of care, an employer accounts the money and pays the benefits as they arise.[96] If a stop-loss plan is utilized, which limits payments for each employee and for the aggregate, the employer can limit its risk but still guarantee coverage for all.[97] This is particularly true for smaller employers, where one catastrophic claim could absorb the entire fund. Additionally, self-funded plans are federally regulated and may be exempt from certain state regulations and taxes. Even if an employee leaves his or her employ, the individual still falls under the COBRA regulations regarding continued coverage for up to 18 months.[98] Another appealing advantage is that the plans can be organized to suit the needs of the individual employees, particularly where preventive services not otherwise covered in a normal plan will help avoid excessive costs in the future. These savings can then be used to provide other specific benefits. While privatization through self-funding may not be suitable for all states and all employers, Alaska's success and flexibility in this area is stirring national interest.

Arizona

Arizona has not operated a traditional Medicaid program since it was granted a demonstration waiver in 1982. Today, Arizona is at the forefront of pioneering successful health care reform. The federal government assists the state in implementing a system of its own design, and thus the state is exempt from such activities as having to cover all persons who are defined as "categorically needy."[99] Instead, the state has implemented a managed-care system that has successfully dissipated costs without compromising the quality of care.

The Arizona plan may not be an ideal standard for all states,[100] but the experience has demonstrated that expensive, sophisticated computer systems, necessary to effectively analyze cost and service data, are imperative to successfully deal with service providers. Also, the plan illustrates that reduced doctor fees, which are a primary target for savings, lead to low-quality care.[101] To sufficiently work through these obstacles and still implement a cost-effective plan takes time and money. With the onset of the new Republican plan to reduce federal spending on Medicare and Medicaid through reliance on managed-care programs, these obstacles will not be easily negotiated by the state. Thus, for states that are not already positioned for managed-care systems, the federal funds to experiment with new facilitation will not be as readily available; consequently, many— if not most—states are left with few options. Some available options are not recommended.

For example, one secondary result of fewer federal funds specifically allocated to health care, and a national reliance on managed-care systems, is that some unprepared states may be forced into, or may even be receptive to, dealing with prematurely facilitated managed-care providers. One health care analyst said that these unscrupulous providers are "people who yesterday couldn't spell HMO and today they are one."[102]

Nevertheless, despite a shaky and fraud-riddled start, in the long run, Arizona's move away from a fee-for-service agenda has proven effective through the access regulation of primary care physicians.[103] The plan—the Arizona Health Care Cost Containment System (AHCCCS) provides comprehensive care to roughly 450,000 participants.[104] Experts say that the ability to effectively service all of its beneficiaries comes from efficient use of the system. That is, resources are utilized in a prioritized manner to counter-balance the obstacles described in this text. States must "take money out of inappropriate use of the emergency rooms, take money out of inappropriate lengths of stay and inappropriate hospitalizations . . . and, for the system to work, you've got to take some of that money and plow it back into physician reimbursement."[105]

Any suggestion of placing priority or value on services will evoke harsh and divergent criticism. Much of that criticism is well-founded. Nonetheless, criticism may be the catalyst necessary to invite people to move from the current postured stance to more active participation in a solution. For instance, as doctors receive higher fees, they provide more quality care and more often opt to participate as service providers in the Medicaid program. This fact evokes criticism, but it is a fact perhaps inviting doctors to volunteer or to work for lower fees. Also, in regard to the elderly, Arizona has all but turned its back on the institutionalization of the elderly and has focused on at-home health care provisions.

Arizona's success may be greatly due to its preparation and its ability to adapt during the managed-care synthesis of the last decade, which is now assuredly going to increase with the onset of the new Republican agenda. Other states may not be as conveniently prepared to keep up with the health care posturing that will be necessary to save the system, particularly states that are home to Medicaid-participating nursing homes, which persistently compete for limited federal funds and now are even more scarcely divided.[106] Clearly, Arizona's success is built on a gradual implementation of a health care system of valuated services in a state that fortunately was prepared for the inevitable breakdown of the traditional system.

Arizona also has a self-insurance program for large employers, which is estimated to save up to $20 million for the state in 1995 alone, and a managed-care leasing system, which should save an estimated $290 million.[107] Both innovative plans cover as many as 45,000 employees, and both have been well-received in other states.

Arizona awaits other legislative proposals, such as using funds received from taxes on tobacco to pay for lung and heart-lung transplants.[108] Such innovative plans hope to save the lives of those over age 21 who do not otherwise qualify for such transplant benefits under AHCCCS. The Arizona legislature had already expanded AHCCCS benefits to include coverage for heart, liver, and bone-marrow transplants and has already saved three lives by raising $64 million on a $.40 per pack tax on tobacco.[109] At the time, lung and heart-lung transplants were considered experimental.[110] Pancreas transplants are still considered experimental and, therefore, remain omitted. It is estimated that the new tobacco tax legislation would allow for 16 lung and heart-lung transplants in the first year and would include approximately $1.7 million in coverage.[111] The legislature also hopes to waive the 90-day waiting period for the law to take effect.

Arkansas

In the face of a projected $42.9 million Medicaid shortage for the 1995/96 fiscal year, Arkansas, which houses the second highest percentage of people over age 65 (Florida has the highest),[117] has struggled to implement a capitated managed-care system, designed after Tennessee's TennCare system.[113] The difference from Tenn-Care would be that the Arkansas' plan would be limited to beneficiaries otherwise eligible for Medicaid, whereas TennCare caps costs and increases the number of beneficiaries. The tactic is to estimate a target cost for service and invite HMO providers to step in and provide the service. If they can do so under the target cost, they keep the difference, but if services exceed the target cost, the provider must suffer the loss.[114]

Arkansas has also adopted the trend of hospital alliance in an added effort to self-reform instead of waiting for federal government reform.[115] Aggressive acquisitions and mergers have increased service effectiveness while maintaining costs and increasing profits. Some hospitals cut costs by implementing a 38-hour work week.[116] Another proposal by Senator Nick Wilson (D) suggested raising the tax on soft-drink cans and bottles from $.02 to $.05.[117] It is estimated that the costs to the bottling companies would run close to

$39 million per year and would raise Medicaid collections from $35.5 million to $67 million.[118]

California

The cost of the Medicaid system in California, known as Medi-Cal, has quadrupled since 1985, reaching annual costs of $156 billion, $67 billion of which is provided through state taxes.[119] Without dramatic reform, these figures are expected to double in just seven years.[120] These skyrocketing figures are especially troublesome to California, which has a greater influx of poor immigrants than most states. Some say that block-granting the system will stabilize the increasing costs in California by providing more flexibility to the state under a more diverse managed-care system. California's small hospitals are particularly sensitive to the threat that as the number of uninsured increase, the surge of nonpaying patients will saturate hospital finances, which results in closings.[121] Consequently, as hospitals downsize due to the growing managed-care system, smaller hospitals are relying on private alliances to remain afloat.

In the broad, national debate of health care reform, California has focused its attention on HMO reform. California Governor Pete Wilson is expected to pass a recently proposed bill that improves governmental oversight over complaints filed against the growing health care maintenance organizations.[122] Complaints against HMOs have risen as states have sought to use them for the very important task of saying no to patients, costs, and hospitals. Other proposals, however, have been set aside.[123] This is not surprising, however, since San Diego claims the highest percentages of HMO participation in the nation—nearly 75 percent.[124] Less than 20 percent of San Diego residents participate in a traditional fee-for-service plan.

San Diego is a unique market with 59 percent of the city's population under age 35, which, along with the elderly population who are now shifting to managed-care systems because of less government Medicare distributions, is a lucrative market for HMO providers.[125] These rates of participation are said to be a glimpse of the future for health care participation in America. Experts who have experienced such high rates of participation have forewarned other cities and states that ambivalence about the effects of managed-care systems, particularly on those most in need of specialized services, will not be tolerated for long. Experts claim that because the system is designed to offer incentives to doctors to minimize treatment, those who cannot afford to purchase costly services with other resources are not served.[126] Consequently, in San Diego, more services are required by the uninsured, whose population is rising, particularly due to the great influx of Mexican immigrants, and medical costs have risen by 105 percent between 1984 and 1994. Nationally, the increase has averaged around 98 percent.[127]

San Diego is a microcosmic representative of the national trend in health maintenance organization developments. Mergers and alliances of smaller hospitals, clinics, and physicians have resulted in a HMO dynasty dominated by a handful of highly consolidated providers. The competition that has emerged in California thus far, has already driven premiums down by as much as 20 percent and satisfaction by participants as high as 62 percent.[128]

Despite a bright outlook for the managed-care system in California—at least in San Diego—there are roadblocks ahead as health care posturing takes its effect on other areas. Examples would be the medical technology field, which is slowly becoming subject to more restrictive HMO standards for cost-effectiveness, and hospital vacancies, caused by unanticipated shifts to managed-care systems by formerly nonparticipating patients. Also, as less expensive HMO premiums attract private patients, specialists with dwindling patient lists are forced to seek out jurisdictions less saturated by managed-care systems.

A study by the Health Access Foundation predicts that San Diego alone would lose $3.3 billion over the seven-year Republican reformation—$2.4 billion in Medicare and $928 million in Medi-Cal (Medicaid).[129] Los Angeles would suffer the greatest loss at $12.3 billion. The entire state will lose more than $44.1 billion, including $16.5 billion in Medi-Cal and $27.5 billion in Medicare. A combined $1.2 billion loss will be experienced in the first of seven years.[130] These cuts are expected to be absorbed most by the more prevalent acute care than long-term care, but much will depend on how much flexibility states obtain through block grants of federally provided funds.

Colorado

Colorado has experienced similar reform in the managed-care system, focusing on information-system upgrades, and this has resulted in a reduction of costs without reduction in quality of care and in increased revenues for highly consolidated providers.[131] The focus, however, has been away from in-patient, crisis-oriented care and more toward a continuum of coordinated care.[132]

In the past several years, Colorado has focused on tort reform as a means of responding to the health care crisis. State legislators most recently attempted to introduce House Bill 1255—a proposal to limit liability for health care providers treating noninsured patients.[133] The sponsor of the bill, Representative Phil Pankey, feels that the Medicaid crunch will have severe effects on free-care providers. Thus, the bill proposes to exempt from liability any provider who provides free care unless a negligent act is gross, willful, or wanton. By quelling the fear of litigation, it is hoped that nonprofit organizations and retired physicians who can no longer afford the high costs of malpractice insurance will provide services to the noninsured, thereby alleviating reliance on limited Medicare and Medicaid funds.[134] Others think that the threat of litigation is a deterrent to the provision of substandard care.

Another proposal expected to find its way to the election ballot in 1996 is a resolution to implement a Canadian-formatted, single-payer health care system—a proposal that only California has ever considered, but rejected.[135] If accepted, the tax-funded system would be implemented in 1998, and the costs of this system would be restricted to between 90 and 120 percent of 1996 costs under a traditional plan.[136] Implementation under a conservative, Republican regime is not likely, however, especially when opposed by the insurance industry.

Connecticut

Once it became clear that President Clinton's health care reform efforts had failed, Connecticut took matters into its own hands with its own effort at stabilizing costs. The state established a new State Office of Health Care Access, proposals for standard benefits, and school-based health centers. Subsidies for the uninsured became the focus of legislation.[137] Despite the federal failure that stimulated such initiatives, the managed-care system in Connecticut made steady advances in recent years, in great part due to a massive direct telemarketing approach to the HMO systems and collaborative service efforts by small groups of service providers.[138]

The leading HMO plan, Oxford Health Plans, Inc. took in revenues in 1994 between $650 and $680 million.[139] Until late in 1994, Connecticut was insufficiently lagging in the rush toward a managed-care system, but was leading the nation in health care costs; in 1991, residents spent $12.75 billion on health care.[140] As of May 1994, only 19 percent of the Connecticut population was enrolled in a managed-care plan.[141] The average hospital stay per 1,000 patients was 350 days—almost twice that of California's average.[142] Connecticut was faced with the reality that if hospital stays are cut in half, so too is the need for hospitals.

In an effort to thwart Medicaid spend-down planning by persons seeking to become voluntarily poor, Connecticut applied to the federal government for a waiver on the look-back period. The state wanted to extend the period to 60 months and apply a penalty cap for transfers.[143] The state also cooperates in planning assistance from the Robert Wood Johnson Foundation, which will rely on Medicaid eligibility for reinsurance after an individual's private long-term health care insurance benefits have been exhausted.[144] This is called dollar-for-dollar protection and allows a person with a policy limit of $100,000 to become eligible for Medicaid once he or she has spent-down assets to $100,000.[145]

Delaware

As with most states, when proposed federal health care legislation failed to materialize in 1994-1995, residents in Delaware focused on the state for individual initiatives to stimulate reform. The Delaware Health Care Commission wasted no time accepting that federal initiatives had failed and the future of health care rested on the shoulders of the states. Thus, it considered several alternatives in 1995, which included the implementation of a statewide managed-care system.[146]

The proposed program focuses on access for the indigent, which will reduce Medicaid expenditures for the state. Also, the state plans to assess the effectiveness of House Bill 331. The Bill implemented the certificate of need, which requires a public need for any health care expansion or addition.[147] The purpose of the initiative is to reduce costs spent on duplicating expensive medical equipment.[148] The state also focused on tort reform, data effectiveness for beneficiaries,[149] children's health, and the effect of insurance reform on small businesses.[150] With national health care concerns in mind, the state is developing its own method of cost-effective reform by implementing initiatives that benefit the specific needs of state residents.

District of Columbia

Approximately 25 percent of District of Columbia residents are uninsured. This number increases to 40 percent of all residents if those counted are uninsured or rely on Medicaid for health care services.[151] Since 1990, Medicaid expenditures have increased by 66 percent, totaling $668 million in 1993.[152] Legislation was proposed that would establish a $30 million trust fund, which would help pay the hospital bills of uninsured District residents.[153] The bill would "enable more low-income residents to participate in the Medicaid program, to compensate hospitals for the millions of dollars a year in free care they are providing to poor patients and to encourage doctors to work in medically underserved areas of the city."[154]

Funding for the trust would be derived from taxes paid by health insurance companies, licensing fees paid by all professionals, and other unidentified sources.[155] Other proposals in the District include a Multiple Employer Health Insurance Pool for employers with less than 100 employees. "By pooling the health care resources of Medicare's 31 million beneficiaries, and keeping the administrative cost at a minimum (only 2%), we could meet the need for long-term health care coverage."[156] Health Care Trust Funds are also suggested as a resource for paying the premium balances for low-income residents who buy into the Medicaid program according to their income level. Other suggestions range from "cutting the bloated military budget" to "rolling back the tax giveaways to the big corporations."[157]

The District of Columbia is, of course, at the heart of the national posturing that is occurring as a result of federal initiative proposals in Washington. Nevertheless, the District spends far more money on health care than most large cities, yet lags far behind in the percentage of residents who obtain adequate care.[158] The District received $1.3 billion in federal and local health care assistance; still, services remain scarce in many areas.[159] On average, the District spent $852 per resident in 1994; Boston averaged $335; New York $473; and San Francisco $743. These figures include average outlays on AIDS services, which is the nation's most populated area of need.[160] Such disproportionate figures are said to be due to the District's poor health care management and duplicative service provisions.[161] Also, the city's hospital employee-to-resident ratio is 91 per 10,000—larger than most, and has three times as many hospital beds as are needed.[162]

The problem for the District seems not to be a lack of funds, but rather the inefficient use of funds. To correct the situation, the District has attempted to separate the fiscal management aspect of health care from its actual delivery of services by increasing its hospital regulation.[163] The future does not look good.

With increased hospital regulation, the District has also focused on the effects associated with insurance reform, resulting in severe hospital staff cut-backs.[164] The problem from the outset is that insurance companies tend to shy away from those who are the highest risks—who happen to be those who are most in need of insurance—by either denying coverage or offering unaffordable premiums.[165] Hospitals in the District provide up to $200 million in unreimbursed services.[166] Insurance reform, therefore, attempts to force insurance companies to more equitably distribute the costs in a method of prioritization. Geographically, however, for cities such as Washington, DC premiums remain higher for inner-city residents, who are less likely to be able to afford the premiums and more likely to require expensive and more frequent services.[167] Thus, the District must concern itself with an even premium distribution within the insurance market to promote cost-effectiveness. To date, the one source of savings has been hospital layoffs due to the proliferation of managed-care insurance. Nationally, the reduction of hospital beds reached 10,000 in 1994.[168]

Medical Savings Accounts are another option being more closely considered in the District, created by the Archer-Jacobs Health Reform Bill to preserve individual choice.[169] Under this proposal, an insured individual or family would be able to deposit a certain amount of money into a medical savings account (MSA) from pretax dollars. This amount would go to meet the deductibility charge levied upon the insured before his or her insurance would commence. MSAs are forecast to be a more effective means of savings since they are controlled by those with the most incentive to use them efficiently. "Nobody spends somebody else's money as carefully as he spends his own."[170] They also provide the only hope to endow a fee-for-service system with some measure of counter-vailing accountability.

One company in Memphis, Tennessee, has cornered the commercial market on Medical savings accounts by marketing them to employers.[171] Darrell Burnett, Chief Administrative Officer of Medical Savings Corp., says that "the task of choosing health care would best be left to the recipient through an MSA."[172] Consumers who purchase the accounts pay a one-time fee of $400 for a primary physician and $1,000 for a specialist, and the consumer can choose which doctor he or she wants to visit.[173] Since 90 percent of medical expenditures per one million claims are under $2,000, participation is expected to be worthwhile. While the budget may be tighter, the company offers choice to the patient and flexibility to the physician—something HMOs do not offer.

Florida

The Governor of Florida, Lawton Chiles, has been waiting for Washington to conclude its debate of block grants and implement his reform for Florida in a special legislative session.[174] Chiles' proposal has already been rejected three times, so he is reconsidering the proposal to see if any Republicans will discover a new interest in his plan before placing the proposal before the legislature. The plan consists of a concerted effort for managed-care coverage by expanding poor working beneficiaries by nearly one million with government subsidized insurance.[175] Large business corporations are supportive of Chiles' plan, but Republicans are not.[176]

The federal government already awarded Florida a Medicaid waiver in 1993, wherein $1.6 million Medicaid patients may be transferred to a managed-care system while Florida retains the savings, which is estimated to equal $8 billion by 2000, and then passes the savings on to the working poor.[177] The problem, however, is that the reform needed to generate $8 billion in savings requires $6.3 billion in state capital, which the state does not have, and will not know if it will have until the Medicaid block-grant debate is concluded.[178] If the block-grant proposal is accepted, Florida will lose $4 billion in Medicaid funds over five years, which essentially obfuscates the effect of the 1993 waiver.[179] Combined with other state fiscal pressures, the outlook for Chiles' reform does not look promising.

Georgia

Georgia governor Zel Miller has prepared to maneuver the state into a position of reliance on block-grant reform.[180] Many feel that less expenditure-conscious states, especially those with growing populations—such as Georgia, which population is the eleventh largest in the nation[181] and expected to rise 7.9 percent per year—are setting themselves up for disaster. Estimates predict that Georgia could lose up to $6 billion in Medicaid funds over the next seven years.[182] Only Florida and West Virginia would lose more, per capita.[183]

In order to account for the gross losses, Georgia would have to cut 227,000 beneficiaries from its Medicaid participation by the year 2002.[184] For the past four years, the state's Medicaid enrollment has increased by as much as 17 percent per year.[185] State Republicans in support of the block-grant proposal say that the resulting reduction in health care cost will make up for the difference. Democrats respond, however, that "[t]his is easy fodder for political posturing and blaming the victim."[186]

It is anticipated that state block-granting will force Georgia to move Medicaid patients to health care management systems. Such maneuvers will only produce 25 percent of the savings required by the reform. Thus, the state is straddled with 75 percent of the bill. Legislative plans to reduce even fractions of the costs have been rejected by health lobbyists who hope to attack the problem from the perspective of less federal regulations.[187]

In terms of health care delivery reform, Georgia has taken advantage of technological advancements to regulate the delivery of prescription drugs.[188] A bill proposed by Senator Charles Walker (D-Augusta)—Senate Bill 309—proposes to update the generic substitution requirements for prescription drugs, which have not been reviewed since 1977 when the Drug Substitution Law was passed.

Regulation of the drug industry was subjected to judicial scrutiny when a group of independent pharmacies from 15 states filed suit against the larger drug manufacturers for various antitrust and patent violations.[189] The claim asserts that larger drug manufacturers are selling products to selected buyers at reduced prices, with which independent manufacturers cannot compete. The action will have tremendous repercussions for the health care industry: "The success or failure of these suits may well determine whether independent pharmacies in this country survive or die."[190] As a direct result of price fixing by large drug manufacturers, Georgia loses ten independent pharmacies per month, which compares with the national average.[191] The attorney for the group of independent pharmacies commented:

> This case represents real health care reform that the court can enforce. Drug manufacturers are destroying retail pharmacy and the brunt of the pricing scheme is falling on the poor, elderly and those who don't get pharmacy benefit insurance coverage.[192]

Hawaii

As long ago as 1974, Hawaii enacted one of the first comprehensive health care laws in the country.[193] The program is based upon an employer mandate that requires each employer to provide health insurance to its workers; employees must also pay premiums unless they are covered for comparable services by another provider.[194] The plan also incorporates successful Medicaid benefits and reduced spending, such that there are sufficient savings to universalize coverage for those that are unemployed, do not qualify for Medicaid, and cannot afford private insurance.[195] As an example of separation from the federal system, Hawaii had to obtain a waiver from the federal government under ERISA so that it could regulate employee health benefits on its own.[196] Hawaii has been the only state to be granted such a leave since its Prepaid Health Care Act was enacted prior to ERISA.[197] That part of the population not covered could still receive protection through a combination of state health insurance programs and Medicaid.[198]

But state efforts are often thwarted. It took nine years for Hawaii to receive the waiver, and when it was received, it applied only to Hawaii's plan as it was written in 1974.[199] This had the effect of freezing the state in time.[200] Furthermore, more current efforts to restructure the system have been stymied by various private and public interest groups.[201] Business leaders complain that the plan would "detract from the coverage already provided by multistage employers" and prevent employers from "providing a uniform compensation package nationwide."[202]

Although Hawaii has the highest rate of health insurance coverage of any state in the nation,[203] several categories of employees are not covered and there is no requirement that dependents be covered.[204] Also, while per capita health care costs are on a par with the rest of the nation,[205] insurance premiums are lower in Hawaii. In order to provide Hawaii with the flexibility it needs to respond to the shortfalls, additional waivers must be obtained from the federal government. This is not without opposition.[206]

Nevertheless, despite the consistent growth of health care costs, Hawaii, with its near universal coverage of its 1.2 million residents, is ranked near the top of the nation in its level of provisional health care and controlling costs.[207] In fact, it is predicted that by the year 2010, Hawaii's health care will overtake tourism as the state's primary industry.[208] In the struggle between a fee-for-service plan and a capitation plan,[209] "[t]he health care environment is changing very, very rapidly both here and on the Mainland. The economic forces have been too significant to ignore."[210] However, Hawaii has adapted to the benefits and pitfalls of both plans. "Without huge bureaucracies, Hawaii administers a system providing superior care to more than a million people and does it almost entirely through the private sector."[211] In addition to the success of its employer mandate over the past 20 years,[212] the state recently initiated the "HealthQuest" program, which was designed to close the "gap group" by combining services for the poor and the unemployed, for whom health care was not immediately available.[213]

Despite its unique approach to health care reform, Hawaii still suffers from fiscal restraints, that result in budget cuts which affect the health care system. A $20 million reduction in the Department of Health is causing Hawaii to join the national trend for consolidation of facilities and services.[214] Despite the reduction in funds and services, however, the restructuring is hoped to focus state administration of the health care system where it is most effective and shift many of the provisional functions into the community.[215] As a result, it is hoped that there will be more home and preventive services provided to the elderly and less reliance on medical care in the future.

Hawaii is also home to litigation involving federal preemption policies, such as those in other states.[216] Since 1993, the policy for Hawaii has been that a new employee must be covered by his or her employer's health insurance for "preexisting conditions" with no waiting period. Opposing the policy, Foodland Super Market, Ltd., has laid recent claim that the state has approved many health plans under the Prepaid Health Insurance Act of 1974, which excludes preexisting conditions.[217] Currently, Foodland's costs for employer health insurance per year is about $3 million. The inclusion of "preexisting condition" coverage would increase the costs by as much as 2 percent. Thus, the suit has consequences for employers as well as employees with health conditions who may be considering new jobs. Oddly, however, Hawaii is out of the norm on the low end of the scale in terms of the number of state-accepted plans that exclude preexisting conditions.[218]

Hawaii is also coming to grips with the effects of escalating health care costs by addressing, or at least acknowledging, the effects of cost shifting, especially as it relates to workers' compensation insurance. In response to the $152 million bill to cover uninsured Medicare and Medicaid service recipients, which costs were passed on through higher premiums, Richard E. Meiers, president and chief executive officer of Hawaii's Healthcare Association said: "Cost shifting is the thing running up health care [costs] in the state."[219] Proposed reforms to account for such losses, such as a

50 percent reduction in payments to providers, are often illogical because the cost-shifting effect is ignored.

Idaho

In 1993, one of Idaho's greatest concerns was the effect of proposed health care reform in Washington on job losses in the state.[220] The higher the costs of the benefits in employee plans, the greater the risk to Idaho's job rate, that is, because employers would have to pay higher costs for employee insurance, employers may well reduce the labor force to compensate. Such concerns exist in other states as well.

Health benefit plans consisting of employer mandates, like the Managed Competition Act of 1992; comprehensive insurance plans, such as those proposed by California Insurance commissioner John Garamend; Senate proposal 1227, introduced by Senator George Mitchell (D-Maine), which requires employers to participate in federally defined plans or pay a payroll tax; and managed competition plans, which require employers to pay for half of the benefits for full-time employees and higher payroll taxes for part-time employees, all affect the way employers change their business practices in order to accommodate the new plans. However, "[a] mandate does not make a struggling business able to afford insurance, it just increases the cost of having employees. If the national priority remains jobs, an employer mandate is not the way to go."[221] There are pros and cons to this assessment and only through comparing the costs associated with such plans can an accurate picture be established.

Illinois

Illinois legislation has been introduced by State Representative Carolyn Krause, which focuses on pooling small business resources to effectuate more affordable health insurance and greater portability for employees with preexisting conditions.[222] Under the current Illinois law, a preexisting condition is not covered under the insurance provided by a new employer for up to a year. Under Krause's bill, service at an old job can be carried over as time on the new job for purposes of coverage for preexisting conditions.[223] The Bill also broadens coverage for children's immunizations up to age six.[224] Major insurance providers applaud legislation that enhances portability since, nationally, millions of employees otherwise covered under employer group health plans are faced with "job lock" because of nonportability of insurance coverage.[225] In 1993, approximately 57 percent of workers at large companies participated in health policies that excluded preexisting medical conditions for some period of time.[226] Greater portability "level[s] the playing field so that one company doesn't end up with all the medically needy."[227]

United States Representative Bill Thomas, of California, introduced similar legislation at the federal level, which was said to be an "incremental approach that would break the gridlock on federal reform efforts to date. . . ."[228] Blue Cross/Blue Shield Association Vice President Mary Nell Lehnhars testified before the health subcommittee of the House Ways and Means Committee that:

> [the] bill supports the revolution in health care that is already well underway in the private sector and the states. . . . It preserves an appropriate role for the states in the regulation of insurance. And it avoids the pitfalls inherent in attempting to enact grand, comprehensive, federal solutions—the reef on which health care reform foundered last year.[229]

Within the private sector, some large employers have taken it upon themselves to discontinue restrictions on new coverage and have opened the doors to new employees with preexisting conditions.[230]

As with many other states, despite advances in one area of health care reform, Illinois is severely lacking in others. Restricted distribution of services due to lack of Medicaid coverage is one lacking area. The Medicaid program in Illinois does not cover services provided by ambulatory surgical treatment centers, of which there are 87 in the state.[231] As a result, patients in need are either treated for free, turned away, or referred to a hospital, where they will pay higher costs. The state's Medicare system, however, does pay for these services for the elderly.

Besides Illinois, Michigan is the only other state in the nation where the Medicaid system does not cover payments to such facilities.[232] As the move toward managed care increases, ambulatory surgical centers will increase, but lack of coverage by the Medicaid system could defeat the purpose of these centers. Lower costs and greater accessibility are the sticking points for Medicaid patients, few of which are accepted at the ambulatory centers; the few that are accepted are charity cases. Ironically, the costs to Medicaid for coverage of the same procedures at a hospital, which it does cover, are several times higher than if it were done at an out-patient center.[233] Studies in North Carolina and Florida revealed that out-patient procedures can costs up to half as much as similar in-patient procedures.[234] The hospital industry, however, opposes legislation directed at the competing facilities.

Illinois also faces bleak realities concerning Medicaid's coverage for the disabled and elderly. A study from the University of Chicago's Center for Urban Research and Policy Studies reveals that in the state's 1994/95 budget year, Medicaid expenses for the disabled and elderly reached $3.2 billion—nearly 66 percent of the state's $4.7 billion total Medicaid bill.[235] The study suggests that the state's proposal for a move to a managed-care plan, which awaits federal approval, focuses on welfare beneficiaries, who account for only one-third of Medicaid costs.[236] When calculated using the 5 to 15 percent savings realized by other states from the switch to managed care, the total savings for the Illinois Medicaid system is only about 2 percent. The authors of the study conclude that "reform of the health-care program must go further than a managed-care program for welfare families. . . . For the elderly. . . the most promising strategy for Illinois may be to join with other states in advocating a program of federal long-term care coverage."[237]

Indiana

Much of the focus in Indiana has been toward the advantages and disadvantages of medical savings accounts. While politicians hail the accounts as a great idea, many doctors are skeptical of their implementation and the transition to a new health care provision.[238] A major concern is that a significant number of uninsured persons who live below the poverty line will have no participation in the system. Nevertheless, many companies have initiated pilot projects wherein employees are afforded savings accounts and control over how the account is utilized. If the account is depleted, medical insurance becomes effective; if there is an excess of funds, the employee keeps the difference. Of course, many questions remain unanswered, such as whether the system will be mandatory and, if not, how are nonparticipants insured? The American Medical Association will not approve the system until these questions are answered.[239]

Medical Savings Accounts (MSAs) are advocated by many health care industry lobbyists, including small insurance companies such as Indiana's Golden Rule Insurance Co., which proposes that retirees should be permitted to opt out of the Medicare system for catastrophic insurance coupled with medical savings accounts.[240] Republicans have historically touted MSAs as an important factor in free-market reform and the idea has played an increasingly important role as one of several alternatives in the ongoing health care debate. Medicare's average per-patient cost is about $4,800; the combined federal outlay for a catastrophic policy and the MSA is presumably less. However, critics fear that the MSAs would be attractive to only healthy, younger retirees, which will raise the cost of insuring the more populated, unhealthy elderly class of retirees.[241]

Indiana has recently become more reticent of the importance concerning individual state initiatives in the area of health care reform. For instance:

> Last year, many employers were waiting on the outcome of health care reform. We got so caught up thinking in terms of legislative reform when all around us reform was taking place anyway.[242]

> The situation might be described as a race with the federal government. Legislators in Indiana, among other states, are feeling pressure to pass health care reforms that would eliminate the need for reform by the federal government.[243]

Richard W. Worman, Chairman of the Senate Committee on Insurance and Financial Institutions stated:

> The fear that the passage of a federal plan would not take into account the individual needs of states is paramount. State legislatures that don't pass health care reforms . . . have only

themselves to blame. . . . We could be criticized heavily if we don't.[244]

Many in Indiana foresee a move toward a capitated system that focuses on preventive care and places the burden on health care providers to keep patients healthy.[245] It is anticipated that as much as 50 percent of the nation will work under a capitated system by the year 2000.[246] Until such a transition takes place, however, Indiana is responding to the dichotomy of two diverse delivery systems.

Despite a 20 percent annual increase in costs for a traditional fee-for-service delivery system, Indiana has not embraced the managed care system wholeheartedly. Still, the trend in Indiana is a 5 to 12 percent shift toward managed care, annually.[247] Point-of-service plans have also become familiar in Indiana because they allow for out-of-network coverage.[248]

Indiana has also received proposals for exemptions to preexisting condition waiting periods in new jobs if the employee has already been covered for one year and has already experienced a waiting period in their current job.[249] Portability of coverage continues to be a difficult issue for the Indiana legislature. So, too, is the price of premiums. As the expense of portability and comprehensive care increases, the debate over premium prices will surge to the forefront of the legislative debate.[250]

Iowa

In Iowa, many elderly retirees—more than 14 million—are concerned over an Eighth Circuit Court of Appeals ruling, which held that even though an employee has a contract that provides lifetime health coverage, the benefits are only viable until the labor contract is renewed.[251] The case is being appealed, which should help other courts clarify the other 35 outstanding retiree health benefit cases.[252] Nevertheless, Iowa retirees still face the reality of rising health care costs,[253] particularly as the retired population continues to increase and live longer. Unfortunately, the only alternative for many retirees who are dropped from coverage is to spend money otherwise saved for nursing home insurance to buy necessary health care, like prescriptions, which are no longer covered.

Despite difficulties for retired employees in Iowa, the state did make progress in 1994 when several of the state's hospitals collaborated in a health partnership, similar to an HMO provider, in an effort to coordinate resources, develop an integrated health care delivery system, and better regulate costs.[254]

Kansas

1994 was not a good year for legislative health care reform in Kansas. With the exception of a tort-reform initiative, which was later vetoed by the governor, and other minor administrative reforms, every comprehensive health care reform measure proposed to the legislature in 1994 was rejected.[255] Kansas thus still confronts many of the issues faced by many other states: portability of insurance plans, preexisting condition waiting periods, stabilizing premiums, and most important, cutting costs.[256]

Representative Henry Helgerson thinks that the legislature dealt with the "no-brainers" and left the major health care issues to the whim of federal reform: "Kansas is sometimes viewed as a leader in health care issues, but we're now behind other states on health care reform."[257] Representative Helgerson urges the state to consider a comprehensive package that incorporates a community rating system, which mandates that insurers offer similar premiums to participants of similar demographics.[258] Nevertheless, the state legislature has rejected several comprehensive proposals, including a plan to encourage small businesses to participate in a state employees' insurance plan,[259] and a plan to privatize the state's Medicaid system and establish a tax-free medical savings account program.[260] To some, however, who would prefer to wait for federal reform, the state legislature's hesitancy was acceptable.[261]

Kentucky

Kentucky is also taking steps to restructure its Medicaid program and cut health care costs.[262] The plan is to turn more of the responsibility over to service providers, such as doctors and hospitals, to determine rates, develop networks, and administer the plan. This increased role is incentive for providers to join. The proposal, which has been approved by the federal government, establishes eight regional alliances of public and private health care providers, who will then phase-in a managed-care delivery system by the end of 1997.[263] The plan is expected to save an estimated $171 million per year.[264] The savings from the plan will be placed in a fund to service the uninsured.[265] Although the state has passed a Health Care Reform Bill in the past, previous attempts to extend Medicaid coverage by obtaining federal waivers have failed.[266] Nursing home patients covered by Medicaid would not be covered by the plan.

Also under consideration in Kentucky is a new reform plan: KentuckyKare, a state-funded plan, to be offered to the state's 130,000 state and school employees.[267] The purchasing alliance promoting KentuckyKare hopes to offer the plan on a voluntary basis to individuals and small businesses, but the insurance industry argues that state law restricts the plan to the public employee sector. The insurance industry has sought court intervention to prevent KentuckyKare's introduction into a new purchasing alliance because it places the state in a position to involve itself in the private insurance business. KentuckyKare, however, offers much less expensive premium rates than private HMOs.[268] Members of the state's General Assembly feel that KentuckyKare's implementation is a crucial incentive for private insurers to maintain competitive rates.

Louisiana

In 1995, Louisiana's legislature debated more than 100 health care related proposals and more than 600 bills that affect access to care for women and children.[269] Such proposals have included employer mandates,[270] access for women,[271] product liability,[272] the Nurse Practice Act,[273] abortion,[274] and suicide prevention.[275]

Despite numerous proposals for restrictions, HMOs have continued to expand in Louisiana. Six new HMOs were licensed in 1994 and were added to the existing ten, which number had not increased in the past seven years.[276] Now, it is estimated that as much as 10 percent of the Louisiana population—some 400,000 people—participate in HMOs.[277] Still, managed care in Louisiana is a virgin concept. Commenting on the tardy reform in Louisiana, Mike Manes, Director of the Louisiana Managed Health Care Association stated: "[H]ealth care is one of the most tradition-bound systems that we have in our country. . . . It has been the most sacred. Managed care and other factors are causing significant change in that industry. People are reluctant to change."[278]

Nationally, one-fifth of the population—some 50 million Americans—are enrolled in HMOs.[279] This figure was only 42 million in 1992. By the year 2000, it may reach as high as 56 million.[280] Such growth is attributed to the Medicaid crisis, which is expected to reach a deficit of $3 billion for the state, and the privatization of reform.

The changes and administrative restructuring in the health care field have changed drastically in Louisiana over the past four years. In 1991, Louisiana instituted a massive marketing campaign to promote nursing, which was suffering a severe shortage. Now, in 1995, many nursing graduates who accepted the challenge in 1991 cannot find jobs.[281] "There really does seem to be more and more of a trend nationally and locally of decreasing hospital censuses. . . . The shift really is to outpatient versus inpatient. That, long-term, is going to have an effect."[282] As the home health care industry increases, nurses who leave already scarce hospital jobs will find greater opportunities in the out-patient sector.

Maine

In 1994, the Maine legislature opted to defer approval of a single-payer health care plan until the federal government adopted a national plan with defined state options.[283] Instead, the state continues to study several options, including a multipayer managed-care system, and anticipates initiating some reform by 1997. As in Louisiana, 1994 also witnessed a proposition that nurse practitioners receive more authority at rural service facilities, but the bill was vetoed when doctors demanded malpractice immunity.[284] Nevertheless, Maine has followed suit in the move to a managed-care system by producing increased affiliations of private health care providers with hospital administrations. Such affiliations are attractive to managed-care insurers because a broader spectrum of services can be provided.[285]

The private organizations often sacrifice financial autonomy and take on administrative regulations not otherwise experienced, but insist on retaining authority on treatment decisions. Many of the details of the affiliations will differ according to local needs.[286] Many use a PHO (Physician-Hospital Organization), wherein private doctors retain ownership, but agree to take on managed-care patients according to a specified service agreement.[287] "There's a movement now away from using specialists and back to the primary care doctors. In the drive to cut costs, the insurance companies want as many patients seeing the less-expensive generalist."[288]

In 1983, the Maine legislature authorized the Maine Health Care Finance Commission to oversee hospital restructuring. This authority was repealed as of July 1, 1995, and now enables much more flexible consolidation and integration of hospitals with private service providers.[289] Some think, however, that the monopolization of health care will lead to the degradation of care because of tighter control by hospitals over doctors, who are pressured to avoid otherwise necessary treatment and tests.[290] "Hospitals in other states are several years ahead, and reporting results so far are mixed. Of Maine's 42 hospitals, there's no definitive list of who's doing what and how far along they are."[291] Others disagree: "Maine is a fairly self-controlled state that likes to address and correct its own problems. . . . There is a lot of money in health care, and a lot is taken out to manage various health care plans being offered."[292]

> [M]ost of them are either beginning to restructure or are at least looking into it . . . because the way health care is financed is changing under managed care. The old fee-for-service health plans are giving way to prepaid care at fixed rates and restrictions on which hospitals and physicians patients can go to. Under the traditional system, inefficiencies and duplication of services benefitted the provider economically . . . but restructuring rewards streamlining. It's a complete turnaround in economic incentives.[293]

Maryland

Uniquely, Maryland has attempted to control health care costs and increase access to health care coverage through greater government regulation of the private insurance market.[294] Because of Maryland's geographically diverse population, a managed-care sys-

tem is impractical,[295] yet health care reform was grossly necessary.[296] This necessity was of particular concern to the Maryland
legislature in the early 1990s, when President Clinton's federal
reforms loomed large and Maryland legislators scrambled to implement state-specific change before a national reform took priority.

Traditionally, since 1976, Maryland has implemented an all-
payer hospital prospective payment system and, in fact, has been
the only state to successfully maintain such a system.[297] The system
is designed to integrate a prohibition on hospitals from offering
discounts to any insurer or managed care organization; maintaining
a certificate-of-need program; and mandating certain health benefits.[298] In April 1993, Maryland enacted further two-tiered legislation to increase access and cut costs. One initiative in this plan,
which is unique to Maryland, is limiting the premium rate of the
standard health benefit plan to a percentage of wages. To regulate
these initiatives, Maryland created the Maryland Health Care Access
and Cost Commission. The purpose of the commission, in conjunction with the Maryland Health Services Cost Review Commission,
established in 1971, was to create a database on all health care
practitioners and compare fees and practices to organize a more
comprehensive benefit package for patients.[299] The Commission
was given broad authority to revamp the claims and forms process
in an effort to reduce administrative costs.

The Maryland program further provides for a fee-regulation system, which factors in three criteria: The first is based on the
resources needed by a practitioner to provide services, such as
malpractice costs, debt, education, and overhead. The second factor
is procedure specific and considers the complexity of the service
provided, including skills involved, time, and effort. The third factor converts the procedure provided into a dollar figure.[300] The
Commission has the authority to adjust the conversion method if it
determines that a particular specialization is receiving excessive
levels of payments, or it may even implement mandatory rates.[301]

The legislation also provides for the establishment of an Advisory Committee on Practice Parameters, which will analyze and
recommend procedures for the standardization of Maryland's medical practice.[302] To do so, three criteria must be met:

(1) 60 percent of specialists in the state, whose practices will be affected, [must] vote to adopt the guideline; (2) it [must be] determined that the guideline will reduce unnecessary use of services; and (3) the guideline [must] maintain high quality standards.[303]

Any guideline adopted by the commission will remain effective for a term of three years, but is subject to amendment or readoption. Critical to malpractice litigation is the fact that there are no enforcement provisions codified in the law and the commission's guidelines may not be introduced in legal proceedings as an affirmative defense. Therefore, depending on the degree of deviation from one's practice, statewide adoption of the commission's parameters is unlikely.[304]

Maryland's reform bill integrated insurance reform by mandating employee coverage with a comprehensive package for all employers with 2 to 50 employees working 30 hours per week, beginning July 1, 1994.[305] Preexisting condition exclusions were prohibited as of 1995 and rates are currently set by a community rating system that may be adjusted for age and geographic region. By October 1, 1998, the commission is to report on the possibility of implementing a community rating system that is not subject to adjustment.[306] Under this system, the average premium is limited to a specific percentage of the average annual wage in the state. If the community rate exceeds the specified percentage, the commission is authorized to alter the benefit package. Thus, the rate of increase and contributions are directly tied to the beneficiaries' income, which is unique to the United States, but standard in other countries.[307]

Finally, the Maryland legislation allows for expansion of the small business reforms to large businesses and individuals if ERISA is amended to give states more autonomy in regulating its specific health insurance needs and procedures. Clearly, the success of the Maryland system in the future will depend on continued autonomy for the states as federalism increases.

Massachusetts

Massachusetts has also experimented with health care services.[308] In order to escape the travail of seeking a waiver from the federal government, Massachusetts designed a play-or-pay system, which was "framed as an exercise of the state's taxing power; all employers subject to the requirement must pay the tax, but they are permitted to take as a credit the expense of providing health care insurance coverage."[309] In addition, the state established a separate program for persons not covered by Medicaid, which included expansion of Medicaid eligibility, mandatory health insurance for college students, a Health Security Plan for the unemployed, and a Center Care Program for low-income residents.[310] The plan also provides for cost control and other policies that would result in hospital closings and elimination of excess hospital beds.[311] The Massachusetts plan was implemented in 1995. Obviously, it shall have implications for Medicaid estate planning[312] and shall complement an effective estate recovery program already in operation.[313]

As of 1995, the community hospital in Massachusetts is all but extinct. Affiliations of small and large hospitals in the managed-care market have increased in an effort to compete in the health care market by cutting costs and integrating cradle-to-grave health services. These affiliations rely on a capitation payment system, in which specific procedures are no longer considered a source of payment, but a cost of keeping a patient healthy.[314] Those hospitals and long-term care facilities that do not consolidate usually downsize as the need for acute care diminishes and in-home care increases.[315] "[T]he mergers, closures, affiliations and other strategic moves among industry players are part of market-driven forces demanding greater efficiencies and lower costs from an industry that, up until only a few years ago, considered itself immune from change."[316] Consolidation has spread even to the insurance and biotechnical industries,[317] but many are skeptical of such radical and free-flowing consolidations:

Many institutions appear to be teaming up with each other for the sake of teaming up. They're doing so under the assumption that there's strength in numbers, particularly at a time when the industry faces an uncertain future . . . . 1994 began, on some level, a process of real paranoia . . . . There has been almost a frenzy to move into something.[318]

Michigan

According to the Office of Policy, Planning and Evaluation at the Michigan Department of Public Health, the state of Michigan spent $30 billion on health care in 1993.[319] Consequently, state legislatures have recently focused on small markets, much like the federal reform sponsored by Senator Ted Kennedy (D-Massachusetts) and Nancy Kassebaum (R-Kansas), in anticipation that President Clinton's failed national program will soon shift responsibility to the states. Presently, "Michigan is one of the few states in the country without true small-market reform."[320]

Nationally, an average of 15.3 percent of the population under age 65 remains uninsured. In Michigan, this percentage is more than 11 percent.[321] According to the employee benefits Research Institute in Washington, DC, 22.7 million employed Americans between ages 18 and 64 remain uninsured, the largest percentage of which is employed by companies of 25 to 99 employees.[322] Michigan continues to struggle with these figures but the long-standing policy for small businesses in Michigan has been a stale one. Because beneficiaries' histories are extensively considered and have a significant effect on premiums, the only small businesses that can afford insurance are those that do not need it. Thus, the Chamber of Commerce proposes to move to a community rating system, such that insurers could only classify groups by geography and industry instead of assessments of individual beneficiaries.[323]

Because Michigan is one of only 12 states without a health care database or a law requiring medical providers to disclose information, legislation was proposed in June 1995 to establish the Michigan Health Data Institute, which provides local data analysis to help providers and purchasers compare the quality and value of hospitals, services, and insurance plans.[324] This is called "outcome-based" or "results-oriented" performance.[325] In conjunction with this proposal is the increased use of Community Health Information Networks (CHINs), which coordinate care and reduce costs by electronically coordinating administrative information.[326] These collaborative efforts are hoped to integrate care and, at the same time, improve the status of community health. Michigan has one of the nation's highest rates of chronic disease and death.[327] "If we reduce the cost of care, but do not improve the health status of the community in the process, health reform will have failed."[328]

Minnesota

In 1987, Minnesota implemented the Children's Health Plan, which provided services for pregnant women and children under the age of six who were not covered by Medicaid.[329] The Plan was funded by a minimum annual fee and a 1 cent-per-pack cigarette tax. In 1991, the Plan expanded to cover all low-income children under 18 years of age. Still, between 1985 and 1990, Minnesota increased its total spending on medical assistance by 41.4 percent to $1.403 billion.[330] By 1991, Minnesota was the ninth highest spender in the nation in average family payments, which reached $7,252 per family.[331] The political atmosphere in 1991, and its effect on health care reform, was very similar to that of the present federal climate: health care was of major concern and importance, the state suffered under a huge deficit, and reform was a public mandate, yet the governor snubbed public opinion and rejected a promising Health Care Access Bill, which provided hope of universal coverage for the state.[332]

Then, in April 1992, the governor announced a bipartisan proposal—HF 2800, called HealthRight (now called MinnesotaCare)—which would reform the state's health care system completely and serve as yet another model of successful reform. The model incorporated five major issues: cost, access, insurance, data collection, and particularized problems of the state. As in Maryland's plan, the Minnesota plan organized a Health Care Cost Containment Commission. The commission's purpose was to slow health care cost inflation by a target deadline, regulate total spending, encourage regional planning, monitor technology expenditures, and promote individual wellness.[333] The plan also subsidized insurance coverage for the 7 percent of the uninsured population and continued to expand on its uninsured coverage through 1994. Still, because the plan lacks employer mandates and comprehensive incentives for participation, it is estimated that by 1997, the plan will only apply to 40 percent of the state's uninsured population.[334] Further, the law's only rating restriction is gender based; with the exception of small employers, rates can vary based on occupational and health status.[335]

Another limitation, like in Maryland, is Minnesota's large rural population, which has a high uninsured percentage and consequently causes an imbalance in the distribution of resources.[336] These limitations are symbolic of the legislative compromises necessary to initiate reform, however. The law also favors a state-sponsored insurance pool, which allows more affordable access to businesses. The plan was initially funded by a hotly contested income tax surcharge and a 5 cent-per-pack cigarette tax.[337]

Mississippi

Despite the fact that the Mississippi legislature is more attuned to health care reform issues than most state legislatures, much of the health care reform proposed in Mississippi rests with the state Insurance Department, which hopes to literally walk legislators by the hand through reform proposals and initiatives that would not otherwise be considered.[338] Despite its late arrival in the last two years, overall, the state is favoring a move to managed care, with expanding regulation and market assessment of managed-care providers.

For example, state law authorizes the state Insurance Department to restrict rate increases to 25 percent.[339] A capitated system is in force in Mississippi—a plan which was considered amidst the fading federal reformation.[340] Like many other health care experts and concerned legislators in other states, one health care advisor in Mississippi commented: "In the hysteria last year of the possibility of health care reform, I decided, on my own, to say, 'Okay, I can't worry about what happens in Washington. Let's see if we can't put a little logic to the madness of what's going on here in our backyard.'"[341] Since almost half of the insured residents of Mississippi received federally transferred funds, as opposed to privately funded insurance, a capitated system will bring drastic changes to Mississippi. Just like Maryland and Minnesota, however, Mississippi's rural configuration is a limitation to change.

Other proposals include portability of coverage for preexisting conditions, guaranteed renewal of existing coverage, and a one-time guaranteed window of access to any qualified plan. Changes to the Mississippi Comprehensive Health Insurance Risk Pool Association were also proposed, such as allowing access to Medicare for recipients under age 65 and allowing severely ill employees of small business to utilize the pool.[342]

Missouri

Much can be learned about the difference in state perspectives on health care reform by comparing the Missouri perspective to its neighbor, Illinois. In 1994, the 600,000 Medicaid beneficiaries in Missouri moved from a traditional, cost-based reimbursement Medicaid program to a managed-care system.[343] The transition started in localized areas and will encompass the entire state of Missouri by 1997.[344] At the same time, Illinois opted, instead, to push proposals to slash its Medicaid budget.[345]

In light of the Republican-proposed Medicare cuts over the next seven years and the push toward managed care, Missouri hospitals are postured to suffer significant losses. Nationally, 34 percent of hospital revenues are generated by Medicare reimbursements.[346] Presently, Missouri hospitals average a loss of $177 per Medicare case. Should any Republican plan become effective, that loss will soar to $1,000 per case.[347] Overall, Missouri hospitals expect to experience a 25 percent reduction in revenues over the next seven years. Some experts think that further reductions for Missouri and expansion of the managed-care system will require cost reduction at the expense of quality of care.[348] Particularly, the referral system mandated by managed care is designed to reduce unnecessary visits to more expensive specialists and restrict the number of diagnostic tests—but often, these are necessary tests.[349]

In fact, a study of 70 patients conducted by physicians in Colorado and released at the American College of Allergy and Immunology revealed that referrals to allergy specialists for moderate to severe cases of asthma reduced costs by $145,000, decreased hospital stays by 68 percent, reduced sick care office visits by 46 percent, and minimized emergency room visits by 56 percent.[350] Less severe cases of asthma were adequately treated by primary physicians. Thus, a cost-effective managed-care system, with primary care physicians serving as gatekeepers, is dependent on physicians recognizing their own service limitations.

To help alleviate the Medicare squeeze, the state will rely on provider-sponsored networks (PSNs), to offer comprehensive services to Medicare recipients. As collaborative efforts like these increase and obtain a firm handle on service delivery, HMOs will become less relevant. Still, the emphasis on managed care in Missouri is significant.

Montana

In 1993, the Montana legislature passed Senate Bill 285, which created the Montana Health Care Authority, which was given $1.3 million for the purpose of creating initiatives to provide universal coverage to Montana residents.[351] The results were a proposal for a single-payer Canadian-style plan, which boosted state taxes by $1.1 billion per year, and a proposal for a multiple-payer system, wherein the state required $100 million to subsidize the uninsured.[352] Both proposals were deemed too sweeping; neither was affordable. Still, 1 out of every 12 people in Montana is uninsured.[353] Subsequently, the state has cast its legislative eyes on less drastic reform.

Some commentators have proposed abolishing the Health Care Authority itself and utilizing the savings for universal coverage through employer mandates. Other proposals are to implement individual mandates by requiring insurance for motor vehicle registration, school enrollment, job applications, and tax return filings.[354] Mostly, however, as federal health care reform wanes, the Montana legislature is relying on private sector initiatives and preventative health planning by the public. Said Senator Bob Brown: "The legislature will be cautious in its approach. . . . [y]ou won't see anything bold, far-reaching or Clintonesque coming out of the Montana legislature."[355]

The Montana Hospital Association, however, is taking measures to prepare for the future of health care—what it refers to as "Navigating Mega Change." That change is a drastic reduction in the need for hospital services.[356] The increase in total expenses for Montana hospitals increased by only 4.5 percent between 1993 and 1994, which has been the lowest increase in seven years.[357] Medicare and Medicaid are the largest payers of health care in Montana.[358] As efforts continue to prepare for further Medicare and Medicaid cuts,[359] downsizing and layoffs are often the only source of savings. "[C]hanges in Medicare and Medicaid programs will drive changes in the entire health care system because those government programs are such a large part of all health care."[360]

Nebraska

In Nebraska, group health insurance increases have minimized recently.[361] Some estimates show an average increase of only 2 percent, down from an average 6 percent between 1993 and 1994.[362] Experts attribute these savings to efficient managed use throughout the state. "Nebraskans have been slower than some to adopt managed care plans . . . [b]ut rising health care costs and greater knowledge about how managed care works have encouraged businesses to make the shift."[363] With the rise in managed care comes collaborative efforts of physicians and hospitals forming organizations (PHOs) that hope to expand service provisions to nursing homes, pharmacies, and other medical providers in the future.[364] These affiliations "allow the medical community to control health care costs based on local needs, rather than on what is taking place somewhere else."[365] However, the price of controlling costs in Nebraska is less autonomy for the physician and less choice for the patient. This is particularly pertinent for states such as Nebraska, where rural geography plays a major role in the effectiveness of health care delivery.[366]

Nevada

In 1991, Nevada was considered the most expensive place in the nation to get sick. In response, Nevada has focused on reducing the utilization of services through managed care in an effort to reduce the rising costs of health care.[367] Nevada is not unaware, however, that the financial aspects of managed care threatens the quality of, and access to, services and care. As a result, in 1991, Nevada passed a law that limited the annual increase of medical bills to 5 percent.[368] The law makes Nevada the only state in the nation since 1988 to have an increase cap under 10 percent.[369] Still, Nevada, which is one of the least populated states but growing rapidly, is one of the costliest states for health care. Experts attribute this to the fact that most of Nevada's hospitals are for-profit.[370] Administrative efficiency and cost cutting, therefore, has been the focus of Nevada's health care organizations and hospitals.

Despite Nevada's concern for hospital efficiency and cost-effectiveness, it still leads the nation in percentage of uninsured population—23 percent—85 percent of whom are employed.[371] The annual cost to the state for caring for indigents has reached $23 million, which includes only the cost to the hospitals, not to the doctors.[372] Some legislators would like to see Medicaid expanded to include the "medically needy," to absorb some of these costs, but such a reform is not likely.

The Nevada State Medical Association has, in the past, proposed "Health Access Nevada," which is a market-approach legislative package of tort reform ($275,000 cap on noneconomic or "pain and suffering" damages and sliding-scale contingency fees), medical savings accounts, portability, and purchasing pools. This package is hoped to provide universal coverage.[373] The reform also offers a basic health care package, as opposed to the 20-benefit package now mandated by state law.[374] Many feel that the plan too closely resembles the Medical Insurance Comprehensive Reform Act of 1975, which many feel had negative results. Similar versions of the plan were introduced by the 1993 legislature, but it received little attention because of the anticipated federal plan, which has since failed.

New Hampshire

Like most states, New Hampshire hospitals get most of their funding through Medicare—for New Hampshire—70 percent.[375] New Hampshire houses a greater percentage of the elderly population and could suffer more significantly from federal cutbacks. For example, in 1993, Medicare reimbursed the 26 hospitals in New Hampshire only 87.8 percent of the cost of treating Medicare patients, resulting in an average loss of $781 per patient for the hospitals. A $250 billion reduction over seven years will drop the reimbursement to 82 percent, resulting in a loss of $1,561 per patient.[376] Historically, these losses were shifted to private insurance payers (employers). Because of the increase in competitive managed care, cost shifting to employers is more difficult and the shift will now change to a reduction in hospital services, like end-of-life interventions.[377] To compensate, hospitals hope to coordinate services with long-term care facilities and private service providers, but only 9 percent of Medicare patients have switched to managed care.[378]

Typical of what is occurring for hospitals in many states is expressed by Alyson Pitman, CEO of New London Hospital, which has reduced its operating expenses by $1 million:

> We looked at what's going on around the country with mergers and acquisitions. . . . When we saw what was going on in this state, we decided that we should take a really proactive stand on health reform. We didn't want to wait and have another group decide the fate of this hospital.[379]

Nationally, in 1992, there were approximately 15 hospital mergers; in 1993, there were about 20 more.[380] As the state moves toward a capitated system of managed care, more mergers will occur.

New Jersey

New Jersey has led health care innovation in many areas, including pharmaceuticals, research, and telecommunications, but has ironically lagged behind in establishing a managed-care system.[381] Currently, New Jersey is picking up the slack.

In 1971, New Jersey passed the New Jersey Health Care Facilities Planning Act, which employed a certificate-of-need and a rate-control system.[382] Further legislation in 1978 provided for the inclusion of uncompensated care as an allowable cost in an effort to control cost shifting.[383] By the mid 1980s, many hospitals were providing so much uncompensated care that the allowable rate setting grew uncontrolled and hospitals providing more uncompensated care placed themselves at a significant competitive disadvantage because their rates were higher to account for the difference. To make up for this competitive edge, in 1987 the state employed an Uncompensated Care Trust Fund for hospitals with a larger portion of uncompensated care. By 1989, however, the New Jersey reform rates were far exceeding the Medicare prospective payment rates adopted by the federal government in 1983, and New Jersey's waiver was finally withdrawn. Cost shifting again became the norm.[384]

By 1990, New Jersey still struggled to provide health care to more than 900,000 uninsured residents. The continued funding of the Uncompensated Care Trust Fund discouraged the purchase of private insurance and commanded overuse of hospital services. Statistically, the uninsured use hospital services 47 percent less than the insured. In New Jersey in 1990, the uninsured used 30 percent more hospital care than the insured.[385] In fact, recent surveys show that New Jersey still ranks the highest in hospitalizations for otherwise preventable care by primary physicians.[386] Further, the Trust Fund offered little incentive for hospitals to regulate its expenditures from the fund because any bad debt was fully reimbursed. Finally, in 1990, Governor Jim Florio appointed the Commission on Health Care Costs to evaluate the health care system's failing reliance on hospital-based services and rate setting.

In 1991 came the Health Care Cost Reduction Act, which shifted the focus from hospital-based care.[387] However, the plan extended the Trust Fund, and the state still faced the growing problem of financing uncompensated care. Union groups finally brought suit under ERISA, and in 1992, it became clear that New Jersey's hospital rate-setting laws, which were preempted by ERISA, needed reform. That reform would come via the Health Care Reform Act of 1992, which employed significant deregulation of the hospital rate-setting scheme and implemented a ceiling on rate increases for hospitals. The act also tapped the Trust Fund for $500 million, with remaining funds to help promote a managed-care insurance program for the uninsured.[388] The growth of the managed-care system has continued since that time.

In 1983, a little more than 200,000 residents participated in HMOs; in 1995, that figure reached 1.3 million.[389] When added to other forms of managed-care participation, the total reaches 3 million. By the year 2000, it is expected that 85 percent of New Jersians will have health insurance through a managed-care plan.[390] Governor Christine Todd Whitman obtained approval from the federal government in June 1995 to mandate that all state welfare recipients—except the elderly, disabled, and chronically ill—participate in an HMO.[391] In 1993, 27 percent of businesses offered managed-care coverage to employees; in 1994, 38 percent offered such care while the total cost dropped 1 percent.[392] HMO costs dropped 2 percent from 1993.[393] Overall, 89 percent of employers offered some form of health insurance to employees—an increase from 87 percent in 1993.[394] Seventy percent offered family coverage—an increase of 8 percent from 1993.[395] Eighty-two percent of small companies (less than 20 employees) offered coverage (52 percent to families) while 98 percent of large companies (more than 20 employees) provided benefits.[396]

The cost of conventional, fee-for-service plans rose by 15 percent, but the rate of increase for conventional policies decreased from 59 percent to 50 percent.[397] The attrition rate for employer coverage dropped from more than 2 percent in 1993 to only 1.4 percent in 1994.[398] Many think, however, as do many other states who are new to the managed-care field, that the quality of care may suffer because doctors fear termination from HMO participation for providing needed, but expensive, care.

There are other consequences faced by New Jersey as a result of increasing managed care; such consequences are not unique to New Jersey. For example, New Jersey has a surplus of hospital beds—30 percent of the state's 30,000 beds are empty.[399] This surplus, coupled with managed care and the passage of the Health Care Reform Act of 1992,[400] which deregulated hospitals and applied a revenue cap on a hospital's annual income, has led to many alliances and collaborations between hospitals in New Jersey.[401] In fact, more hospitals became affiliated in 1994 than in the entire previous decade.[402] In 1993, 4,000 physicians started their own HMO group—the Physician Healthcare Plan of New Jersey—which hopes to include 80 percent of the state's physicians by 1997.[403] Thus, unlike Maryland's reform, which is grounded in regulation, New Jersey has relied on deregulation to expand its competitive market.

New laws have also helped to quell the push for short hospital stays, particularly for childbirths. In 1988, the average length of stay for childbirth was 3.45 days; in 1993, it dropped to 2.87 days.[404] Soon HMOs began the practice of covering only 24 hours for hospital stays after childbirth. In response, New Jersey passed a bill requiring insurers to cover at least two days after a childbirth and four days after a Caesarean section. HMO supporters retorted by having the bill amended to waive the two-day rule if medical service was provided to the home.

Enrollment in New Jersey's Individual Health Coverage (IHC), which was created by the New Jersey Individual Health Insurance Reform Act of 1992 to provide access for those with no accessible insurance through an employer, increased 21 percent from 1994 to the first quarter of 1995. Thirty-one percent of new enrollees were previously uninsured.[405] The IHC plan has built in a requirement that carriers pay a minimum of $.75 in benefits for every dollar they receive in premiums. Eligible applicants cannot be denied coverage, and all recipients must be covered at the same community rate.[406] There are approximately 26 carriers in the program, whereas, historically, Blue Cross/Blue Shield had been the sole provider.

Despite the continuing use of the more expensive and conventional fee-for-service health plans, the statistics in New Jersey show that there is a trend of moving toward managed care and that the move is quite successful. New Jersey has enabled employers to offer a choice of plans at lower costs. The history of New Jersey's reform demonstrates "what can happen when a state attempts to "piggyback" a universal access scheme on a fragmented system based on private employment insurance, Medicaid, and Medicare."[407] In applying the lessons of New Jersey to long-term care for the elderly, the following question remains pertinent:

> Can a system in which people's access to care is determined by where they work and live, their age, or their income ever be rationalized by trying to bring these pieces together into a coherent whole? A paradigm based less on filling gaps, and more on universality and equity in access to basic services, may have a much better chance of succeeding.[408]

New Mexico

In 1994, the population of the state of New Mexico was 1.6 million. As a result of the high number of illegal immigrants migrating into the southern part of the state, it is expected that within 40 years, just the population south of the Rio Grande, alone, could exceed that figure.[409] Unfortunately, this "corridor" historically has been overlooked by legislators when considering health care reforms.

Now, however, it has become a focal point, and delivery and access—both financial and geographical—have become key issues.[410] Still, health care costs in New Mexico have passed the $3 billion mark, which far exceeds the state's income from one of its more lucrative industries—tourism.[411]

Like most states, New Mexico takes a reactive stance to the failing federal health care reforms by cutting back on procedures and services in the hospital setting and restructuring its delivery system with a capitated managed-care format.[412] After failed attempts in 1993, by which the legislature sought to implement a statewide insurance program, legislators in New Mexico concluded the only other viable alternative other than capitation is one employing price controls, which results in an unwanted rationing of services.[413] In order to make a capitation system work, however, hospitals must eliminate waste and effectively budget resources. Given that 20 percent of health care costs in New Mexico is attributed to administration and paperwork, these endeavors will be focused on the information resources of the service providers.[414] Nationally, it is expected that the computerization of the health care system will result in an annual savings of $100 to $200 billion.[415] As with other industries, what will be the effect on employment?

Says Ray Barton, President and Chief Executive Officer of Albuquerque's St. Joseph Health Care System: "Any health care reform proposal—state or national—will work best if [the hospital, medical, and payer] components are unified and integrated."[416] Because a health care system such as St. Joseph is already very well integrated in these areas, it is postured in such a way that any national mandates, e.g., employer benefit packages, can be easily implemented. Bill Johnson, Chief Executive Officer of the University of New Mexico Hospital says, "Instead of trying to gut the current system and rebuild, maybe we need to take the existing delivery system [and] nurture it . . . ."[417] As with other states, this is the most likely course of action.

New York

New York stands to suffer more than most states if the failing federal health care system surrenders to a block-grant arrangement to the states because the present formula extracts money from New

York and disperses it in the southern section of the nation.[418] Under the much-anticipated federal budget reform cuts, New York would expect to lose $21 billion in Medicaid funds over the seven-year span of the reform.[419] Because of a series of deals made among states, the total expected loss will be up to $30 million. The federal grant received by New York would only increase by 2 percent each year beginning in 1997, whereas other states' increases may rise as much as 9 percent annually.[420]

As Republican and Democratic legislators alike reluctantly posture their states for these losses, hospitals and health care providers, in turn, scramble to affiliate cost-cutting efforts and maintain quality service despite the reform.[421] In mid-1995, Governor George Pataki revealed a 16-point plan to save the state $101 million by reducing the micromanaging tasks of the health care system and focusing on patient care.[422]

As part of its own cost-saving effort, New York has similarly increased its reliance on the managed care system. However, the results of a 1995 pilot Health Plan Employer Data Information Set, which is an increasingly accepted resource for rating managed-care systems and developing industry standards across the country, indicated that the only participating New York City area managed-care system—Health Insurance Plan of Greater New York—had the lowest rate of patient satisfaction, 72 percent.[423] This rating system appears to be developing a nervous, albeit subjective, trend throughout the industry for managed-care providers to maintain accreditation and quality care. Despite mediocre satisfaction in New York City, more than 4.5 million New Yorkers remain enrolled in some form of managed-care system.[424]

Within the next several years, nearly a million more enrollees are expected to migrate from their present fee-for-service system.[425] Unfortunately, managed-care systems are reluctant to become reputable insurers for long-term or chronic care patients, such as the elderly and persons with HIV, who do not fit the profile for healthy HMO candidates who minimally utilize the organization's services.[426] Still, "[u]nless managed-care providers integrate these consumers and strike an appropriate balance between patient health and corporate wealth, costs will escalate for everyone, sick or not."[427]

Consequently, New York legislators have proposed a Health Care Bill of Rights, which guarantees uniform and comprehensive access standards to ensure quality, choice, fairness, and affordability.[428] Fifteen other states have employed similar consumer protection standards and have met great success. Thus, cries from HMO providers that such high standards will drive up costs and, therefore, premiums are skeptically received by advocates of the bill.[429]

Most important to New York and to other states was the United States Supreme Court's decision allowing states to use financial incentives to create health care reform packages that ensure coverage for the poor—a decision stemming from New York's surcharge on all commercially insured hospital bills.[430] New York's surcharge was initiated in 1988, despite insurer's complaints that the surcharge was preempted by ERISA. Now, 21 states have similar regulations, and with the Supreme Courts' holding, more are likely to initiate similar regulations. Said one lawyer representing the National Governors Association, "[t]he decision was of vital importance given Congress's failure to regulate in the health-care area. . . . It would have been a disaster if the case came out the other way . . . because the states would have been paralyzed in their efforts to try new forms of regulation."[431]

North Carolina

The breakdown of the federal health care plan has left North Carolina physicians in a tumultuous professional environment. Says Dr. Neil Howell, chairperson of the Mecklenburg County Medical Society: "I have never seen a group of people so well trained and so knowledgeable so confused and insecure. . . . We don't really know what's coming."[432] As managed care continues to take root throughout the country, all that is known is that business trends will continue to force the integration and affiliation of service providers.[433] Between 1994 and 1995, the number of HMOs in North Carolina increased from 10 to 16. Many more have been approved in 1995, with still others awaiting approval.[434] As the number of organizations increases, so does the competition for the market share. "We will see fierce price competition and we'll see winners and losers. . . . [T]he market forces are all in play to cause for that kind of revolution. . . .

[T]hat kind of change [will drive] the health care industry for years."[435]

But the growth of the affiliation rate will decline as integrated systems develop and begin the operating process, and a shift in emphasis toward cost-effectiveness will ensue.[436] Some affiliations are not successful.[437] Data collection will play an integral part in surveying the effectiveness of the various affiliations taking place.[438] Commenting on the effects of reform on the practice of medicine, Dr. Howell states:

> People are still getting sick and we're still trying to help them get well. We'll keep doing that though we find frustrations at every turn—to make sure we do it in the place that's okay with the insurance company and that method that's okay with the insurance using the drug that's okay with the insurance company. We're having to learn about that sort of thing that takes away from the active practice of medicine.[439]

North Dakota

In 1993, U.S. Department of Health and Human Services Secretary Donna Shalala called the Heart of America Medical Center, in Rugby, North Dakota (also considered the geographic center of North America), "a model for rural health care delivery."[440] These were profound words as the managed competition of the health care industry began growing exponentially throughout the rest of the country. For the rest of the country, where there are enough large cities and hospitals to effectively create more than one health care network to compete in the insurance plan market, managed competition is feasible; in rural North Dakota, where the entire population did not exceed 650,000 in 1993, however, it is not.[441]

In 1993, 38 of the 53 counties in North Dakota experienced physician shortages. Sixteen counties had no hospital beds. Five even lacked a satellite clinic.[442] Similar problems arise in most rural areas in all states,[443] but North Dakota is especially prone to geographical hurdles when it comes to the delivery of health care. It is especially telling, therefore, that North Dakota has so successfully regionalized its health care delivery system. Authorities attribute effective delivery management to an emphasis on preventive care, control of administrative costs and overutilization, and mostly a high percentage of private-provider cooperation.[444] The administrative reforms in North Dakota are hoped to be a standard by which other states can format a flexible and comprehensive system that suits their own needs.

Ohio

Ohio has taken its own initiative to salvage the failing federal recommendations for Medicaid reform by implementing OhioCare, which requires Medicaid recipients to enroll in one of the 33 HMOs now in Ohio,[445] thereby expanding coverage to thousands of uninsured residents without federal or state budget increases.[446] The 13 HMOs that already service Medicaid recipients are expected to participate in the system, but the balance will have to weigh the advantages of taking on a large amount of rural enrollees, which entails a wider range of services and expenses.[447] The plan is hoped to be financed by the Hospital Care Assurance Program (HCAP), which taxes hospitals 1 percent of yearly operating expenses, to be redistributed according to the amount of uncompensated care offered to patients.[448] Sixty cents in federal funds is also contributed for every $.40 contributed by the hospitals, but as the number of HMOs increase, each taking a small share of the federal pie, hospitals will begin to see smaller and smaller portions on their plates. Possibly, other taxes may absorb some of the blow, but legislators are hesitant to reach into the pockets of other social programs.

The problem with the system, however, is that it will have devastating effects on hospitals and service providers that do not historically service Medicaid clients nor offer traditional services more frequently utilized by Medicaid patients. Consequently, when the plan is fully effective, these providers will lose that segment of the patient population.[449]

It is the opinion of many of the employers in Ohio that the failure of the federal government to organize and control the health care crisis is a positive step for individual health care reform.[450] One proposal for state reform of the insurance accessibility problems in Ohio, which are faced by most states, includes introduction of the "any willing provider" legislation, which restricts the ability of managed-care companies to selectively contract with doctors, hospitals, and other service providers.[451] The legislation, however, is severely opposed by the Coalition for Managed Care, which includes several of Ohio's largest employers, labor groups, and managed-care companies. Supporters think, however, that managed-care advocates merely wish to shift the costs to smaller providers.[452]

Regardless of the success or failure of legislative initiatives, market forces are clearly at work in the health care reformation. The home health care industry has expanded significantly in Ohio and continues to be a growing delta in the health care industry.[453] For example, one home health care provider, St. Elizabeth's Health Resources, Inc., which made approximately 17,000 home visits in 1993, increased its total number of visits in 1994 to more than 40,000.[454] Nationally, some 15,000 home care providers service more than seven million residents suffering with acute, long-term, and terminal illnesses.[455] Estimates reveal that the industry has grown by 10 percent each year between 1986 and 1991 and by 12 percent since 1991.[456] The field of home health care aide services has been reported by the Department of Labor to be the fastest-growing job field in the 1990s.[457]

Authorities think that the growth of the home health care industry has been attributable to advances in medical technology, increased demand, and a universal push in the industry to control costs: "dealing with a medical condition in a home setting costs a tenth of what the expense would be in a hospital."[458] Added incentive to expand has been the fact that Medicare has gradually enlarged the scope of in-home services for which it will pay.[459] Conversely, however, the expanding home care market has forced drastic downsizing and restructuring for hospitals. This, in turn, eventually has a secondary effect on the number of nurses entering the home health care workforce who have not obtained necessary experience through previous employment in hospitals.[460]

The human dimension of the aging population is a factor often overlooked. Most persons needing assisted living care would wish to remain in their homes. Others would nonetheless like to keep the home in which they have lived. Their expectations, the experiential level of the nurses, and the growing component of home care market entities provide a human patchwork of expectations that is not completely understood or explainable.

Oklahoma

Oklahoma is not unique to the effects of the growing managed-care industry. Like most states, one noticeable effect has been the crunch placed on local pharmacists who are gradually becoming inundated with HMOs' control over prescription prices.[461] Thus, as managed care continues to become the norm across the country, Oklahoma legislators desperately search for other creative ways to balance the shortcomings of this expanding industry.

For several years, Oklahoma legislators have continued to encourage support for Medical Savings Accounts, which many have viewed as an alternative version of the successful Individual Retirement Account.[462] A panel was created in 1992 by the Governor, David Walters, to assess the benefits of the accounts. A comprehensive plan to implement the idea for the state was designed to include financing through employer contributions and supplemental Medicare and Medicaid payments, as well as through private financing.[463]

The accounts are designed to allow the consumer/patient to control his or her own spending, but opponents of the plan, including Vermont Governor Howard Dean—who is also a physician—argue that this is the very flaw in the concept, since health care is not controlled by the patient, but rather by the service provider.[464] As a result, it is argued, the most frugal of consumers' efforts will result in only minimal savings at best. Further, critics contend that the accounts offer incentives to save money by avoiding much needed and, in the long run, cost-saving preventive care. There are no assurances that patients will be receiving the full range of appropriate care.

The argument follows that most healthy Americans will resort to using their savings accounts, while sickly, needy Americans will rely on traditional insurance plans and, thus, will continue to inflate premium prices.[465] Advocates of the accounts respond with the positive aspects of the accounts, which include flexible and efficient utilization of limited resources and transferability with new employment. When consumers begin to experience the reality of spending their own money and not just insurance resources, health care may begin to be seen as a benefit, not an entitlement. "If you want the system to be efficient and answer the needs of patients, . . . you need to transfer the money from bureaucratic institutions to individuals and families."[466]

Oregon

Another state at the forefront of health care reform is Oregon. In 1989, Oregon extended health care to most uninsured residents through the Oregon Health Plan.[467] It did so by (1) reducing services offered; (2) implementing, by July 1995, a play-or-pay mandate that requires employers to pay into a state insurance pool if they do not provide health insurance; and (3) establishing a risk pool to protect those unable to obtain medical insurance because of a preexisting medical condition.[468]

In the same year in which it mandated health care, 1989, Oregon also created the Health Services Commission to draft a medical care priority list and to supervise its implementation.[469] The list ranks approximately 1,600 medical procedures and attempts to measure the cost of each treatment against the benefits to the patients in years of extended life and improved quality-of-life categories.[470] The state legislature would then decide the level of services that would be provided by assessing the level of funds available.[471] Services that fell below this level would not be funded by Medicaid.[472] Service providers are encouraged to participate in the plan through the waiver of Medicaid reimbursement rates, which Medicaid providers feel are too low.[473]

The rationing of health care services allows Oregon to provide greater allowed Medicaid coverage to more state residents. The state expects to decrease the number of uninsured residents from 15 percent to 3 percent of the population.[474] In order to ensure access to services and health care providers for these newly covered people, Oregon is recruiting managed-care providers and implementing a new cost-based reimbursement system.[475] Such severe changes in the Medicaid system required a waiver from the federal government, and the Clinton administration granted that waiver in 1993.[476] The waiver expires in 1998.[477]

One of the harsh realities of this rationing of resources is captured in the death of seven-year-old Cody Howard.[478] The child suffered from lymphocytic leukemia, and his parents were only able to raise $80,000 of the $100,000 needed for a bone marrow transplant, a service not allowed under the state's new Medicaid policy restrictions.[479] The child died. Nonetheless, the reality of the situation is clearly explained by the following comment, by former Governor Neil Goldschmidt: "How can we spend every nickel of support for a few people when thousands never see a doctor or eat a decent meal?"[480]

The Oregon plan has been criticized at many levels.[481] Commenting on the plan's infamous "list," two authors write:

> [S]pecificity (the infamous "List") can become a political albatross. No state has emulated the list or seems likely to do so soon.
>
> The final lesson of Oregon is ironic. As a result of debates about rationing, Oregon lawmakers backed into defining a minimum basic package of services. In doing so, they showed that it is possible to design and implement a plan that puts a floor of coverage under everyone in the state.[482]

But there is truth to the response by John Kitzhaber, President of the Oregon State Senate: "What we've done [in Oregon] is articulated what's going on right now. We just have the intellectual honesty to admit it. These choices are being made every day in America."[483]

Pennsylvania

In 1987, Pennsylvania was one of eight states that had over 1 million people over the age of 65.[484] Philadelphia maintains a higher percentage of people over 65 than the national average.[485] These eight states[486] domiciled almost half of the country's older population.[487] During the same year, Pennsylvania was 1 of 18 states in which persons over the age of 65 constituted 13 percent of the total population.[488] Pennsylvania ranked fourth of all states in persons over the age of 65, having over 1.7 million in 1987.[489] It ranked third of all states in percent of persons over age 65 at 14.8.[490] By 1995, Pennsylvania had moved to second in the nation in percentage of people over the age of 65.[491]

Part of the high proportion of elderly in Pennsylvania is due to the heavy migration of younger people out of Pennsylvania and a low fertility rate of those remaining in the state.[492] Another significant factor is "countermigration," which occurs when the elderly who move to another state at retirement move to a state in which their family members are located. Pennsylvania was one of four states that received a high percentage of migrant elders from Florida.[493] Faced with the heavy influx of the elderly population who are perfect targets for Alzheimer's disease, Pennsylvania is blindly aligning itself with an economic storm that no legislative proposal to date has been able to weather.

Currently, more than 70,000 elderly, many of whom are middle-class, live in nursing homes and depend on Medicaid.[494] In 1980, the federal government spent approximately $400 million on nursing home care; in 1995, it spent approximately $7 billion.[495] The Commonwealth of Pennsylvania has experienced a proportionate increase.[496] In 1988, Pennsylvania incurred a $695 million bill for Medicaid expenses. The bill for 1995/96 more than doubled this amount to an estimated $695 million.[497] An increase of nearly 18 percent will be seen in 1996/97. Ironically, however, because the ever-expanding Medicaid system pays for patients whom it was never intended to cover (like the elderly), the system itself is an incentive for nursing homes to raise costs. Because the government reimburses the homes for servicing Medicaid patients, the homes make more money by increasing costs, thereby increasing their reimbursements.[498]

In 1986, the elderly in Pennsylvania paid $52 million in doctor bills that exceeded the reasonable rate set by Medicare. This figure reached $4 billion nationwide.[499] Consequently, courts have actively taken part in the effort to limit the costs of health care for the elderly. For example, a U.S. District Court judge in Pittsburgh upheld a state law that prohibited doctors from exceeding the rates set by Medicare for services for the elderly.[500] Under Medicare guidelines, there is a set fee for certain services for the elderly that is determined by Medicare.[501] Generally, Medicare will finance 80 percent of this fee, and the patient pays the remaining 20 percent.[502] The state law prohibiting doctors from charging more than the designated fee for respective services will save an estimated $50 million annually.[503]

Pennsylvania also suffers the expense of being one of the largest prescription drug purchasing states in the country.[504] Since 1984, the state has undergone a 113 percent increase in the costs of prescription drugs.[505] Nationally, the elderly spend $10 billion a year buying drugs.[506] The Government Accounting Office reports that millions of elderly Americans are hospitalized or die every year due to the use of unsuited prescriptions.[507] Reports reveal that of the 30 million medicare recipients who are not in hospitals or nursing homes, about 17.5 percent were receiving prescriptions that were unsafe for their age group or were duplicative of other prescriptions. Resulting health problems account for approximately $20 billion in hospital bills.[508] One-fifth of Pennsylvania prescriptions is paid for by the Pharmaceutical Assistance Contract for the Elderly (PACE) program, which is funded by the Department of Aging.[509]

In an effort to alleviate this dramatic increase in costs, the Pennsylvania legislature has introduced a bill that would force pharmaceutical companies to cut costs by over $3.5 billion.[510] Without this reduction, each one of the 387,000 PACE participants, who average an annual bill of $700, will suffer the financial effects of the escalating prescription costs.[511] Participants in the program are generally low-income individuals who depend on financial support for their prescriptions. "In most cases, if they were not in the program, they would have to make a choice between food and medication."[512] Pharmaceutical companies warn, however, that refunds may only serve to "undermine the health and growth of the pharmaceutical industry, which currently is a vital corporate presence in the state of Pennsylvania."[513]

Faced with this restriction, pharmaceutical firms may be forced to cut back on research and development, which is arguably the reason for increasing costs,[514] or even withdrawal from the program altogether.[515] Should they relinquish their participation in the program, however, participants could be left without medication.[516] Some doubt that such a drastic result would follow because of the proven success of similar legislation at the federal level. As a result, other states, such as Maryland, Massachusetts, and Maine, have considered the institution of similar laws.[517]

Pennsylvania currently houses the second highest percentage of elderly in the nation—nearly 2.5 million. One out of every five Pennsylvanians is over the age of 60.[518] This figure will grow significantly in the next five years. As a result, Richard Browdie, Pennsylvania's Secretary of Aging, called for "policy and programmatic approaches" to posture Pennsylvania for the year 2000.[519] The first priority, said Browdie, is to encourage alternatives to expensive nursing homes.

The State Department of Public Welfare in Pennsylvania also plans to require all Medicaid recipients to participate in a managed-care health plan.[520] The objective is to save money and to provide better care. Presently, the sicker the individual, the more money doctors and hospitals make. Because managed-care companies prosper by reducing individual care costs, there is economic incentive to keep beneficiaries healthy and deinstitutionalized. Presently, one out of every seven Pennsylvanians—nearly 1.75 million— receive Medicaid and one-third are already enrolled in a managed health care plan.[521] Only 9 percent of all senior citizens are enrolled, however.[522]

The shift is hoped to provide the state a more definite price on its bill for health care while affording the recipients an opportunity for more regular personal care. The yearly Medicaid tab in Pennsylvania is approximately $6 billion, with Pennsylvania picking up slightly more than the federal government does. New Jersey and Maryland did not hesitate to follow suit with Pennsylvania and approximately half of the other states in the country in requiring managed health care planning. Experts forecast that the surge toward managed care in Pennsylvania, which increases participation by as much as 18 to 20 percent per year, has not even begun to be realized.[523] Consequently, throughout the state, hospitals are posturing for restructuring and downsizing.[524]

Under a managed-care system, Medicaid would pick up a standard monthly tab for the benefits received by all its members, who would subscribe to a primary care physician to oversee all of their service needs, as in a typical HMO system. In doing so, Medigap insurance, which can cost more than $1,000 per year and which many elderly buy to cover the $763 deductible and 20 percent copayment required by Medicare, could be eliminated.[525] Currently, however, the system also works under a traditional fee-for-service policy. Welfare Secretary Feather Houstoun predicts that Pennsylvania cannot afford to operate under both systems.

The switch to managed-care networks is also critical to the continuation of Medicare. In order for Medicare to remain solvent, the number of Medicare recipients who are enrolled in a managed-care system must increase by 450 percent, or one of every two senior citizens.[526] By the year 2002, it is hoped that 19 percent of Medicare beneficiaries will be enrolled in a managed-care program. If this is unattainable, the alternative to preserve Medicare is to raise the current 3.8 percent payroll taxes by at least half.[527] Bill Clinton's plan is to save $124 billion in ten years by paying less to hospitals and doctors.[528] Rather than reducing benefits, Clinton proposes a push for less expensive managed-care services. Part of the Republican plan will be to change from fee-for-service plan to a less expensive managed-care plan. Seniors may have to pay more to retain the fee-for-service option.[529]

Rhode Island

Disparity in support for the GOP's proposed reform of the Medicare and Medicaid systems between Rhode Island Republican Representative Peter I. Blute and Democrats Jack Reed and Patrick J. Kennedy has stirred a political dustbowl in this state.[530] Blute claims that the Democrats' proposal is merely a Band-Aid for Medicare/Medicaid wounds, asserting that the Medicare bill "will put Medicare on a sound footing for long enough to let Congress decide how to cover the wave of Baby Boom retirees after about 2010.[531] Reed claims that the GOP proposal is destined to fail because it disproportionately benefits only the rich and that insurers will cover only the healthiest applicants, leaving the sickest elderly Medicare patients to survive on a traditionally expensive fee-for-service system.[532]

Commenting on why the Republicans are "all of a sudden" so interested on saving Medicare, Reed likened the GOP to the famous bank robber, Willy Sutton, who, when asked why he robbed banks, responded, "Because that's where the money is."[533]

Because the elderly comprise 17 percent of Rhode Island's population (third in the nation after Pennsylvania) and health care is the state's largest private industry,[534] federal posturing affecting the Medicare system will have a significant effect on Rhode Island. However it postures itself, the federal reform is apt to inspire a move toward managed care by either raising premiums for Medicare participants who remain in a traditional system—a scheme which is estimated to save some $80 billion—or by minimizing reimbursements to service providers who treat medicare patients, which is predicted to save an even greater $110 billion.[535] The latter could have devastating effects for local private hospitals, of which all but two receive 50 percent of their revenue from Medicare.[536]

Some health care lawyers predict that mergers and affiliations will soon level off and downsizing and network development will take their place.[537] The result will be continued downsizing, which has spread throughout the country,[538] and a diminished quality of delivery of care. Presently, there are only two Medicare HMOs in Rhode Island, which service 8.4 percent of the 150,000 Medicare population.[539] However, as the managed-care industry takes hold in Rhode Island, many more Medicare HMOs will move into this market.

As the market grows, a new proposal called Aging 2000 is being designed to help the elderly obtain accurate information and data on the market players and their various plans, so that insurance shoppers can be more informed about which plans are best suited for their needs.[540] The plan originated in Cleveland, where corporate leaders bullied their way to obtaining a quality report on various hospitals as a means of gathering information on the quality of care and suitability of several insurance plans.[541] The Cleveland plan's vice president, Ed Zesk, is now the Executive Director of Aging 2000 in Rhode Island and plans to initiate the same quality assessment system in this state for the elderly. Robert DiCenso, President of Aging 2000, said the following:

> Our objective for Aging 2000 is to represent the medical consumer, working with insurers, providers and public policymakers to develop a health care and social service delivery

system that is consumer-oriented, community-based and emphasizes preventive and primary care.[542]

The group's emphasis is on maintaining health rather than treating illness by organizing and assessing "outcome" data, and thereby keeping check on the effectiveness of care. The group may request federal waivers in order to obtain necessary information from the HMOs and to act as a purchasing cooperative for Medicare patients.[543]

South Carolina

South Carolina has played the middle of the road in terms of its response to health care reform. Like most, if not all states, it has experienced the market force of managed care and has responded with hospital restructuring and provider affiliations.[544] Despite this growing trend, however, which really began to take root in South Carolina in 1993, competition between hospitals and service providers remains fierce. Commentators agree that it will take years before the market in South Carolina neutralizes its own payment incentives for service providers to create a more integrated delivery system. Unfortunately, the state seems to be awaiting federal reform to implement any plans.

By the end of 1993, South Carolina was home to approximately 3.6 million residents.[545] About 400,000—11 percent—over half of whom are children—relied on Medicaid for their health care benefits.[546] More than 300,000 residents are uninsured. The percentage of uninsured residents under age 65 in 1991 was 15.5 percent, compared to the national average of 16.6 percent.[547] Although in years past, per capita spending on health care remained under the national average, in 1995, Medicaid accounted for 25 percent of the state's budget, while high school and secondary education accounted for only 22 percent.[548] South Carolina contributes about $300 million to the system, obtaining $3 from the federal government for every dollar contributed.[549] Legislators hope to alleviate the access and cost-control problems associated with these figures by helping small businesses pool together to purchase insurance, an option which is not yet available for small businesses,[550] and by a gradual move to a managed-care system.[551]

In 1991, however, only 2.8 percent of the state participated in an HMO. Now, with a focus on primary care, the state hopes to significantly increase its access and reduce costs, such as its $96 million expenditure on emergency room care.[552] The state is not alone in these concerns.

South Dakota

Rural South Dakota naturally falls prey to one of the most troublesome hazards of health care delivery—geography. The state simply suffers from a shortage of rural doctors. Nationally, there is one doctor for every 400 people; in South Dakota, there is one for every 600 persons.[553] Fifty years ago, doctors were located at 165 different locations throughout the state. Now they are found at only 69 locations.[554] Fourteen percent of rural families in the state are uninsured.[555] In total, 100,000 residents are without coverage. Because of rising health care costs, even employers are cutting back on their provision of health benefits to retirees.[556] Thus, in states such as South Dakota, while there are alliances between insurers,[557] there is very little market competition or alliances among hospitals. Downsizing is not a factor. Thus, there are very few areas wherein minimal reforms are going to make a difference. Accordingly, South Dakota has little to learn from states such as New York and Hawaii, and little to teach. Rural states must struggle with the basics of health care delivery just to survive.

Tennessee

In 1993, Tennessee obtained federal approval to revamp its health care system and became one of the first states to employ a managed-care plan—TennCare—to replace its Medicaid system.[558] At the time, TennCare was at the national forefront in terms of reform; now, some feel it is struggling for survival among the perspectives of doctors and patients alike. The General Accounting Office reports that hospitals have been financially hit the hardest,[559] and critics warn that TennCare may just be a preview to the national disaster of allowing states to administer block-granted funds. At present this does not seem to be the case. Indeed, *The Washington*

Post reports that "In less than three years, TennCare has stopped the hemorrhage of money in Tennessee's Medicaid program, saving the state and federal taxpayers about $1 billion. It has cut the growth of state spending on health care for the poor to about 5 percent a year."[560] Furthermore, the uninsured were about 12 percent of Tennessee's population in 1993 and about 13 percent in the country as a whole. "Today, TennCare pays for the health care of the state's 800,000 former Medicaid patients and heavily subsidizes the coverage of an additional 420,000 formerly uninsured people."[561] There are still about 304,000 uninsured people in Tennessee—about 6 percent of the population.[562]

Prior to TennCare, health care costs accounted for as much as 25 percent of the state's $12 billion budget, yet much of the state was ineligible for Medicaid. Many were left without access to care.[563] Within a year after obtaining a five-year waiver from Medicaid regulations, a dozen managed-care organizations had insured more than 1.2 million people—800,000 of whom were previous Medicaid participants and 400,000 of whom were previously uninsured—and held cost increases to under 1 percent.[564]

Soon after, however, doctors and patients became dissatisfied with administrative aspects of the plan and began to resist participation.[565] One study revealed that 45 percent of former Medicaid participants who switched to the TennCare plan felt their health care had diminished.[566] Several of the participating managed-care plans suffered tremendous losses in the first year.[567] Consequently, participants suffered a rise in premiums, and there were initial premiums for participants living under the poverty line. A premium change went into effect on January 1, 1996, seeking to produce an additional $28 million if everyone required to pay does so.[568] The result is an $82 million federally matched fund that will go toward coverage for 60,000 other uninsured residents.

As predicted, Tennessee's public hospitals are not functioning well under TennCare. "Memphis' public hospital, for example, is trying to survive on TennCare fees that are even lower than those Medicaid paid but must still carry a large burden of 'charity cases,' whom it treats for free."[569] Because of this financial effect, some administrators warn of what the future of TennCare may hold, particularly if a block-grant system is installed:

The problem . . . is that urban public hospitals, without federal oversight of social programs, will fall victim to the realities of state politics. We have a Legislature which, like every other state, is dominated by the rural representatives. It's very hard to make a case for funding public hospitals before a rural Legislature. . . . [] [E]very public hospital in this country needs to think about that when we look at block-granting.[570]

Proponents of the plan, however, assert that the early problems have been ironed out and that TennCare is once again taking its place at the forefront of reform. Since TennCare's institution, the percentage of the population left uninsured dropped from 11 percent in 1993 (550,000 residents) to 5.8 percent in 1995 (304,000 residents), which officials claim puts Tennessee just slightly ahead of Hawaii as the leader in the nation.[571]

By the end of 1995, plans like those in in Oregon and Hawaii were finding wide acceptance as innovative reforms to serve as models for other states while TennCare was inundated with problems and confusion.[572] Experts contributed the contrast between the systems to three factors: (1) human factors, such as preparation (Oregon had included doctors in its plans from the initial stages of planning—Tennessee did not; Oregon's plan took years to design—Tennessee's took months);[573] (2) natural factors, such as geography (Oregon has a diverse managed-care system, whereas Tennessee's managed-care system is minimal in comparison); and of course, (3) financial factors, such as lack of funding (Oregon implemented a $.10-per-pack cigarette tax to help fund the reform; TennCare has been described as "a managed-cost program rather than a managed-care plan").[574] Some experts felt that TennCare was, in fact, a model of reform—on how *not* to reform.[575] Others viewed TennCare as a symbol of the pitfalls associated with implementing managed care.[576]

Some feel that TennCare's most disappointing feature is its inability to provide treatment for substance abusers.[577] Many addicts are discharged prematurely only to return to their habits because they are uninsured. One addict, who had weaned herself from drugs for a short interval, attempted to enter a TennCare treatment program for continued treatment, but claims she was told by the program official that she would not qualify for TennCare coverage unless she started using drugs again.[578] TennCare officials deny such a policy and point to the new behavioral health organizations (BHOs), which will service 1.2 million mental health and substance-abusing TennCare recipients, with no limits on either the number of treatments or the number of days of treatment, but with a lifetime limit of $30,000.[579] Comparatively, California's Medi-Cal does not pay for hospitalization or residential treatment for substance abusers, but has no lifetime limit on outpatient coverage, and sees $7 in savings for every $1 spent on treatment, due mostly to a reduction in drug-related crimes.[580] Others refer to statistics showing that, under TennCare, funding for alcohol and drug treatment services under Medicaid was cut from $60 million in 1993 to $20 million in 1995.[581] Tennessee hopes the move to managed care will pick up some of the slack.

Other states have experienced significant savings in the treatment areas of mental health and substance abuse. Massachusetts, for example, saved $47 million in substance abuse treatment between 1992 and 1993 under a new managed-care system;[582] however, Massachusetts has no lifetime limit and pays 40 percent more for each enrollee than does TennCare.[583] Thus, Massachusetts officials warn against unrealistic comparisons. It is feared that such false expectation will only result in inadequate payments and planning in Tennessee, which, in turn, results in unsuccessful treatment. Experts predict that inadequate treatment of alcohol and drug abuse in Tennessee will lead to increased costs for addicts who end up on the street, in the hospital, or in jail. Thus, in the area of substance abuse treatment, TennCare is not the model of reform that states like Massachusetts and Oregon have proven to be.

Successful reform plans, such as the Oregon plan, have not always been a harbor of safety in the struggle for effective and efficient health care. Every year, many "low-ranking" treatments are ousted from the Oregon plan's umbrella of coverage because of a lack of funding. Consequently, many physicians and patients were dissatisfied with the plan at the outset. And so it was with the debut of TennCare—many doctors felt the plan was painfully underfunded, which resulted in poor payment rates to physicians.[584] Critics of the Tenncare program still lodge the same complaints.[585]

Supporters of the program point to successful statistics, such as a 50 percent cut in the uninsured population and a small increase in rates, which will alleviate funding problems.[586] "Despite all the negative concerns, after two years of implementation, [TennCare] is running about as well as it can for such a radical plan."[587] A report presented to the legislature's TennCare Oversight Committee reveals that emergency room visits for people under age 21 went from 900 visits per 1,000 people in 1993—prior to TennCare—to 360 visits per 1,000 persons by June 1995.[588] The number of days spent in the hospital for people under age 21 went from 490 days per 1,000 people in 1993 to 265 days per 1,000 people by June 1995.[589] Similar figures apply to the 21- to 64-year-old age bracket.[590] The number of physician visits has increased by 20 percent since 1993, which, in turn, has decreased the number and costs of subsequent services.[591]

One continuing problem, however, was getting the federal health care Financing Committee to approve the requirement that Medicaid-eligible patients make small copayments. By June 1995, health care providers were being paid $107 per month, per patient.[592] It was hoped that the rate could increase to as high as $128.20 per month, per patient, but that that figure was doubtful. The TennCare Roundtable hoped to compromise at $118 per member, per month.[593] Other recommendations included requiring private health plans to pay claims within 30 to 45 days; restoring funding for physician training; moving to a managed-care, gate-keeping system more quickly; and paying more reimbursement to primary care physicians rather than specialists.[594] Governor Sundquist also hoped to raise premiums to non-Medicaid patients and charge premiums to patients below the poverty line for the first time.[595]

These recommendations were earmarked as indicative of the unique undertone of TennCare to inject a balance of equity between provider and patient, but skeptics felt the compromises would only alienate thousands of medically needy patients from the system and send them hobbling to the emergency room for uninsured treatment. In defense of the compromise, state Finance Commissioner Bob Corker responded:

The goal is not to reduce enrollment but to replace those people with people who are willing to pay. . . . All of us involved in TennCare realize that the ultimate best thing would be for everyone in Tennessee to have health insurance . . . But people who are getting this tremendous benefit should pay a little for that.[596]

Under TennCare's proposed premium increases, by implementing the highest premium raises at the highest income levels, wealthier recipients may opt to purchase private insurance at similar costs, thereby opening enrollment to those in need.[597] One hospital vice president commented:

They're making some logical, reasonable efforts to make sure the people on the rolls are actual people who need care. Eventually, it may result in more real people being covered.[598]

Rusty Seibert, Director of TennCare, summarized the bottom line by stating: "[TennCare] is not an entitlement and it never was an entitlement. . . . If you let people get on the rolls for nothing, you're just asking to get punched in the head."[599]

Despite its initial shakiness,[600] TennCare is now postured to protect the state from the Medicaid caps that loom over most states that have not yet taken some sort of reform initiative to save costs. As of June 30, 1995, TennCare had approached $1 billion in savings by cutting expenditures to about 7 percent.[601] Before TennCare was initiated, the state was averaging an annual growth in Medicaid expenditures of 15 percent.[602] In September 1995, TennCare contracted with a data-processing firm founded by Ross Perot and now owned by General Motors Corporation to manage information for the program and hopefully to cut even more administrative costs.[603] These savings have helped to put TennCare on the managed-care track. As of June 1995, 94 percent of Tennesseans had health insurance because of the introduction of TennCare.[604] The number of residents enrolled in the 12 existing managed-care organizations increased from 6 percent to 35 percent after TennCare was introduced.[605] This percentage will grow as managed care takes root throughout the state.[606] It is predicted that by the year 2000, 65 percent of Tennessee will participate in a managed-care plan.[607] In neighboring Southwest Virginia, which is more rural, however, managed care is virtually nonexistent. It is anticipated, therefore, that Virginia will soon adopt a program designed much like Tenn-Care to replace its Medicaid program.[608]

While Tennessee's preparation for managed care may appear to some to be a speedy and drastic one, it appears that it is one which effectively postured Tennessee for the pending block-grant system now threatening wasteful welfare programs in every state. The adjustments made by Tennessee for this potential change, however, are praised as "a win for the state and a win for enrollees" by Tenncare Director, Rusty Siebert.[609] Still, the Republican block-grant agenda has met with much opposition by northeastern states such as New York, New Jersey, and Pennsylvania, which tend to offer a broader scope of services at a greater expense than does Tennessee.[610] Still, while Tennessee would find itself with the flexibility and fairness it needs under a block-grant system and would increase its federal receipt from $1.8 billion in 1994 to $3 billion in 2002 (a 62 percent increase, compared to the average 30 percent in the northern states), it will still fall $1.2 billion short of what it would realize under Bill Clinton's system by the same date.[611] Presently, Tennessee must front $.33 for every $.67 funded by the federal government.[612] The House GOP plan does away with Tennessee's matching requirement but requires that at least 40 percent of the grant funds still be designated as health care funds.[613]

Whatever federal plan is implemented will have significant effects, not only for hospitals,[614] but for nursing homes. There were 57 new nursing homes with nearly 10,000 new beds established in the state between 1985 and 1995.[615] During this time, the costs of nursing homes increased from $280 million to $745 million per year, of which the federal government paid 67 percent.[616] Congressional budget cuts will, no doubt, severely undermine this growth.[617] Richard Sadler, Executive Director of the Tennessee Health Care Association, predicts that there must be a balance between sufficient funding and adequate care: "If there is going to be less money, there will have to be less patients so those that are there will receive adequate care."[618]

Presently, Medicaid pays for nearly half of the nation's nursing home bills; long-term care accounts for 37 percent of all Medicaid expenditures.[619] Under the Republican proposals, individual states could require adult children to pay for some of their Medicaid-eligible parent's nursing home bills.[620] Many doubt the social and economic viability of such an option in Tennessee as a means of supplementing long-term care funding.[621] Now, the state spends $1 billion a year on 30,000 nursing home residents, $800,000 of which is paid directly to the nursing homes.[622] TennCare, on the other hand, spends considerably more—$2.4 billion—but it insures 1.2 million members. Experts expect that the difference is because the Medicaid nursing home program still works on a fee-for-service basis, so providers are paid for each procedure and there is no incentive to avoid added expenditures.[623] Under the TennCare program, providers are paid a flat fee of approximately $1,600 per person and are inspired to design treatment plans geared toward savings, which equal profits. Commenting on the relationship between nursing home care and TennCare, Rusty Siebert stated: "Long-term care has never gone under managed care. It is the only kind of 'free-floater' we have."[624] The hope for Tennessee, therefore, is that long-term nursing home care can somehow be squeezed under the cost-saving protection of the TennCare umbrella.

Tennessee has slowly accepted the philosophy of TennCare. While there was much skepticism at first, many critics have resolved themselves that there is hope for the program. Most of the health care industry in Tennessee, however, still holds its breath to see what effect TennCare will have on the industry, now that its managed-care roots have taken hold. One executive vice president of a major health care system in Tennessee states:

> TennCare is with us. Conceptually, it's the right thing to do, but we still have concerns about how it performs. That's something that providers and state officials will have to work on together.[625]

One legislative effort that is indicative of the collaborative philosophy of the TennCare program, and which is expected to assist the growth of managed care, is a new law in Tennessee, passed in June 1995, wherein hospitals can now hire physicians as employees and set their own costs for procedures.[626] In turn, physicians acquire the right to greater independent medical judgment.[627] Even so, mergers and acquisitions will continue to be the trend in Tennessee as the managed-care program of TennCare continues to grow.

As the managed-care system of TennCare continues to expand, so do its effects. Already, TennCare has experienced a legal intervention that is destined to arise at some point in every managed-care state, if not already in every health care provider's thoughts, who has the final say on what treatment will be received?

And who will pay for it? Take, for example, the case of three-year-old Brandie Hinds, of Maynardsville, Tennessee, who awaits major surgery to have her small intestine and half of her colon removed in order to save her life.[628] Unfortunately, Brandie was initially denied coverage by TennCare for her operation, which cost nearly $600,000.[629] Testimony in court revealed that, at one point, Blue Cross/Blue Shield agreed to pay for the operation, but only in Tennessee, where no hospitals were capable of performing it.[630] Later, they offered to pay for the liver transplant, but not the bowel transplant, on which the liver transplant was dependent. Finally, they denied coverage for both transplants, labeling the operation a "nonemergency service . . . not medically necessary . . . and experimental."[631] In a December 28, 1995 decision filed in January 1996, however, U.S. District Court Judge John T. Nixon issued a ruling entirely contrary to the premise of managed care—that managed-care organizations will determine which procedures are financially viable for coverage—and ruled that TennCare and Blue Cross/Blue Shield must pay for the surgery.[632] In his opinion, Judge Nixon writes:

> While the court is cognizant of the need to contain health care costs in order to distribute benefits among the widest number of recipients, the law is clear that necessary medical treatment must not be sacrificed in an effort to contain costs.[633]

Commenting on the effect of the decision, attorney Neil McBride stated: "Under TennCare, all the incentives are to deny services. That may be necessary, but it would only work if people have a way to question the denial of services."[634] Lenny Croce, lead counsel on the case, commented that people do not want "a bureaucrat in government or private corporations . . . to decide who dies or who lives."[635] Brandie is now scheduled for surgery in Pittsburgh.[636] While Brandie awaits suitable organ donors, the health care industry awaits to see the effect of Judge Nixon's decision on TennCare's coverage of other questionable procedures. Blue Cross spokesman Ron Harr stated: "There are broader implications to Judge Nixon's ruling than just this one case and that is what we are considering at this time."[637]

Since the ruling, it has been decided that TennCare will now pay for high-dose chemotherapy with stem cell transplantation at selected study sites—a procedure denied coverage just a year ago because of its controversial nature.[638] The treatments will cost TennCare about $60,000 per patient.[639] TennCare will cover treatment for several thousand qualified patients at a total annual cost of about $8 million.[640] Pursuant to Tennessee law, because TennCare has now opted to cover the procedure, other private insurance carriers must also pay.[641] The decision has fared well with the public.

> The decision by TennCare administrators to cover the treatment means an important option will be available for patients. But in broader terms, its an indication that the TennCare program is gaining sound footing. It shows that the system, launched in 1994, is now in position to grow and offer new services. It also shows that TennCare officials are willing to listen and learn.[642]

The next hurdle for TennCare will be coverage for AIDS drugs, which more and more are being approved by the Food and Drug Administration.[643] If accepted for coverage, the two latest drugs could cost TennCare between $24 and $120 million a year.[644] The treatments cost about $5,000 per patient per month.[645] The expense of the drugs could put many smaller health plans out of business[646] and may severely restrict the program's ability to accept new members.[647] TennCare covers approximately 2,000 to 2,500 Tennessee residents who have AIDS or HIV.[648] Karl Kovacs, Chief Executive Officer of the TLC Family Care Health Plan in Memphis says that there are more than just financial factors to consider: "We're dealing with a finite amount of resources and we have to, in a rational way, determine what we can cover and what we can't. It's not just a TennCare issue. It's a societal issue."[649] TennCare officials fear if the drugs are now covered, the expense could jeopardize other needed services.[650] If TennCare does pay for the treatments, it will again be left with the same question: What does this mean for other new procedures? "This time, it's new AIDS drugs; next time it's a cure for cancer or a new heart procedure. Ultimately, we'll have to face the (rationing) issue nationally, but because of TennCare [Tennessee will] be the first to face the crisis."[651]

Enrollment in TennCare has expanded so much, so quickly, that now enrollment is closed for only uninsured residents to join, by either being Medicaid-eligible or failing to qualify for insurance because of preexisting conditions.[652] What frightens TennCare officials and threatens to bankrupt the system, especially in light of the expanding procedures now covered by TennCare, is that there is no requirement to establish one's residency in the state before qualifying for coverage. Officials fear, therefore, that Tenncare will be a resource for out-of-state uninsurables using in-state addresses to obtain coverage.[653] Many feel the difficulty of discovering the fraud could be mitigated by requiring proof of residency before acquiring coverage. At some point, officials will have to balance interests[654] and determine at what point TennCare will become a reform plan no different from many other states—a sinking ship taking on more passengers.

Texas

On September 1, 1995, the Texas Legislature effectuated the "guaranteed-issue provision" of a 1993 law—House Bill 2055—which stated that all health insurers must provide coverage to all small businesses, regardless of the presence of employees with costly health problems.[655] To make up for the added risk and expense, however, insurers are charging small firms with potentially unhealthy workers as much as 67 percent more for coverage.[656] Until the law was passed in 1993, increases for risky businesses had seldom gone beyond 20 percent. In 1994, rate increases resulting from the law were incorrectly expected to go no higher than 15 percent.[657] As one commentator noted, "[t]he new law is going to give you accessibility, not necessarily affordability."[658]

The founder of the law, Senator Mike Martin, did not anticipate that insurers would take advantage of the law's language,[659] but the Department of Insurance found the law to be vaguely worded. Even businesses with healthy workers have been hit with a 6 percent raise in premiums to make up for the mandatory higher-risk participants. Still, most businesses are apt to be willing to pay more to ensure coverage for potentially unhealthy employees.

The legislature initially passed the law in 1993, at which time it guaranteed coverage in firms of 3 to 50 employees who were not otherwise insured. Preexisting conditions can be excluded for 12 months, however.[660] Now, the law has sparked intense competition between insurers, who fear a flood of sickly applicants if they offer the most affordable premiums. Since its introduction, opponents have criticized many aspects of the law as "socialized medicine," claiming it is too similar to Bill Clinton's failed plan for reform.[661] Many fear smaller insurers will not be able to compete by spreading the risk of unhealthy participants among fewer clients. Other states that have employed a guaranteed issue provision,[662] such as Florida, however, have not experienced the fallout that is expected by many.[663]

Other new initiatives proposed by Texas legislators include the Archer-Jacobs Family Medical Savings and Investment Act of 1995, which provides for the institution of Medical Savings Accounts for catastrophic plan participants.[664] Contributions are excludable for the employer and deductible for the individual.[665] Also, former President George Bush's son, Governor George W. Bush, is trying to obtain a waiver from Medicaid regulations to adopt a plan allowing counties to match federally funded programs.[666]

Utah

Utah also hopes to minimize the rising costs of health care through the institution of a managed-care system.[667] Its ability to effectively integrate the capitated managed-care system has made it one of the nations leading states in terms of reducing costs, according to some.[668] One Vice President of Intermountain Health Care noted:

> Market pressures and public policy are moving managed care to a cornerstone position in a reformed U.S. health care system. . . . In the next five years, managed care plans are expected to account for more than 90 percent of all health insurance, as

businesses and consumers seek more cost-effective alternatives to traditional insurance.[669]

As insightfully noted by Charles J. Kofoed, however, regardless
of the proposals for reformed health care, most, if not all proposals,
have one common missing link—a lack of individual responsibility.
Kofoed states, "[M]ost of us are sitting idle, waiting for final details
from Congress."[670] Thus, while many state initiatives may be effective, most lack the integration needed if health care is to be locally
efficient and universally beneficial.

Some states, such as Utah, have dealt effectively with narrowly
focused reforms that address specific glitches in the state's delivery
of health care. Some feel, therefore, that drastic, comprehensive
reforms—overhauls—may not be beneficial for the uniqueness of
some states.[671] The competitive market forces create all the change
that is necessary to slowly refurbish and already workable system in
some states. "[One] concern is [that] a federal level plan will end up
creating a big thing that is already solved by the market."[672]

Vermont

Vermont is uniquely postured to maintain a successful health care
reform that provides universal coverage at an affordable rate under
the Vermont Health Care Act of 1992.[673] The act was a phase-in
plan that involves a tradeoff with physicians, who accept greater
state involvement, but are freed of the burden of the normal administrative demands of insurance companies and the confines of malpractice litigation. The Act is clearly a move toward a managed-
care system, but the state must still assess how it will be financed
and what minimum care it can afford to universally deliver. The
uniqueness of the state's posture lies in its size and small population, its nonprofit hospital system, its physician-oriented governor,
and a medical community supportive of state intervention.[674]

Under the Vermont plan, a family of four that does not qualify for
Medicaid (earns less than $30,150 annually) may receive free medi-
cal care for its children.[675] Overseen by the Vermont Health Care
Authority, the plan expands access by offering a safety net for group
beneficiaries who lose coverage, and cuts costs by developing uniform health insurance forms and standardized processing, which

decrease administrative costs, particularly in the area of malpractice claims.[676] Insurance rates are determined by a community-based rating system, which assures equality between group versus individual purchasers. Significantly, the plan imposes a global budget, including hospital spending caps, to control costs.

As long ago as 1979, the state implemented a certificate-of-need program, the regulation of which became more focused in 1987 and which expanded to physician practices in 1990.[677] Unlike many states, this program has proven successful. A similar process of review was established in 1983 called the Hospital Data Council, the purpose of which was to conduct budget reviews of hospitals and make cost control recommendations. This council has helped in molding regulations for reform.

In 1987, the state created the Vermont Health Insurance Plan to help address the growing uninsured population. The plan attempted to initialize an employer pay-or-play method and a state subsidy for a basic health care package for the uninsured, but the plan's implementation proved too expensive.[678] By the following year, the plan was restructured as the Prenatal and Children's Health Program (Dr. Dynasaur) and became a successful tool for insuring children up to age seven and pregnant women with restricted incomes. The success of the plan spurred the implementation of Act 52 in 1991, which mandated a community rating system and small group eligibility guarantees.[679]

Political changes in Vermont in 1991 brought about the new reform of 1992, spearheaded by a new governor, Dr. Howard Dean, who has commented on the effect of federal involvement in Vermont's health reform as follows:

> My biggest fear has been . . . that the federal government would impose Medicare for everybody, and that would be national health care. . . . And in that case I think you would see the end of decent health care in this country. I didn't want to see that in Vermont.

At the time, however, the state had a tremendous debt, and a push toward a single-payer system was gaining momentum.[680] Eventually—and controversially—the two proposals were compromised to develop the Act of 1992. The act leaves the state the task of integrating a single- or multipayer system and developing a basic health care package, which, as Oregon has discovered, is no simple task. Most important, the state must find a way to finance the plan effectively and efficiently.

Virginia

As federal and state efforts to improve health care while cutting costs increase, so do the number of Virginians relying on Medicaid.[681] Medicaid enrollment has increased by as much as 75 percent, in large part due to the federal government's directive that the state be more flexible in its Medicaid enrollment criteria.[682] With increasing enrollment comes increasing costs; Medicaid expenses for the state nearly doubled between 1990 and 1993, from $1 billion to $1.9 billion.[683] Under Bill Clinton's plan, some experts expect the state to lose more than $1 billion by the year 2000,[684] but many feel that the Clinton plan is so convoluted that it is fruitless to try to assess or predict the financial effects.[685]

Instead of waiting for comprehensive federal reform, Virginia has taken small steps to alleviate the growing uninsured population, such as the creation of a managed-care program called Medallion, which groups certain Medicaid patients under the care of specific primary care physicians to reduce individual reliance on emergency room treatment for nonemergency illnesses. The Medallion plan seeks to increase accessibility to insurance through cost reductions.[686] In 1994, the Medallion Program increased its enrollment from 160,000 to 260,000. Despite opinion polls showing a loud cry for reform,[687] comprehensive universal care and increased regulation is not on the agenda for Virginia legislators; that is being left to the federal government by some[688] and the free-market system by others.[689]

In the meantime, as the managed-care industry spreads throughout the state, albeit at a slower pace than most, hospitals have been feeling the effects of the need to affiliate, much like most other hospitals in most other states.[690] Affiliation and cooperation among providers will prove significant, especially for rural areas, as the prospect of federal reform, oblivious to the specialized needs of specific states and counties, looms large.[691] "Health care reform will be through groups."[692]

In 1995, Virginia began a phase-in plan to increase the number of general practitioners across the state by focusing incentives on medical school graduates to locate in rural areas.[693] However, even specialized plans like these have been daunted by budget restraints. The state's health care commission requested $10.3 million to fully integrate the initiative plan, but received only one-third of their request from the legislature.[694]

Washington

The state of Washington is another leader of health care reform as a result of political posturing and a history of failed reformation attempts.[695] Its comprehensive reform began with a focus on the uninsured. Such focus led to the introduction of the Basic Health Plan in 1987—much like New Jersey's Individual Health Plan—which is independently operated and state subsidized and which allows participants to choose from several managed-care plans. Eventually, contested debate and a collaborative vision of universal care led to the Washington Health Services Act of 1993, which implemented certified health plans (CHPs) in an effort to deliver a uniform health package to four regions of the state. Businesses may still employ their own individual plans, but they must conform to the standards regulating the CHPs.

As with most successful reforms, a state regulatory commission—the Health Services Commission—was created to oversee the market.[696] Its function focused on cutting costs through regulating managed competition, capping premium increases, and simplifying other administrative burdens, particularly the structure of tort reform.[697]

The plan affords expanded accessibility by integrating an individual and employer mandate and expanding state subsidization for the uninsured.[698] Individually, the mandate requires participation in a CHP by 1999. The employer mandate will be phased-in, beginning in 1995 for large firms (more than 500 employees), and by 1999 for smaller firms. The employer is mandated to contribute 50 percent toward the cost of qualified plans.[699] An assistance fund of $150 million—similar to that in Hawaii—will be established by 1997 to assist smaller firms (less than 25 employees) that are otherwise burdened by the mandate. A 1998 tax credit for firms with less than 500 employees will also soften the blow.[700] For the uninsured, a revamped Medicaid system will now cover all children below 200 percent of the poverty level in a managed-care plan. Similarly situated adults may be joined with employer subsidies.

It is expected that once in full force, approximately 100,000 Washingtonians will still be excluded from state and employer subsidization and will fall under the individual mandates.[701] Insurers are subject to community rates and exclusion prohibitions. Accessibility for providers was enhanced by free participation in a CHP, with particular guarantees and restrictions. For example, a CHP may limit the number of its providers, but a physician may not be terminated without notification of the criteria for termination and the opportunity to correct the terminating behavior.[702]

Having structured its accessibility, the success of the plan lies in its focus on delivering preventive clinical services. Funding is obtained strictly through hospital, insurance, and tobacco and alcohol taxes.[703] Minimal drawbacks have been raised, such as the exclusion of seasonal workers, who are mainly Hispanic, but strong efforts are being made to integrate this demographic into the reform. Long-term care provisions, which are also omitted from the plan, must be discussed legislatively to be integrated into the plan by 1999.[704] The impact of rural areas on the success of a competitive system must also be further addressed. As with any comprehensive state reform, there are risks, restrictions, such as ERISA,[705] and unanswered questions, but for Washington, there are none so severe that the individual initiative of the state is restricted.

West Virginia

Rising costs have taken a serious toll on health care in West Virginia, which has consistently lagged behind the rest of the nation.[706] In 1991, West Virginia was spending $4.3 billion on health care, averaging expenses of $2,400 for every resident.[707] The state has the second highest rate of Medicaid use in the country.[708] Although health care spending increased at an annual rate of 9.5 percent—twice that of inflation—one in three West Virginians could not afford insurance, according to a 1992 study, and the state has long been noted as one of the unhealthiest in the nation.[709] As much as 70 percent of the illnesses treated in West Virginia are considered to be preventable illnesses.[710] Because of the high rate of poor health habits recorded by West Virginians, many feel the legislature should implement health reforms that are designed to cut costs, while at the same time, promote health, such as implementing "sin taxes" on tobacco products.[711]

In 1992, 86 percent of the state's insurance coverage occurred through employment.[712] Of these, 76 percent contribute to the costs of coverage; 57 percent of these contributors paid more for premiums in 1992 than they did in 1989.[713] These costs have taken a large toll on local hospitals, which charge patients as much as $500 more per day to compensate for unreimbursed services provided to the uninsured.[714] The rural areas of West Virginia suffer even more as a result of a shortage of doctors.[715]

Despite West Virginia's poor track record for overall health, there is still a sufficient push for preventive and primary care that hospitals not suited to adapt to future reform will find it difficult to stay competitive within the market.[716] Unless hospitals are equipped to specialize and to provide outpatient services, they will not integrate well into the new and changing health care market.

Wisconsin

Health care delivery is the focus of Wisconsin, particularly in counties wherein swooping federal reforms will have little effect because of the specialized needs of the state.[717] Health care networks are making efforts to gather data regarding the health care concerns of the residents in order to more effectively service those needs. "Community involvement is crucial . . . to any reform movement."[718] Hopefully, commercial interest will be sparked in the "community-oriented" reform plans once savings become noticeable.

A significant contribution to controlling costs in the state has been the success of employer alliances forming insurance purchasing cooperatives.[719] Purchasing agents have begun not only to weed out expensive plans and point clients in the less expensive direction, but agents are now processing and evaluating outcome information to make comparative assessments of the quality and efficiency of insurance plans as well.[720] For the outcome data to be useful, however, employers must remain faithful to their alliance and maintain a strong collective bargaining voice in the market.

Like many other legislators in many other states, some Wisconsin legislators are less optimistic about universal reform and are more hopeful that less ambitious reforms will augment the already existing health care system in the state.[721] As in other states, the market forces of the growing capitation system create reform.[722] "Many of the efficiency-related changes in health care have come in reaction to increases in health care costs and the related health care reform debate."[723] Even the natural market reforms can seem monumental, particularly for hospitals. "By the year 2000, it will be difficult to say what a hospital is. Having a wing where people are horizontal at night may not be that important."[724] The state saw 25 hospitals close their doors between 1980 and 1993, particularly in rural areas.[725] The remaining Wisconsin hospitals, however, have proven their efficiency in hospital service by substantially decreasing their number of inpatient admissions and inpatient days spent in the hospital.[726] Meanwhile, both nationally and locally, outpatient visits drastically increased.[727]

Experts think that Wisconsin's ability to maintain a leading edge in hospital efficiency will depend on its ability to minimize costs, regulate competition, maintain quality care under a capitated payment system, and integrate effective employee-purchasing coalitions.[728]

Wyoming

Wyoming is home to a large percentage of uninsured residents: reports reveal that in 1993, 15 percent of its residents were without coverage, ranking the state thirty-fifth in the number of uninsured residents.[729] Other studies place the state twenty-third in the percentage of uninsured population, but second in the nation when considering also health care costs and quality of care.[730] Insurance groups report that the state's health care system is doing well. The state spends a small percentage of its gross state product on health care due to similarly small percentages of residents with AIDS, the elderly population, and immigrants.[731] In addition to the $1.2 billion state residents spend on in-state health care, they also spend $300 million a year on out-of-state care.[732]

STATE PENUMBRAS

While the states tend to be more reticent to foster truly innovative proposals for long-term care—perhaps because of the political ramifications—individual commentators have freely given advice. For instance, one commentator offers a bifurcated system of reform.[733] First, he suggests the creation of an expanded health insurance plan for low-income elderly financed through targeted revenues. Second, he suggests a universal program funded by all members of society. These approaches incorporate a mix of "public, familial, and individual responsibility emphasized by society."[734] He also incorporates a long-term care insurance program to be paid for by the federal government; this is a social market solution that would provide for those unable to provide for themselves. Children aiding their parents would be given a tax deduction for private long-term care insurance premiums and an elderly parent-care tax credit for in-home custodial care.[735]

Dr. Daniel Callahan suggests that health care resources should be equitably allocated according to practicality and usefulness, somewhat similar to the bill proposed in Oregon,[736] establishing prioritization. Any such proposal is certain to provoke controversy because such a hierarchy of health care benefits would allocate less resources to the elderly as age approaches and extends beyond what would be considered a reasonable life expectancy. For example, a heart transplant for a 100-year-old man would not be economically, and possibly even socially, practical; however, the same transplant may be resourceful for a 50-year-old man. Although this allocative structure entails line-drawing problems as to age limitations and economic usefulness, Dr. Callahan suggests that conditions such as Alzheimer's disease would be placed very high on the hierarchy of benefits because of the severely dehumanized condition in which it leaves its victims.[737]

Certainly voting patterns and vested interests will have a strong voice in any prioritization plan, indeed any plan which would seek to determine value and economical distribution. Countries such as Canada have been allocating resources—rationing services—as a part of a national health care system for a long time:

> We [Canadians] ration according to the severity of the disease . . . For us, those who need care most get it first . . . . regard-

less of economic status. That's a fundamental philosophical difference between Canada and the United States. Both sides ration.
[The states] have got thirty-seven million people who don't
have diddley-squat for an insurance plan. They're rationed,
too.[738]

When polled, only 3 percent of Canadians preferred the American system over their own, concluding almost certainly that their
own system of allocation was preferable over the American plan of
rationing by ability to pay.[739] Also, the comfort of knowing that
needed care will be affordable takes priority over concern about
waiting.

The goal of allocation would be to add to or maintain a minimum
quality of life for *all* people rather than extension of the quantity of
life for only those who can afford it.[740] Therefore, as there is

no current law directly prohibit[ing] the rationing of health care
based on chronological age . . . it may be appropriate to discrimi-
nate on the basis of age when it would not be appropriate on the
basis of sex or race. . . . If people receive equal treatment at the
same chronological times in their lives, we can achieve age
equality.[741]

Such a goal opens the door to a common question: "If we can't
afford everything medicine has to offer, then how and where do we
draw the line?"[742] And what good does it do to win the Nobel Prize
for a great medical breakthrough if you bankrupt Medicare, Medicaid, and every patient who has to pay for it?

The states are grappling with the issues; this is evident from the
survey of the states. Most seem more intent on solving the immediate need of medical insurance for the growing numbers of persons
without the ability to pay for even minimum service.

By June 1993, eight states have enacted comprehensive measures designed to provide universal health coverage: Hawaii,
Massachusetts, Oregon, Florida, Minnesota, Vermont, Maryland
and Washington. Only Hawaii has [in 1994] an operational
system. Four other states—California, New Jersey, New York,
and Iowa—have undertaken major demonstration projects.[743]

States have expanded financial access, portability of coverage, cost limitations, tort damage caps, improved delivery systems, computer tracking of costs and patients, and naming commissions to recommend future health reform legislation. Employer-mandated insurance and even "sin taxes" to pay for coverage of the needy have been successful in some states. Others like Tennessee's TennCare and Kentucky's KentuckyKare have developed model programs.

The point is that the states are seeking solutions to the most pressing needs of those without insurance and those without minimum medical care. The inability to pay has closed hospitals and cost both the state and federal governments millions in Medicaid costs that would be borne by private individuals, HMOs, or cooperatives with advanced planning. The Medicaid dilemma is forcing the states to act.

Only time will tell whether the many reforms that are proposed and instituted prove effective. Furthermore, health care reform is only a part of the problem. With the aging of America and what is sure to become a trend of institutionalized care for the elderly, the dilemma of long-term care is just around the corner. Whatever the nature of the current reform, the primary goal must be long-term care as this is the end toward which we are going. The end must encompass some of the dignity we possess as humans:

> Refocusing the Medicare coverage from an acute care to chronic care orientation which provides for service in the least costly setting will be more effective, more humane and more affordable. We must redesign the Medicare system so that it enables individuals to remain at home where they are able to maintain their independence and dignity.[744]

Said one scholar, testifying before the Senate Finance Committee:

> Every meaningful . . . reform . . . will cause some children to suffer. . . . So will a continuation of the status quo. You are engaged in a necessarily brutal calculation, trying to estimate what strategy will result in the least net suffering.[745]

Federal policymakers should consider the diversity among the states as they develop a national reform proposal and determine how much flexibility should be given to states in adapting the national approach to meet their unique needs and circumstances.[746]

Finally, the effects of the various state initiatives are uncertain. Comprehensive state reform may, in fact, be dependent on federal reform, which will be forced to play its hand as state budgets continue to pour expenditures into failing Medicare and Medicaid systems. Everything seems to suggest that the future lies with "providing states with expanded discretion, but in fashioning a partnership that both respects the diversity among the states and provides a federal reform framework."[747] Both governmental entities must be involved.

As long as the shape of federal reform remains in flux, states have a good reason (or at least a good excuse) to delay moving forward. States that read the tea leaves correctly and accordingly proposition themselves correctly for federal reform will have the jump on other states for implementation. On the other hand, states that head off in the wrong direction may encounter substantial effort and expense in correcting their course.

Reform is politically contentious and often costly. On the other hand, the problems of access and cost . . . exist in every state just as they do at the federal level. A handful of states have stepped out boldly. Their efforts may light the way toward reform at the national level.[748]

Chapter 6

Assessment for the Future

POLICY CHANGES

Affordability Confronts Expectations

Historically, health care reform has taken a prioritative backseat to budgetary concerns.[1] Now, on the eve of health care dismantlement, it has become apparent that the broad range of congressional ideologies with regard to welfare reform and health care is merely a microcosm of society's skepticism about successful reform in these areas. No one disputes that change is necessary, but everyone disagrees on how much change is needed and who should absorb the cost of change.

The expectations confronting long-term care abound. Who should pay? For how long? And generally, When life and health are at stake, how might we determine that a given sum of money spent on health care would give greater value were it used on things *other* than health care?[2] Much has changed since this last question was asked in 1983, but the question is still very relevant. Pope John Paul II asks the same in his encyclical *Gospel of Life*. So does Bruce Nussbaum when he writes about AIDS in 1990,[3] and so does Professor George P. Smith when he states that: "The challenge of the New Biology . . . is to seek and maintain quality in purposeful living, both in the early potential for life and its subsequent continuation, yet at the same time protect the recognition of sanctity of life—again at its conception through its natural conclusion."[4]

Health care itself is very expensive and it has grown more so as technology and expectations expand. In 1980, Americans spent an average of $2,590 per family on health care, or 9 percent of family

177

income. In 1993, the figures jumped to $7,739 per family, which is 13.1 percent of family income.[5] The average American family spent 11.7 percent of its income on health care in 1991, up from 9 percent in 1980. This figure is expected to reach as high as 16 percent by the year 2000.[6] It will thus come as no surprise that, in 1991, America led the way in spending per capita and percentage of its gross domestic product for health care by spending $2,868 per capita, or 13.2 percent of its GDP. During the same year, by comparison, Germany spent only $1,659 per capita, or 8.5 percent of its GDP; Japan spent $1,307 per capita, or 6.8 percent of its GDP; and the United Kingdom spent $1,043 per capita, or 6.6 percent of its GDP.[7] The cost to the federal government in health care costs rose as well. Between 1965 and 1991, federal revenue spending on health care grew from 3.5 percent to 20.5 percent, while state and local revenue spending grew from 8 percent to 21.4 percent.[8]

But what is the point: Money is not the operative word for long-term care; value is. "Value is the life-giving power of everything."[9] What Americans value most is the ability to make decisions for themselves from alternatives that are both understandable and affordable. Technology has given us alternatives that we never had before. This has, in turn, created a monetary problem because the alternatives are expensive. They are so expensive that the federal and state governments have positioned themselves through history so that they have provided the money necessary to pay for these alternatives. These same governments are now victims of success, that is, the paid-for medical alternatives are keeping people alive longer and thus we are right in the crux of long-term planning. But so do we face the inevitable, that long-term care and health care itself are intertwined.

If government retreats to an affordable level of care, the expectations of many will die with them. Only the most affluent will be able to afford the treatments necessary to stay alive. The expectation that all should have equal access to fundamental care is built into the American dream; thus, the opportunity to retreat is limited. Expectations have eliminated any retreat; this is a dangerous predicament. And should the government run out of money and go to extended families or to the savings of those seeking care and ask for payment, the cry would become a wail. Machiavelli's assertion in *The Prince* is appropriate: "[W]hen neither their property nor honour is touched, the majority of men live content."[10]

This is the dilemma of affordability . . . confronting expectations today: to acknowledge the seriousness of long-term care planning; to be precise as to what it is costing and shall cost in the future; and to lay out the alternatives from which the able, the disinclined, and the disabled may choose so as to provide for the most affordable alternatives each can expect regarding long-term care. This will entail many, if not all of the following: (1) regulation of fee schedules, such as Medicare's physician services;[11] (2) a managed competition within what is available to the sick and elderly;[12] (3) cost sharing among insurance groups and perhaps employers or wealthier persons or savings plans or withholding. This will incorporate deductibles and even tax incentives for both employers and savings plans.[13] As it is, business health care expenses now exceed after-tax profits; in 1980, health care expenses equalled only 44 percent of after-tax profits.[14] There also needs to be a reduction in administrative costs through electronic billing, malpractice reform, and fraud and abuse regulations.[15] An economist at Brookings Institution in Washington stated: "[t]he question is whether [these] expenditure[s] [are] going for services that are worth what they cost. If that were the case, this would be just fine."[16] For instance, the General Accounting Office estimates that over the next five years, fraud in the billing procedures by doctors will cost Medicare $4 billion.[17]

Alternatives to Nursing Home Care

The private sector must become involved with long-term care in the manner in which it has become involved with elementary education. Just as we provide elementary schools, tutors, day care, busing, parent-teacher associations, lunches, Head Start, and local control, so must the same be implemented for the elderly, those most likely to enjoy long-term care.

Tax incentives must be built into construction and maintenance costs and inasmuch as home care is both desirable and cost-efficient, this form of long-term care must be supported. Some estimate that the home health care industry could expand by 140 percent between 1992 and 1997.[18] The home infusion therapy market has grown by 16 percent a year. As with elementary education on a public scale, the public must be educated as to what is required to maintain a quality program.

Public Policy Necessity

What is lacking is an understanding of the "integrating" component among the various factors affecting long-term care. Too many people are doing too many things separately and without consultation or cooperation. Duplication abides. Of course, this breeds contempt for the system, manifested in ethical inquiries about Medicaid estate planning and the actual transfer of assets through Medicaid spend-down. Congress and President Clinton speak of reduction in the deficit and a balanced budget. Block grants to the states through which they would be able to establish their own eligibility levels command the most vociferous comments. Yet the point is not getting across: Every American will face the dilemma of long-term care for himself or herself, or for a family member or friend. There is a necessity for public policy.

During the fall of 1993, President Clinton gave a speech in which he asked for "America to fix a health care system that is badly broken."[19] Congress eventually rejected the Clinton proposal, and it seems that the loss of reform could be attributed to a preference for the status quo rather than any reform proposal offered.[20] At present, the suggestion is made that new efforts at reform should be on an incremental basis, perhaps starting with children and then, with added education, progressing to broader coverage.[21] Long-term care is part of this incremental approach; it deserves immediate public policy recognition and education.

Elements needing consideration in proposing long-term care changes would include those already adopted and working within the states. Specifically, attention should be directed toward long-term care insurance, home- and community-based services, and matching grants to states to encourage development of programs. Recently enacted tax incentives should be strengthened. Nonetheless, it seems most reasonable to suggest that education of the American public is a decisive factor. Perhaps the graying of America will make a difference, and the first-hand experience of growing older will be the best of teachers. Presently, however, most Americans do not understand the difference between health care and long-term care, and Medicaid spend-down will not be available much longer to forgive their ignorance. Education is needed as a public policy necessity.

Sheer numbers and costs provide incentives for long-term planning both at a private and a public level. In 1965, 19 million elderly had no health insurance and one third of them lived in poverty. Times have changed. Today, 97 percent of 35 million elderly have Medicare cards. This number shall expand rapidly with the baby boomers aging. They shall need care, as is demonstrated by the statistic that people over the age of 65 consume 2.3 times the health resources as those under the age of 65 and account for 35 percent of the annual growth in health care costs.[22] Notwithstanding Alzheimer's disease, "between ages 65 and 70, one out of eight Americans suffer from a disability. But by age 85, the odds have shortened to four out of five. . . [T]wo out of three need help with such basic daily activities as dressing, bathing, walking and cooking."[23] The United States and South Africa are the only two industrial nations in the world not to offer a comprehensive health care program to take care of its people.[24]

In Canada, health care coverage is available to anyone who carries a plastic Care Card. The card is available for a $55.00 per month premium, which covers both spouses. The system is not perfect and the American health care delivery system is quick to point out the shortcomings. Nonetheless,

> Canadians . . . spend $7 on medicine for every $10 [Americans] spend. They live longer than [Americans] do. Fewer of their babies die. Everyone has full health coverage. No one is denied insurance because of an expensive illness. No one pays a deductible for a doctor's care. People pick their own doctors. Their family doctors see them quickly, either in the office or, when necessary, at home.[25]

Private insurance is illegal in Canada; the government also places strict limitations on hospital expenditures. The American health care industry claims that such restrictions only serve to lower the standard of care to a point that would be intolerable to the American public. Most discouraging, however, is the time one must wait to receive care, especially major surgery. For instance, one 63-year-old

Toronto man, Charles Coleman, received extended publicity because his heart surgery was postponed eleven times to accommodate more seriously ill patients. Eight days after he finally received his operation, he died. Shortly thereafter, plans were made by the Canadian Ministry of Health for potential heart surgery patients to flock to the United States. The University of Washington in Seattle concluded a deal with Canada whereby the hospital would accept bypass cases en masse (50 patients at a time) for a reduced rate. When the time came to institute the plan however, only 9 percent of the 720 bypass patients on the waiting list signed up to go to Seattle for their surgery.[26]

Because long-term planning remains nascent—especially in regard to insurance—there is maneuverability. It is politically, and maybe even socially, inspiring to hear the marching cry for health care reform. The rhetoric of managed-care programs whisper consistency of service and uniformity of treatment. Block-grant proposals hint of federal regulatory surrender and the greater flexibility of state control. Illusions of surplus benefits in Medicare and Medicaid look grand on paper, but there is always a proverbial fly in the ointment. No matter how grandiose the ideas and promising the proposals that are offered to Americans, Mr. and Mrs. John Elderly are never going to be inspired to back the system if so many others are still bucking it. Thus, the only way to inspire a grassroots reform in support of affordable long-term care is through incentives and education. Barbara J. Collins, an elderlaw attorney, suggests that the present situation is brought on in part by a failure of information. Many persons do not understand their exposure to catastrophic long-term care costs; they also do not understand the value of or inadequacies of insurance plans.[27]

Just as the fly in the ointment of welfare reform is the punitive nature of the proposals,[28] there are also drawbacks to the privatization of long-term care financing. The opportunity for spend-down presently available to the average American serves as a sufficient disincentive for any elderly American to find middle-of-the-road reform worthwhile. And while society may be on the verge of long-term financial disaster absent drastic reform, it may be that for most individuals, such drastic measures are not necessary. Therefore, in order to force Americans to "take their medicine," incentives for

privatization must be sufficiently magnetic▮
drastic reform.

NATIONAL INSURANCE PROGRAM

Sooner or later America will adopt a program of national hea▮
insurance that mirrors those in other countries. Perhaps it will mir-
ror a "mega" managed-care plan. States are already debating the
policy alternative; some have enacted plans. For instance, in 1994,
seven states enacted legislation regarding medical savings accounts:
Arizona, Colorado, Idaho, Illinois, Michigan, Mississippi, and Missouri. Eight other states requested the adoption of medical savings
account legislation. In 1995, an additional 27 states considered
medical savings accounts legislation. In 1996, Congress passed the
Health Insurance Portability and Accountability Act of 1996, which
created limited savings accounts, resembling IRAs, that allow people
who have only catastrophic coverage to set money aside for medical
expenses.[29]

While the states and the federal government are debating medical
savings accounts, however, a 1992 report of the Employee Benefits
Research Institute found that the number of uninsured Americans
reached a record 38.9 million persons, an increase of two million
since 1991 and 4.2 million since 1989.[30] At one point, four states—
Louisiana, Oklahoma, Texas, and Nevada, as well as the District of
Columbia—have left more than a quarter of their populations uninsured.[31] During 1992, the fluctuating number of uninsured reached
as high as 50 million during its highest interval, but the figure never
dropped below 25 million at any given time during the year. Also,
between 1991 and 1992, the number of nonelderly covered by
employer health plans decreased by two million, while public
health plan participation increased by 1.7 million.[32] Clearly, reform
proposals advocating employer mandates may not be entirely well
received by employers, large or small. In fact, the American Medical Association has restricted its support of employer mandates
since 1991, which some say "suggests self-interest over health
interests."[33]

It will be an effort to bring about long-needed health care reform,
and thus encompass far more than long-term care for the elderly.

.strative. And even though it
foreign programs are guides,
gets older, the element in the
, taken care of will find in a
.m arms of long-term protection.

4RE INSURANCE

ong-term care, he or she may private
pay, th... ᴐort funds from existing assets. If not,
then perhaps u... 1-down or involuntary impoverishment,
the individual may qu... y for Medicaid's payment of all costs.
Finally, there is a growing movement toward long-term care insurance, a private contractual arrangement between an individual and
an increasing number of carriers. With the recent change by Congress to allow long-term insurance to receive the same tax treatment
as accident and health plans, there is certain to be greater interest in
such plans.[34]

For instance, a 70-year-old couple each bought a policy of long-
term care insurance providing that if either should become significantly disabled, the policy will pay $100 a day (increased 5 percent
a year for inflation) for three years toward nursing home or home
care.[35] Combined premiums for the two policies were $3,649 a
year, but financial planners say this makes sense for "people over
60 with assets of $100,000 to $1 million (maybe more for a couple)
and a desire not to dissipate the assets on long-term care."[36]

To buy a policy, you must be in good health. Some companies
will disqualify you for conditions such as Alzheimer's, and if you
are 72 or older, Amex Life Assurance Co., the largest seller of these
policies, will send a nurse to your home to check for physical
disabilities.[37] The annual premiums are level for the life of the
policyholder, but benefits vary according to the following: (1) the
amount to be paid each day, (2) the day when coverage starts,
(3) the duration of coverage, (4) the definition of disability, (4) the
services covered, and, (5) the treatment by the individual states
regarding Medicaid asset protection.[38]

Types

There is no federal regulation of policies as there is with "Medigap" policies. "The National Association of Insurance Commissioners has devised a model statute, but universal adoption is nowhere near at hand."[39] Experts agree that it is important to compare the following factors: (1) guaranteed renewability, (2) a waiver of premium clause once benefits are required, (3) a premium refund policy if the benefits are never required, (4) payment of partial benefits if there is a lapse of payments, and (5) applicable state law protection and treatment under Medicaid.[40] A few of the states are more experienced with long-term insurance than others.[41]

One variation of long-term insurance is accelerated benefits on life insurance. Long-utilized by people with AIDS, the accelerated benefits option "is a rider on a person's life insurance policy that pays a percentage of that policy's death benefit before the policyholder dies."[42] Treatment under the income tax provisions are important; accelerated death benefits are treated as amounts received on account of death and thus may be excluded from gross income under Section 101(a) of the Internal Revenue Code.[43] But the rules are complicated and require precision for avoidance of taxability.

Analysis and Critique

The issue confronting the increased use of long-term insurance is treatment in conjunction with available private assets and existing Medicaid eligibility rules. Surely the point for estate planners will be to integrate the three—and perhaps even a fourth, the assets of children—to provide safe and comfortable coverage.

This task has not been made easier by the latest changes in OBRA '93. Specifically, the estate-recovery program operates as a disincentive to integration of all assets. The statute provides the following:

> In the case of an individual who has received (or is entitled to receive benefits under a long-term insurance policy in conjunction with which assets or resources are disregarded (under an approved State plan) . . . the State shall seek adjustment or recovery from the individual's estate on account of medical

assistance paid on behalf of the individual for nursing facility and other long-term care services.[44]

Because New York, Connecticut,[45] Indiana, California, and Iowa had granted asset protection to persons with long-term care policies, these states are in a particularly precarious position.[46] Nonetheless, it is through their example that lessons will be learned for a future integration of assets that would provide incentives for long-term care insurance.

Furthermore, the long-term insurance policies themselves are not being given due consideration as instruments of estate planning.[47] Perhaps they are just too recent.[48] Perhaps it is because people avoid thinking about what will occur when they become older and are forced to rely upon government programs as a last resort act.[49] Surely they deserve examination so as to offer a critique of the method that would involve spreading the costs among a broader group of persons, incentives for reasonable use of private assets, health and age factors, and a place for government review, which would ensure reliability and accuracy.[50] As always, the balance must be between private ingenuity and government consistency.

Suggested Payment Schedule

With the projection that 24 percent of 65-year-olds—14 percent of all men and 31 percent of all women—will spend more than a year in a nursing home,[51] the urgency of long-term care is evident. Medicare and Medicaid are the subject of political budget reduction, medical expenses continue to mount, and people continue to rely upon the American belief that government will take care of them whenever catastrophe occurs. What to do? The answer surely results from a combination of private assets, government programs such as Medicaid and Medicare, greater involvement by the states at federal or individual initiative, and long-term insurance coverage working in tandem with health care reform or greater use of managed health care. This seems to be the future, and posturing will likely lead in that direction.

Since Social Security is a foundation for Medicaid and Medicaid, it would seem logical that the Social Security apparatus be used for collection and broad-based support of a national program of long-term care insurance. Despite the onslaught of silencing statistics regarding population growths and economic deficits, Treasury Secretary Robert E. Rubin predicts that Social Security will remain intact well beyond the year 2050.[52] The monies, like the posture of the plan used for Medicare and Medicaid, could be made available to the states or administered as a joint effort. Hearings would need to be held and a program planned.

INTEGRATED PLANNING

Definition: Assets, Insurance, and Medicaid

Posturing must include the factors that allow a person to plan for a life with dignity as he or she grows older. These factors are currently defined as Medicaid, private funding, possible insurance, Medicare for older persons, family funds, and a myriad of state options only currently being adopted. When combined, these factors have come to be termed an integrated plan, and such a plan must be the focus of posturing for alternatives to the present individualized pieces of the puzzle.

At present, the system is grossly unfair. The Medicaid process was not intended to be the provider of nursing home care for America's elderly. Indeed, it would be better if it were explicitly allocated as such, for then at least the poor and uninformed would have an opportunity to learn of the method of escaping multiple jobs so as to assist an ill parent. At present, Medicaid spend-down is most often used by the wealthier heir, with the help of an elderlaw attorney, as the first and foremost method of Medicaid payment.

The states, especially with the economy of block grants, cannot absorb the cost of long-term care. Part of the reason is that the states are struggling so desperately to address the reality of health care, an issue so intimately connected to long-term care. If health care is resolved as an issue, long-term care would be addressed as well. Nonetheless, one need only skim the surface of state initiatives to the health care morass to understand that the states are only at the beginning of a long and difficult process. If states lack definition concerning health care, there will also be a lack of definition in long-term care. Lobbyists and special interests groups may well be the better harbingers of what is to come.

For instance, many states are seeking to provide legal redress through tort reform, fee regulation, consolidation of facilities, or health care cost containment commissions. Some are working with employers through mandates, pay-or-play taxes, or the most popular plan of all, a managed-care (HMO) plan to contain costs. Special "sin taxes," mandated generic substitution of drugs, purchasing alliances (KentuckyKare), prioritization of services, or capitation of costs are used by some states. These efforts are a start. Better education of the public is essential if U.S. residents are to move from the dual elements of individual need and inflated expectations. The education must be incremental, for we saw with President Clinton's 1993 health care initiative, the American voter would not accept a plan that it did not understand, was understood to be a product of "big" government, and sought to replace too quickly the status quo: "The devil you know is better than the one you don't know."

Perhaps the new electronic age will make a difference. This would permit a single-payer system, such as in Canada, computerization of bills, government regulation of the private insurance market, and even provider-sponsored accounts or data analysis of need. Eventually there may be a national Health Care Bill of Rights as there exists in at least one state now. Nonetheless, money today is just as likely to come from Medical Savings Accounts, trust funds, Managed Savings Accounts, or an Uncompensated Care Trust Fund. If the electronic age will allow some humans to understand the system and administer it fairly and in a responsive manner, then this will be a proper and human use of technology. If the electronic age only allows for criminalization of those who abuse an abusive situation, then it will serve no purpose at all. The system produced from posturing is the villain, not those who abuse the system.

Many state options are currently at work, serving as laboratories. Some, like Tennessee and TennCare, are achieving some success and will likely become a model for other state and even federal initiatives. The fact of the matter is that life expectancy is lengthening for most Americans, in part because of the care available through Medicare. The costs are escalating and there are concomitant issues of necessity and risk, and advancing technology promises an increasing dilemma as the years progress. Thus, Americans are living longer and staying alive longer in spite of ailments that would have served as natural and often welcome predators in the past. There simply may not be enough time for states to produce the proper laboratory results. This catastrophe would fall most harshly on those who are poor or suddenly disabled. Thus, the new federalism is not enough; neither block grants nor states as laboratories can be a sufficient national policy approach to the current situation and what we must do now to address health care and long-term care needs.

America needs to start with an examination of Medicare and Medicaid, national programs. To provide care, Medicare is a great blessing and a goal for many. Medicare is simple; a resident turns 65, and he or she qualifies for the named services. Medicaid is the safety net for some, but all too often, it becomes the security blanket for the middle class who are able to circumvent the intent and the letter of the law. Frankly, the more complicated legislators seek to make the entitlement, the more wealthier people able to afford attorneys will be the resulting beneficiaries of a program designed to take care of the truly poor. The present complexity of the system is the most accurate example of this. Also, forcing children to care for elderly and needful parents just seems too far-fetched for even the local governments to do. Although assets are available and usable for care, there is a part of the American psyche which says that something so catastrophic as long-term care should be paid for with government money. Like it or not, in a country of such adamant individuality, socialized long-term care has become institutionalized.

New to the scene is long-term insurance. This is a definite option and would take millions of middle-class people out of Medicaid spend-down and into the respectability of long-term care. Hundreds of insurance companies now offer plans that complement the definition of integrated plans. In 1986, 30 insurance companies were selling long-term care insurance policies to approximately 200,000 consumers. By 1987, a Department of Health and Human Services task force on long-term care insurance stated there were 73 providers writing policies for 423,000 individuals. By 1991, the Health Insurance Association of America discovered more than 135 insurance carriers proving long-term insurance to over 2.4 million Americans.[53]

Long-term insurance seems the most valuable piece of any posturing, especially if the risk can be borne by as many persons as possible. Insurance offers a return to honesty for the thousands of elderly with middle-income resources and assets to resist the temptation to apply for Medicaid benefits, a program designed and funded with the focus of aiding the truly poor.[54] It is also affordable, especially if the risk can be spread throughout many. Certainly, because insurance presently remains with private companies rather than government bureaucracy, there exists the image and the reality of cost control and energetic management.

Statistics show that this image has the potential of becoming a reality with just a little "spring cleaning" in Washington, DC. Historically, as government has grown larger, the economy has grown more slowly. In 1973, the median family income, calculated in 1993's value, was $36,893. In 1993, the median family income was $36,959.[55] Yet, during the same time, government has grown significantly. Presently there are now three million employees of the federal government,[56] which seems to have only added to the overhead expense of nearly $270 billion per year.[57] In 1994, the cost of running welfare programs increased at a rate twice that of the number of people in the program.[58] Between 1987 and 1991, the number of welfare recipients increased by 18 percent, but the administrative costs of providing the extra assistance increased by 43 percent.[59] Since then, American taxpayers have spent as much as $8 billion per year on the administrative costs alone on a welfare system that has completely failed.[60]

Insurance providers are rightly concerned over adverse selection, induced demand, and open-ended liability.[61] Because these are private companies without the open-ended coffers of federal revenues, such issues are and should be of concern. Yet, because these concerns can be examined in tandem with the other elements of integrated planning, they are neither insurmountable, nor should they be viewed as major. Rather, private long-term insurance needs to be examined and studied as a factor to be placed within the spectrum of integrating planning.

Critique and Analysis

Since integrating planning for long-term care is comprised of longevity, costs, Medicare, Medicaid, personal assets, dependent and children's assets, and in some cases, private insurance, the first step is to recognize the interdependence of the elements. Since the federal government is the one paying the bulk of the cost, the initiative should logically come from there, and that initiative would necessarily include incentives for the states and private individuals and enterprises to accept greater responsibility. Because recent rules regarding long-term insurance and estate-recovery programs offer disincentives to private insurance companies, they should be abolished. Indeed, Medicaid eligibility would do well to incorporate incentives for greater private use of private insurance programs.[62]

The government has a decisive role to play in the use of these insurance companies. Minimum standards should be developed with approval ratings. This has been done in New York; the states have acted as a testing forum. In addition, the government should begin plans to increase the risk pool of persons insured so as to lower costs. Incentives or mandatory inclusion such as with Social Security are feasible options. Medicaid and Medicare would not be abandoned, nor would the focus be upon "cuts," but rather upon alternatives, incentives, and complements. Once in place, the 36-month look-back period should be eliminated, foreclosing the most tempting estate-planning tool for inclusion in Medicaid. At present, 36 months is but the blink of an eye to emerging technologies.

CONCLUSION

It was Leon Trotsky who said: "[O]ld age is the most unexpected of all the things that happen to [you]."[63] To date, in the United States, this is true. Perhaps with the baby boomers entering the age of 50 and above, the perspective of Americans will change and old age will be neither unexpected nor unplanned. The one lesson to be learned is that no one can afford to live in the age of "perhaps," the age of "denial," the age of "not me." The United States has come to a pivotal point and, regardless of private interest groups, government bureaucracy, traditional interests, and plain old inertia, dollars and cents will force U.S. residents to face the future of long-term care.

While it would be possible to say that health care is the issue, such an assertion would not take into account the unique status of long-term care. Certainly, health care has a dramatic and casual effect upon any long-term care proposal. But long-term care, particularly as it affects the elderly with their large voting block, the disproportionate number of women, and the existent government programs already in place to assist these persons is unique and deserving of special attention.

Special attention is warranted because of technology, the beast that thrives on longer and longer life, more and more dollars, jobs, and progress. How can anyone suggest a curtailment of technology? Well, there may not be a suggestion but there is a denial of funds from the managed-care industry growing so rapidly in the United States. In a joking fashion, someone once asked: "Why was Jesus born in a stable?" The answer is: "Because his parents were on managed care." The truth of the matter is that managed care serves a very important function when it serves to hold the power of new technology and its irrefragable potential to prolong life without regard for what is or is not extraordinary. The litigation explosion in America fuels the technological advance, and the inattentiveness of so many working-class men and women sustains it. Surely, the politicians are part of the problem. How many times during the most recent presidential election were cuts in Medicare raised to a level of feverish rhetoric. U.S. politicians know how to speak to those who vote.

Thus, American health care is a victim of posturing. Each of the posturing elements has a vociferous following and each a fortress of past or current entitlements. Change will not be easy, but change will come. When it does, change will likely be incremental, perhaps starting with innovative insurance programs.[64] Then change will encompass payment for home care, innovative respite care programs, and other efforts to reduce inefficient overinstitutionalization. Once alternatives appear, reliance on Medicaid spend-down, consideration of assisted suicide, and financing difficulties of Medicaid and Medicare will lessen and reoccupy their traditional roles.

Finally, it is absolutely crucial to remember that long-term care is not simply about money, government, insurance, managed care, nursing homes, deficits, hospice, elderlaw attorneys, doctors, estate planning, meals, deductibles, eligibility, block grants, portability, premiums, and working. Long-term care is about *persons*, real live human persons. In all of our incremental planning, plan for what is best for the human in ourselves.

Notes

Chapter 1

1. See, e.g., *Compassion in Dying v. State of Washington*, 79 F.3d 790 (9th Cir. 1996) admitting that, in considering assisted suicide, courts "confront the most basic of human concerns—the mortality of self and loved ones— and to balance the interest in preserving human life against the desire to die peacefully and with dignity." Id. at 793.
2. See Shawn P. Regan, *Medicaid Estate Planning: Congress' Ersatz Solution for Long-Term Health Care*, 44 CATH.U.L.REV. 1217 (1995) (note).
3. Medicaid was established under Title XIX of the Social Security Act of 1965, Pub. L. No. 88–107 (1st Sess.)(1965)(Title XIX of the Act is officially termed "Grants to States for Medical Assistance Programs"); federal statutes and regulations governing the Medicaid program are found in 42 U.S.C. § 1396 and 42 C.F.R. §§ 430-456; state programs are covered under the federal mandate in 42 U.S.C. § 1396a(a)(10)(1988 & Supp. V 1993), 42 C.F.R. § 435.0 to 435.340. The federal government has wide discretion. See, e.g., *Beltran v. Myers*, 451 U.S. 625 (1981)(state must comply with regulations of the Secretary of the Department of Health and Human Services). Other examples of states being required to comply with federal regulations are the following: *Brown v. Giuliani*, 158 F.R.D. 251 (E.D.N.Y. 1994) (addressing New York's inability to effectively protect the interests of its welfare recipients under a redevelopment plan to cutback government agency workers, yet still meet federal regulations regarding the timeliness of processing claims); *Townsend v. Swank*, 404 U.S. 282 (1971) (finding unconstitutional an Illinois statute prohibiting payment of welfare benefits to dependent college students between the ages of 18 and 20, while allowing payments to trade school or high school students of the same age, in light of a federal statute requiring eligibility for all dependent 18-to-24-year-olds); *R.G. v. Florida Dept. of Health & Rehabilitative Services*, (No. 94-00779) (Fla.Dist.Ct.App. filed June 8, 1994) (discussing the "scheme of cooperative federalism" involving the participation of Florida's foster care system in the federally assisted welfare program [AFDC] as it relates to dependent immigrant children), discussed in Angela M. Elsperger, *Florida's Battle with the Federal Government Over Immigration Policy Holds Children Hostage: They Are Not Our Children!*, 13 L. & INEQ. 141 (1994); *Mullaney v. Woods*, 97 Cal.App.3d 710, 727-728; 158 Cal.Rptr.

902, 911-912 (1979) (Court held that states have no choice but to comply with federal regulations in upholding the constitutionality of the challenged Social Security number requirement); *Coalition for Basic Human Needs v. King*, 654 F.2d 838 (1st Cir. 1981) (Massachusetts ordered to make welfare payments to comply with Federal AFDC regulations, regardless of the state's constitutional ban on the same); *Memorial Hosp. v. Maricopa County*, 415 U.S. 250, 94 S. Ct. 1076 (1974) (Arizona statute imposing a one-year waiting period for new residents to become eligible for state medical assistance held to impermissibly interfere with the Constitutional right to the freedom of interstate immigration). See also, *Uhrovick v. Lavine*, 43 A.D.2d 481, 483-484, 352 N.Y.S.2d 529, 531-532, aff'd, 35 N.Y.2d 892, 324 N.E.2d 360, 364 N.Y.S.2d 890 (1974); *Bunting v. Juras*, 11 Or.App. 297, 300-301, 502 P.2d 607, 608-609 (1972); *Gaither v. Sterrett*, 346 F. Supp. 1095, 1100-1101 (N.D. Ind.), aff'd, 409 U.S. 1070 (1972); *Rosen v. Hursh*, 464 F.2d 731, 734 (8th Cir. 1972) (involving Minnesota statute); *Ojeda v. Yackney*, 3109 F. Supp. 149, 153 (N.D. Tex. 1970), vacated in part, 452 F.2d 947 (5th Cir. 1972); *Solman v. Shapiro*, 300 F. Supp. 409, 413-414 (D.Conn.), aff'd mem., 396 U.S. 5 (1969), all of which address federal regulation 45 C.F.R. 233.90(a)(1), regarding a stepparent's duty to support stepchildren.

4. Staff of House Committee on Ways and Means, 103rd Cong., 1st Sess., Background Material and Data on Programs Within the Jurisdiction of the Committee on Ways and Means: 1994 GREEN BOOK (COMM. PRINT 1994) [hereinafter, GREEN BOOK].

5. Persons may become eligible for Medicare even though not age 65 by being disabled for more than two years or by having a chronic kidney disease. Id. In fiscal year 1994, approximately 32.1 million persons over the age of 65 and 4.1 million disabled had hospital protection; 31.4 million aged and 3.7 million disabled had supplementary medical assistance. Id.

6. Id. at 808.

7. Id.

8. Id.

9. New York City spent nearly $1 billion for long-term care of the elderly in 1993. "Mayor and Pataki Plan $2.2B Raid on Medicaid," *The New York Post*, December 26, 1994, at 1, [hereinafter, "Mayor and Pataki"].

10. In Pennsylvania, the number of elderly requiring nursing home care increases by 2 to 3 percent annually. Malcolm Gladwell, "As Residents Get Older and Sicker Nursing Homes Face Cost Squeeze," *The Washington Post*, May 29, 1995, at A10, col. 1.

11. Joan M. Krauskopf, ELDERLAW: ADVOCACY FOR THE AGING §11.1, 376 (1993).

12. Barbara Collins, *Medicaid*, 239 PLI/EST 55 (1995) (contains background and eligibility requirements for spend-down); Esther B. Fein, "Welfare for Middle-Class Elderly?" *The New York Times*, September 25, 1994, at 39. See also U.S. GEN. ACCT. OFF., MEDICAID EST. PLAN., GAO/

HRD–93–29R; Alexander Bove, THE MEDICAID PLANNING HAND-BOOK: A GUIDE TO PROTECTING THE ASSETS OF MASSACHU-SETTS FAMILIES (1990), Boston: Little Brown; Marshall B. Kapp, *Options for Long-Term Care Financing: A Look to the Future,* 42 HAST-INGS L. J. 719 (1991); Brian Burwell, SYSTEMETRICS, MIDDLE CLASS WELFARE: MEDICAID EST. PLAN. FOR LONG TERM CARE COVERAGE (1991), Boston: SysteMetrics/McGraw-Hill; Linda Koco, "What Planners Look For in LTC Policies," *National Underwriters,* September 11, 1989.

13. *Medicare and Medicaid Budget Reconciliation: Hearings Before the Sub-committee on Health and the Environment of the House Committee on Energy and Commerce,* 103d Cong. 1st Sess. 337 (1993) (statement of Brian Burwell, Division Manager for SysteMetrics/MEDSTAT Systems).

14. Dick Polman, "Old Target May Yet Backfire on Dole," *Philadelphia Inquirer,* August 13, 1995, at E1.

15. See Vanessa Gallman, "Dole Cuts Off Debate on Welfare Reform," *Philadelphia Inquirer,* August 9, 1995, at A3.

16. Russell Gold, "Greenwood to Seniors: Medicare May Fail," *Philadelphia Inquirer,* August 11, 1995, at N2.

17. See Christopher Connell, "GOP Favors Raising Fees for Medicare," *Philadelphia Inquirer,* Aug. 11, 1995, at A18.

18. Id.

19. Id.

20. Id.

21. Id.

22. Id.

23. Id.

24. See "Positioning on Medicare," *The Washington Post,* August 17, 1995, at A28.

25. Polman, supra note 14 (ch. 1), at E2.

26. Peter G. Peterson, *FACING UP,* at 123 (1993), New York: Simon and Schuster.

27. See id., at 379 (chart 5.9).

28. Id. at 123.

29. See Debbie Cenziper, "Conference Focuses on Keepers of Culture," *Fort Lauderdale Sun-Sentinel,* December 3, 1994, at 5B.

30. Reports in 1994 show that 83.4 percent of all Latin American men over the age of 16 born in the United States were participating in the workforce, compared to 74.4 percent of all men over age 16 who are unemployed. See Global Information Network, *United States: New Report Debunks Latin Myth,* May 18, 1994, WL2581457, at 2.

31. Cenziper, supra note 29 (ch. 1).

32. Yeh Ling-Ling, "Perspective on Immigration," *L.A. Times,* April 13, 1994, at B7, col. 1. California receives approximately half of all new immigrants of the United States. See id.

33. Between 1982 and 1992, the reliance on welfare by elderly immigrants increased by 400 percent. See id. A study by the U.S. Department of Labor's Bureau of International Affairs, "Female Predominance of Immigration to the United States Since 1930: A First Look," found that by 1930, a shift occurred in the immigrant demographic. See Janice Mall, "Male Immigrants Are in the Minority," *L.A. Times,* August 4, 1985 at 6. There was less of a surge in male immigrants seeking economic opportunity and an increase in young, female immigration. This is partly due to the influx of family members of immigrants already established in the United States, which accounted for 90 percent of the immigrant gender differential between 1972 and 1979, and natives marrying abroad, whose wives and children accounted for 10 percent of immigration in the early 1980s. Despite the prohibition on preferential immigration quotas by the McCarren-Walter Act in 1952, alien wives, particularly postwar wives, have historically more easily entered the United States.

   The gender differential of immigrants is greatest in the very young and the elderly age brackets. Americans are more likely to adopt foreign females than males, partly due to greater availability. Also, elderly foreign women, who have a greater life expectancy than males, are more likely to reunite with immigrant children after being widowed. See id.

34. Ronald Brownstein, "Immigration Debate Splits GOP Hopefuls," *L.A. Times,* May 14, 1995, at A1, col. 5.

35. See Ling-Ling, supra note 32 (ch. 1), at 137, col. 1.

36. Id.

37. See Peterson, supra note 29 (ch. 1), at 193. Nevertheless, between 1980 and 1990, 87.5 percent of all Mexican immigrants were employed. See Global Information Network, supra note 30 (ch. 1), at 2.

38. See, e.g., 1995 Ca. A.B. 326, Reg. Sess. (1995-96) (regarding the provision of pregnancy-related services to specified aliens); 1994 N.J. S.B. 302, 206th Leg., 2d Ann. Sess. (1995) (requiring certification that persons directly or indirectly receiving state monies or privileges are not unauthorized aliens); 1995 N.Y. A.B. 9114, 219th Gen. A., Reg. Sess. (1996) (excluding illegal aliens from receiving public assistance and care, including home relief, veterans assistance, AFDC, medical assistance for needy persons, institutional care for adults, and child-care granted at public expense); 1995 N.Y. A.B. 9116, 219th Gen. A., Reg. Sess. (1996) (in part, excluding illegal aliens from receiving health care services from a publicly funded health care facility); 1995 S.C. H.B. 4330, Statewide Sess. (1995-96) (directing the Joint Legislative Committee on Aging, in conjunction with other departments, to study the effect of immigration on health care costs and other aging network services and tax policies relative to immigrants).

39. The GOP plan to restrict immigration benefits hopes to save $22 billion over the next five years. The Congressional Budget Office expects that 75 percent of these savings would result from the denial of income and health

care benefits to the elderly and disabled immigrant. See Roberto Suro, "GOP Takes Aim at Legal Immigrants," *San Francisco Chronicle*, December 26, 1994, at A2.

40. Brownstein, supra note 34 (ch. 1), at A1, col. 5. Currently, any person born on U.S. soil is an American citizen, regardless of their parents' status. U.S. Const. Amend. XIV, sec. 1.

41. Buchanan's plan would still allow spouses and children of already existing immigrants to enter the U.S. See Brownstein, supra note 34 (ch. 1), at A19, col. 1.

42. Id.

43. Id. The GOP proposal with regard to legal immigrants exempts two groups of immigrants from the prohibition on welfare distribution: refugees in the United States for less than six years and elderly immigrants over the age of 75 who have resided in the United States for at least five years. See Suro, supra note 39 (ch. 1), at A2.

44. Id. But see David Marzahl and Rob Paral, "Immigrants, Myths and Welfare," *Chicago Tribune*, August 23, 1994, at 15 (quoting Urban Institute statistics that in the 1980's only 2 percent of nonrefugee, working-age immigrants received welfare, while 3.7 percent of working-age natives received benefits).

45. In 1992 alone, America received more than 90,000 immigrants over the age of 55. See Ling-Ling, supra note 32, at B7.

46. See id.; cf. Marzhal and Paral, supra note 44 (ch. 1), at 15, (stating that with the exception of local education services, immigrants pay $25 billion more in taxes each year than they use in government services).

47. Richard D. Lamm and Duane H. Bluemke, "High-Tech Health Care Management and Society's Ability to Pay," *Healthcare Financial Management*, September 1, 1990, at 20 [hereinafter, Lamm and Bluemke].

48. The Office of Technology Assessment of the U.S. Congress and the Institute of Medicine of the National Academy of Sciences defines "technology" as "techniques, drugs, equipment and procedures used by health care professionals in delivering medical care to individuals, and the systems within which such care is delivered." See id.

49. Half of all health care expenditures are devoted to the last few months of a patient's life. See Dick Stanley, "Medical Breakthroughs Prompt Dilemma Over Death," *Austin American-Statesman*, February 6, 1994, at B1.

50. GREEN BOOK, supra note 4 (ch. 1), at 137.

51. Id.

52. See Malcolm Gladwell, "An Uncertain Old Age: The Elderly and Medicaid," *The Washington Post*, May 29, 1995, § A at A1, col. 1.

53. The Health Care Financing Administration reveals that high technology is the most significant reason that health care spending went from $280 million to $620 million between 1980 and 1989. See Lamm and Bluemke, supra note 47 (ch. 1), at 20.

54. *Compassion in Dying*, 79 F.3d at 812.

55. Id. at n.6.
56. "The exaggerated fears of liability risks" cause doctors and nurses to continue futile therapy, overtesting, and overtreatment, which sometimes can even harm the patient. Jack D. McCue, *The Naturalness of Dying,* 273 JAMA 1039, 104 (Apr. 5, 1995). But see Paul A. Gordon, DEVELOPING LONG-TERM CARE AND ASSISTED LIVING (1994) (stating that tort liability against nursing homes has been less prevalent due to factors which would lessen damages, which include the advanced age of the resident, no dependent family members and very short life expectancies).
57. See Dena Bunis, "Costly Errors," *Newsday,* July 27, 1993, at 3.
58. See id.
59. A 1990 Gallup Poll revealed that 73 percent of those surveyed said that they would not want to be sustained if subjected to a terminal illness or irreversible coma. See John Barry, "A Decent Way to Die," *News Tribune* (Tacoma, WA), June 19, 1994, at D1.
60. Authors Lamm and Bluemke offer three major reasons why the costs of medical technology exceed its benefits: (1) the continued use of unneeded or obsolete technologies; (2) duplication of technologies that America cannot afford, which is prompted by competition among hospitals; and (3) the use of marginal technologies, which prolong dying without prolonging life. See Lamm and Bluemke, supra note 47 (ch. 1), at 20.
61. See e.g., *Cruzan v. Director, Missouri Dep't of Health,* 497 U.S. 261, 110 S. Ct. 2841 (1990) (when guardians sought declaratory judgment seeking sanction to terminate artificial hydration and nutrition for patient, state may reject substituted judgment of close family members and require clear and convincing evidence of patient's intent that such life-sustaining treatment be withdrawn); *Quill v. Vacco,* 80 F.3d 716 (2d Cir. 1996) (there is no fundamental right to assisted suicide, but state law prohibiting assisted suicide violates Equal Protection Clause of U.S. Constitution); *Compassion in Dying v. State of Washington,* 79 F.3d 790 (1996) (provision of state statute prohibiting the aid to another person to commit suicide violates due process as applied to terminally ill patients who desire to hasten their death with medication prescribed by a physician).
62. *Compassion in Dying,* 79 F.3d at 793.
63. Id.
64. Id. at 839 (Beezer, dissenting).
65. Id. at 857 (Fernandez, dissenting).
66. See, e.g., id. at 857-859 (Kleinfeld, dissenting, suggesting the democratic institutions as appropriate forums).
67. *Quill v. Vacco,* 80 F.3d 716 (2d Cir. 1996).
68. Id. at 17.
69. Said one internist:

> [A]n average day in an intensive care unit costs between $2,000 and $3,000 . . . the ultimate cost could be five times that when all the

available technology is used. . . . Yet, . . . [I] never saw a case in which cost was the foremost consideration.

[T]he most indigent of the indigent and the wealthiest of the wealthy come in . . . and I've never heard at bedside, 'Hey, we can't afford to do this.'

Stanley, sup. note 49 (ch 1), at B1.

70. Within a recent ten year period, kidney dialysis for persons over age 85 grew 1,278 percent. See Lamm and Bluemke, sup. note 47 (Ch. 1), at 20.
71. Id.
72. McCue, sup. note 56 (ch. 1), at 1041.
73. Id.
74. "In short, the question is not whether recent technological developments have added to health care costs—they have. The real question is whether the benefits exceed the costs, and in at least some instances they may not." Sam Cordes, *The Economics of Health Services*, published by the Pennsylvania State University, Cooperative Extension Service, University Park, Pennsylvania.
75. McCue, sup. note 56 (ch. 1), at 1041.
76. Lamm and Bluemke, sup. note 47 (ch. 1), at 20.
77. McCue, sup. note 56, at 1041.
78. Id. at 1041.
79. Barbara Coombs Lee, "Death With Dignity Act Really Isn't All About Money," *Portland Oregonian*, April 6, 1995, at C9.
80. See Committee for Pro-Life Activities, National Conference of Catholic Bishops, NUTRITION AND HYDRATION: MORAL AND PASTORAL REFLECTIONS, 7 (1992).
81. Gladwell, sup. note 10 (ch. 1), at A10, col. 2.
82. For an excellent appraisal of lessons to be learned in California, see William Alvarado Rivera, *A Future for Medicaid Managed Care: The Lessons of California's San Mateo County*, 7 STAN. L. & POL'Y REV. 105 (1995-1996) (California has saved money and provided a high level of community service).
83. N. Lurie, N.B. Ward, M. F. Shapiro, C. Gallego, R. Vaghaiwalla, and R. H. Brook, *Termination of Medi-Cal Benefits: A Follow-Up Study One Year Later*, 314 NEW ENG. J. MED. 1266-1268 (May 8, 1996). But see Rivera, note 82 (ch. 1), at 105; *The Impact of Managed Care on Doctors Who Serve the Poor and Minority Patients*, 8 HARV. L. REV. 1625 (1995).
84. See Sheryl T. Dacso and Juanita Petty-Hankins, *Practical Aspects of Managed Care from the Standpoint of Providers and Consumers*, C884 ALI-ABA 271 (1994).
85. See Philip Caper, *Managed Competition That Works*, 269 JAMA 2524 (1993)(advocates vouchers and a national system of insurance for health care).
86. Marc A. Rodwin, *Consumer Protection and Managed Care: Issues, Reform Proposals, and Trade Offs*, 32 HOUS. L. REV. 1319 (1996).

87. Id. at 1327-1329.
88. Stephen M. Shortell and Kathleen E. Hall, *The New Organization of the Health Care Delivery System*, STRATEGIC CHOICES FOR A CHANGING HEALTH CARE SYSTEM, 104-105 (1996), (Stuart H. Altman and Uwe E. Reinhardt, eds.).
89. Rodwin, sup. note 86 (ch. 1), at 1380.
90. Shortell and Hall, sup. note 88 (ch. 1), at 127.
91. Spencer Rich, "New Frugality of Health Care Hurts Research Funding, Medical Schools Say," *The Washington Post*, August 18, 1996, at A6, col 1.
92. See Jill Smolowe, "Older, Longer Researchers Are Finding More Ways to Keep Senility at Bay, But How Long Should We Aim to Live?" *Time*, September 18, 1996, at 76.
93. Jim Dawson, "Age-Old Dream," *Star Tribune* (Minneapolis, St. Paul), April 4, 1995, at A1.
94. See sup. text accompanying notes 26-46 (ch. 1).
95. Randolph E. Schmid, "U.S. Births Last Year Lowest in '90s; Deaths at Record High," *Philadelphia Inquirer*, August 1, 1995, at A3. Currently, there are approximately 80 million baby boomers—one third of the American population—who are approaching mortality age. See John Barry, sup. note 59 (ch. 1), at D1.
96. Schmid, sup. note 95 (ch. 1), at A3.
97. Id.
98. Id. (quoting Carl Haub, Population Reference Bureau demographer).
99. See Dawson, sup. note 93 (ch. 1), at 1A.
100. See Peterson, sup. note 26 (ch. 1), at 378 (chart 5.8).
101. GREEN BOOK, sup. note 4 (ch. 1), at 867.
102. Schmid, sup. note 95 (ch. 1), at A1, col. 6.
103. See sup. text accompanying notes 47-93 (ch. 1).
104. See Barry, sup. note 59 (ch. 1), at D1.
105. GREEN BOOK, sup. note 4 (ch. 1), at 870.
106. Id. at 878.
107. Id. at 880.
108. Id. at 884.
109. See Janet Hook, "The Times Poll: GOP Medicare Proposals Win Broad Support," *L.A. Times*, September 21, 1995, at A1.
110. Id. Medicaid funds about 12 percent of the expenditures.
111. CONCORD COALITION, 5 *The Forgotten Numbers in the Medicare Debate*, FACING FACTS, August 6, 1995.
112. Id.
113. Donna St. George, "Women's Groups Hoping To Seal A 75-Year-Old Victory," *Philadelphia Inquirer*, August 13, 1995, at E3. In 1995, however, women made up only 10 percent of the members of Congress, 21 percent of state legislators and 2 percent of governors.
114. Id.

115. Id.
116. See infra text accompanying notes 134-146.
117. For criminal sanctions, see, e.g., MICH.COMP.LAWS § 752.1027(1)-(3) (1993):
    (1) A person who has knowledge that another person intends to commit or attempt to commit suicide and who intentionally does either of the following is guilty of criminal assistance to suicide, a felony punishable by imprisonment for not more than 4 years or by a fine of not more than $2,000.00, or both:
        (a) Provides the physical means by which the other person attempts or commits suicide.
        (b) Participates in a physical act by which the other person attempts to commit suicide.
    (2) Subsection (1) shall neither be applicable to nor be deemed to affect any other laws that may be applicable to withholding or withdrawing medical treatment by a licensed health care professional.
    (3) A Licensed health care professional who administers, prescribes, or dispenses medication or procedures to relieve a person's pain or discomfort, even if the medication or procedure may hasten or increase the risk of death, is not guilty of assistance to suicide under this section unless the medication or procedures are knowingly and intentionally administered, prescribed, or dispensed to cause death.
118. 42 U.S.C.A. §1395cc(f) (West 1992 & Supp. 1995).
119. See R. Sean Morrison, Ellen Olson, Kristan R. Mertz and Diane E. Meier, *The Inaccessibility of Advance Directives on Transfer From Ambulatory to Acute Care Settings*, 274 JAMA 478 (1995), (describing a study conducted in a New York hospital and concluding that 75 percent of elderly patients admitted to the hospital who elicited advanced medical directives were subjected to treatments and decisions by doctors who were entirely unaware of the patient's expressed directives). Dramatically, the study revealed that hospital clerks are responsible for much of the blame. Of all of the cases where the patient filled out advanced directive forms at the hospital, 39 percent of the clerks indicated that there were no directives given, 27 percent said they couldn't tell if directives were given, and another 27 percent simply omitted them from their records. See Terence Monmaney, "Study: Hospitals Often Unaware of Living Wills," *Star Tribune* (Minneapolis-St. Paul), August 27, 1995 at 3E.
120. On January 18, 1991, the Health Care Agents and Proxies Law took effect in New York. It "allows a mentally competent adult to designate another person, often a family member, to make health care decisions in case of loss of capacity. It does not expire but may be revoked." Jan M. Rosen, "Your Money; Preserving Assets of the Old and Ill," *The New York Times*, March 23, 1991, §1, at 30, col. 1. In the alternative, or when health care proxies are not available, it is critical that nursing homes take precautions

to see that complete medical records, which include advanced directives, accompany the elderly patient to the hospital.

121. Committee for Pro-Life Activities, National Conference of Catholic Bishops, NUTRITION AND HYDRATION: MORAL AND PASTORAL REFLEC-TIONS 2 (1992).

122. For some persons, the issue is one of living: "Physical and mental decline, functional impairment and dependence on others, diminishing opportunities to pursue enjoyable and fulfilling activities and inevitable loss of family members and friends." Kapp, sup. note 12, at 719.

123. *Cruzan v. Director, Mo. Dep't of Health*, 497 U.S. 261, 328 (1990) (Brennan, J., dissenting).

124. Id. at 301 (quoting *Rasmussen v. Flemming*, 741 P.2d 674, 678 [Ariz. 1987] [Brennan, J., dissenting].

125. Wendy K. Mariner, *Outcome Assessment in Health Care Reform: Promise and Limitations*, 20 AM. J. LAW & MED. 37 (1994).

126. Alice G. Gosfield, *Value Purchasing in Medicare Law: Precursor to Health Reform*, 20 AM. J. LAW & MED. 169 (1994).

127. Uwe E. Reinhardt, *Rationing Health Care: What It Is, What It Is Not, And Why We Cannot Avoid It*, STRATEGIC CHOICES FOR A CHANGING HEALTH CARE SYSTEM, 63 (1996), (Stuart H. Altman and Uwe E. Reinhardt, eds.).

128. *Compassion in Dying v. State of Washington*, 79 F.3d 790, 813 (9th Cir. 1996) (holding that state statues prohibiting assistance in seeking to end life violated the due process clause).

129. Id. at 820.

130. See George P. Smith, *Reviving the Swan, Extending the Curse of Methuselah, or Adhering to the Kevorkian Ethic?*, 2 CAMBRIDGE Q. OF HEALTH-CARE ETHICS 49, 54 (1993).

131. For an excellent treatment of the Roman Catholic position, see Kevin O'Rourke, *Catholic Teaching in Regard to Two Prominent "Right to Life Issues": A Historical Theological Study*, ST. LOUIS U. PUB. L. REV. 425 (1992).

132. Amy Goldstein, "New Treatments Put AIDS Programs in a Dilemma," *The Washington Post*, August 15, 1996, at A1, col. 3.

133. *Quill v. Vacco*, 80 F.3d 716 (2d Cir. 1996) (law prohibiting assisted suicide violates Equal Protection); *Compassion in Dying v. State of Washington*, 79 F.3d 790 (9th Cir. 1996) (statutes prohibiting assisted suicide violate due process rights of terminally ill patients).

134. See Marie McCullough, "Women's Groups Fight A GOP Spending Bill Restricting Abortions," *Philadelphia Inquirer*, August 2, 1995, at B3.

135. Id.

136. See P.R. Newswire, *Statement by House Democratic Leader Richard A. Gephardt on Republican Plans to Cut Medicaid by One-Third*, September 19, 1995.

137. See *Elizabeth Blackwell Health Center for Women v. Knoll*, 1994 WL 512365 (E.D. Pa. 1994).

138. See Lawrence L. Knutson, "Abortion Funds Cut For Federal Staff," *Philadelphia Inquirer*, August 6, 1995, at A3.

139. See Dan Morgan, "Republicans Jubilant Over Spending Bill," *Philadelphia Inquirer*, August 5, 1995, at A1, A5.

140. See Knutson, sup. note 138 (ch. 1), at A3.

141. See Morgan, sup. note 139 (ch. 1), at A5.

142. See Michelle Conlin, "Greenwood Amendment May Face Floor Vote," *Philadelphia Inquirer*, August 3, 1995, at A1.

143. Id.

144. See Stacey Burling, "Maternity Stay Gets 2d Day," *Philadelphia Inquirer*, August 3, 1995, at A1.

145. Id., at A1 and A16.

146. See generally, Nancy Benac, "Clinton Says GOP Legislators Are Betraying Family Values," *Philadelphia Inquirer*, August 6, 1995, at A3. For an excellent description of the issues of women and children and competition for dollars, see Ruth Sidel, KEEPING WOMEN AND CHILDREN LAST (1996).

147. See John A. Cutter, "The Power of the Ballot Series: Seniority," *St. Petersburg Times*, October 27, 1992, at 12.

148. See *Typical American Voter Is Growing Grayer*, INTELLIGENCER J., August 4, 1994, at A5 [hereinafter *Typical American Voter*].

149. Id.

150. Id.

151. Id.

152. Id.

153. Id.

154. See Thomas McArdle, "National Issue ENTITLEMENT SPENDING GRIDLOCK Washington Still Hooked On Government Largesse," *Investor's Business Daily*, April 13, 1994.

155. But cf. John Hofheimer, inf. note 112 (ch. 5). Statistics show that Alaska will have the smallest percentage of population over age 65, followed by Utah, Colorado, Georgia and Texas. See *Typical American Voter*, sup. note 148, at A5.

156. Statistics in Florida, and nationally, show that "older Americans vote almost twice as often as younger people in primaries and usually up to 30 percent more often in general elections." See Cutter, sup. note 147, at 12.

157. See "Older Legislature Pleas to Continue Its Existence," *Omaha World-Herald*, September 28, 1994, at 12.

158. See id.

159. See id.

160. See id.

161. See Peter J. Howe, "Target: Crime Against Elders," *Boston Globe*, July 18, 1994, at 15.

162. A 1987 congressional study found that the average American woman devotes 17 years to raising her children and 18 years caring for parents. See Ira Mothner, *Take Care*, 10 AM. HEALTH 64, 66 (March 1991).

163. Some studies reveal that Alzheimer's victims usually suffer with symptoms of the disease for over 4 years before the disease is diagnosed. Id. at 20. Typically, for Alzheimer's patients, the time from when symptoms first appear until death is 8.1 years. The time between diagnosis and death is usually 3.4 years. Nevertheless, symptoms may last and intensify for up to 25 years. Id.

164. There are many fine planners to assist persons of any age in arriving at a strategy of financial independence. See, e.g., Peter J. Strauss, *Legal and Financial Issues in Long Term Care Planning*, 219 PLI/Est 203 (1993); David Goldfarb and Nancy R. Stone, *Supplemental Needs Trusts for Disabled Persons*, 67 AUG N.Y. ST. B.J. 32 (1995).

165. *Hearing Before the Subcommittee on Health and Long-Term Care of the Select Committee on Aging: Catastrophic Health Insurance: The Pennsylvania Perspective*, 100th Cong., 1st Sess. 1, 23 (April 10, 1987) [hereinafter *Pennsylvania Perspective*] (statement by E. Joyce Gould).

166. 42 U.S.C. § 1396a(a)(10)(1988 & Supp. V 1993); 42 C.F.R. Part 435, Subpart B, *Mandatory Coverage of the Medically Needy*, (§§ 435.100-435.170 (1993)).

167. 42 C.F.R. §§ 435.100-435.170 (1993).

168. 42 C.F.R. Part 435, Subpart C, *Options for Coverage as Categorically Needy*, (§§ 435.200-435.236)(1993).

169. 42 C.F.R. § 435.230 (1993).

170. 42 C.F.R. § 435.211 (1993).

171. 42 C.F.R. § 435.217 (1993).

172. Id.

173. 42 C.F.R. § 435.201(b) (1993)

174. 42 U.S.C. § 1396a(a)(10)(B)(1988 & Supp. V 1993); 42 C.F.R. § 435.201 (1993).

175. 42 U.S.C. § 1396a(a)(10)(C) (1988 & Supp. V 1993): 42 C.F.R. Part 435, Subpart D, *Optional Coverage of the Medically Needy* (§§ 435.300-435.350)(1993).

176. 42 U.S.C. §1396d(a) (1988 & Supp. V 1993). See also 42 C.F.R., Subpart D, §§ 435.300-435.350 (1993).

177. 42 C.F.R., Subpart I, § 435.851 (1993).

178. 42 C.F.R. § 435.831(c)-(d) (1993).

179. See generally UNITED STATES GENERAL ACCOUNTING OFFICE, HOME CARE EXPERIENCES OF FAMILIES WITH CHRONICALLY ILL CHILDREN, GAO/HRD089-73 20-25 (June 1989); Lusk, *Who's Knocking Now?: New Clientele for Nursing Homes*, GERONTOLOGY NURSING, June 1990, at 8; Zola, *Aging, Disability and the Home Care Revolution*, 71 ARCH. PHYS. MED. & REHAB. 93 (1990).

180. Senator Jesse Helms has received a barrage of criticism for his comments in support of cutbacks under the Ryan White CARE Act in the area of AIDS research and patient care. See Daniel S. Greenberg, "Is AIDS Research Getting Too Much U.S. Funding?," *Philadelphia Inquirer*, July 7, 1995, at A7. The Act authorizes $880 million per year for patient care, 42 U.S.C. § 300ff-1 to 300ff-90 (1996).
181. The federal government establishes only minimum requirements. For example, no state may set an age requirement greater than 65 years (42 C.F.R. §§ 435.406-435.408); recipients must be citizens, lawfully admitted permanent residents, or residing under color of law (42 C.F.R. § 435.540); disability must conform to federal definition (42 C.F.R. § 435.542); and residency must be defined as having an intent to remain permanently or for an indefinite period of time (42 C.F.R. § 435.403(j)(2)).
182. "1,135 New Cases of AIDS Reported in N.J. This Year," *Philadelphia Inquirer*, August 13, 1995, at B2 [hereinafter *1,135 New Cases*].
183. Donna Shaw, "Senate Gets Bill To Assist Hemophiliacs With Aids," *Philadelphia Inquirer*, August 12, 1995, at A2. Ricky Ray was a teenager who died of AIDS in 1992 after receiving an HIV-infected blood-clotting medicine.
184. Id.
185. "Experimental AIDS Surgery Wins Government Approval," *Philadelphia Inquirer*, August 15, 1995, at B6 [hereinafter *Experimental AIDS Surgery*].
186. See Daniel S. Greenberg, "Too Much Money for AIDS Research?" *Baltimore Sun*, July 11, 1995, at 11a.
187. These figures represent 1992 totals; however, estimates show that 1995 figures are roughly the same. See id.
188. Public outrage in recent years over AIDS victim's eligibility for federal assistance, or lack thereof, has stimulated nearly a doubling of federal research grants from the $700 million allotted in 1990. See Greenberg, sup. note 186 (ch. 1), at 11a.
189. As many as 4 million Americans suffer from the degenerative effects of Alzheimer's disease. REPORT BY THE CHAIRMAN OF THE SUB-COMMITTEE ON HEALTH AND LONG-TERM CARE OF THE HOUSE SELECT COMMITTEE ON AGING, 100TH CONG., 1ST SESS., PAYING THE PRICE OF CATASTROPHIC ILLNESS: FROM ACCIDENTS TO ALZHEIMER'S 5, 18 (Comm. Print 1987) [hereinafter PAYING THE PRICE]. More than 200,000 of these are Pennsylvania residents, 35,000 of whom live in Philadelphia, alone. See *Pennsylvania Perspective*, sup. note 165 (ch. 1), at 27. By the year 2000, this number will increase by 60 percent. By the year 2050, as many as 14 million Americans will be afflicted with the disease. See *Alzheimer's Disease More Prevalent Than Previously Thought*, 45 GERIATRICS 14, 14 (February 1990). As many as 250,000 new cases are diagnosed every year. See Thomas Maugh, "Protein Linked To Alzheimer's Memory Loss," *L.A. Times*, April 16, 1991, Sec. A, at 1, col. 3 (Home ed.). These numbers may even be higher as life expectancy increases. OFFICE OF TECHNOLOGY ASSESS-

MENT, CONGRESS OF THE UNITED STATES, LOSING A MILLION MINDS: CONFRONTING THE TRAGEDY OF ALZHEIMER'S DISEASE AND OTHER DEMENTIAS 1, 5 (1987) [hereinafter LOSING A MILLION MINDS]. If, and when, life expectancy reaches 90 and above, it is estimated that one third of the population will suffer from Alzheimer's disease. See Robert Katzman, *Medical Progress: Alzheimer's Disease*, 314 NEW ENG. J. MED. 964, 970 (1986). Alzheimer's is the fourth leading cause of death. See *Pennsylvania Perspective*, sup. note 165 (ch. 1), at 29; LOSING A MILLION MINDS, inf. note 189 (ch. 1), at 20. But cf. "Alzheimer's Ranks Low Among Causes of Death," *The New York Times*, March 21, 1991, Sec. A, at 22, col. 6 (Final ed.) (claiming that Alzheimer's does not substantially contribute to overall mortality and that dramatic increases in the near future are unlikely). The disease becomes twice as prevalent every five years after the age of 60 and the likelihood of succumbing to the disease quadruples every year thereafter. See PAYING THE PRICE, sup., note 189 (ch. 1), at 6.

190. "This disease robs society of the contribution of productive individuals with a wealth of accumulated wisdom and life experience. It also pulls into its eddy friends and family members who give up their own pursuits to look after their afflicted loved ones." LOSING A MILLION MINDS, sup. note 189 (ch. 1), at 11 (quoting Margaret Heckler, former Secretary of the U.S. Department of Health and Human Services). In 1987 alone, 1 million Americans became poverty-stricken as a result of the costs of catastrophic illnesses. See PAYING THE PRICE, sup. note 189 (ch. 1), at 5. In 1986, the cost of caring for Alzheimer's patients was $40 billion. Id. at 5, 18. Annual costs for one Alzheimer's patient may exceed $65,000. Id. at 18.

191. Of all the people in the United States now institutionalized in nursing homes, more than half suffer from Alzheimer's disease. See id.

192. See id.

193. Andrew Purvis, "Alzheimer's Rise: The Disease May be Twice as Common as Doctors Thought," *Time*, November 20, 1989, at 118 [hereinafter "Alzheimer's Rise"]. During the early 1900's, 1 in 25 Americans were over age 65. By the 21st century, due to the "baby-boom" generation born during a period of increased fertility after World War II, this ratio will have dropped to 1 in 5. By the year 2030, when the "baby-boom" generation reaches its peak, there will be an estimated 65.6 million Americans over age 65. See SPECIAL COMMITTEE ON AGING, 101ST CONG., 2D SESS., AGING AMERICA: TRENDS AND PROJECTIONS 1-4 (Comm. Print 1990) [hereinafter AGING AMERICA]. Globally, this figure may be as high as 1.1 billion by the year 2025. See Henry Cisneros, *Health Policy for an Aging Population*, 26 HOUS. L. REV. 787, 787 (1989). Some researchers estimate that in America, by 2040, this figure will be a much higher 86.8 million and the number of Americans over 85 years old will be 23.5 million. See AGING AMERICA, sup. note 193 (ch. 1), at 6-8. In 1986, there were 25,000 centenarians—by the year 2000, there will be over

100,000. Id. at 8. This averages out to be more than 200 Americans per week who reach the age of 100. See Cisneros, sup. note 193 (ch. 1), at 787.

194. PAYING THE PRICE, sup. note 189 (ch. 1), at 1 (quoting Ms. Marion Roach of New York City).

195. Roswell Gilbert, age 76, was convicted of first-degree murder and imprisoned for shooting his wife, who suffered from Alzheimer's disease. See id. at 20. Mr. Gilbert evidences the limited options with which family members feel they are left as a result of the inability to care for the Alzheimer's victim.

Jack Kevorkian has obtained national attention by providing Alzheimer's patient Janet Adkins and others with the option of suicide through the use of a homemade "suicide machine." See Gloria Borger, "The Odd Odyssey of 'Dr. Death'," *U.S. News & World Report*, August 27/September 3, 1990, at 27-28; Melinda Beck and Karen Springen, "The Doctor's Suicide Van," *Newsweek*, June 18, 1990, at 46-48. Despite warnings from Alzheimer's experts that her diagnosis might be incorrect, Adkins, who belonged to the Hemlock Society, which advocates the legalization of assisted suicide, freely submitted to death. See id. at 46. Commenting on the suicide rate of people over age 65, which may be up to eight times as high as that of the general population, Joanne Lynn, who operates a George Washington University hospice said, "[I]t seems more appealing to have people dead than to provide more costly care, than to have them in good housing with good nursing care." See id. at 49. As for Kevorkian, "[h]is peers dismiss him as an oddball fascinated by death. Yet to the desperately ill who resent the medical care that prolongs their agony, he is a hero." Borger, sup. note 195 (ch. 1), at 27.

196. Other catastrophic illnesses would include accidents, Amyotrophic Lateral Sclerosis (ALS—better known as Lou Gehrig's disease), arthritis, cancer, cerebral palsy, childhood disorders, chronic lung disease, chronic mental illness, heart disease, Huntington's disease, Parkinson's disease, premature births, and strokes. See PAYING THE PRICE, sup. note 189 (ch. 1), at 5-14. Although not included in the aforementioned source, HIV would also qualify as a catastrophic illness.

197. See, e.g., Older Americans Act Amendments of 1987, Pub. L. No. 100-175, 100th Cong., 1st Sess., 101 Stat. 926 (1987) (as amended, 42 U.S.C.A. §§ 3001 et seq.); Alzheimer's Disease and Related Dementias Services Research Act, Pub. L. No. 99-660, 99th Cong., 2d Sess., 100 Stat. 3802 (1986).

198. See, e.g., MINN. STAT. ANN. § 145.131 (1983 & Supp. 1990), which states the following:

The legislature finds that Alzheimer's and other dementia diseases occur in recipients of medical assistance. The cost the state pays in terms of human suffering, lost productivity, and medical assistance expenditures are enormous. The legislature also finds that research for the identification, cause, cure and prevention of Alzheimer's and other dementia diseases requires autopsies and pathological studies of suspected victims. Expenses for autopsies and pathological studies are not provided for recipients of medical assistance.

199. In 1987, one million Americans were forced into poverty as a result of catastrophic illness. See PAYING THE PRICE, sup. note 189 (ch. 1), at 5.

200. For example, health reforms by President Reagan fell far short of meeting their goals by protecting less than three percent of the population who needed long-term care. See *Pennsylvania Perspective*, sup. note 165 (ch. 1), at 2.

201. Dementia, in general, may be caused by any one or combination of 70 different diseases. Dementia associated with Alzheimer's, Pick's, and other similar diseases, is inevitable because these are progressive degenerative diseases by nature. Other diseases which may cause some form of dementia include: amyotrophic lateral sclerosis (ALS), Parkinson's diseases, Huntington's disease, cardiovascular disease (which decreases the blood flow to the brain), depression, drugs and alcohol, and metabolic and nutritional disorders. Also, researchers now agree that most persons with AIDS will suffer some form of dementia as a result of their illness. See OFFICE OF THE TECHNOLOGY ASSESSMENT, CONGRESS OF THE UNITED STATES, CONFUSED MINDS, BURDENED FAMILIES: FINDING HELP FOR PEOPLE WITH ALZHEIMER'S AND OTHER DEMENTIAS 1, 9 (1990)[hereinafter CONFUSED MINDS]. For a more complete list of dementia causing diseases, see LOSING A MILLION MINDS, sup. note 189 (ch. 1), at 13-14.

Very often identification of the particular disease that causes dementia can only be diagnosed upon an autopsy following death. See id. Autopsies in the United States have decreased, however, and will effect the accuracy of diagnosis and medical counseling should they continue to decrease. See id. at 21. Despite this decrease, however, clinical diagnosis of Alzheimer's has gone from a 10 to 50 percent error rate to a 90 percent assurance of accuracy over the past decade. See Katzman, sup. note 189 (ch. 1), at 964.

In *Camilli v. Immaculate Conception Cemetery*, 244 N.J. Super. 709, 583A.2d 417 (Ch. Div. 1990), the plaintiff sought a court order to exhume her mother's body and to conduct an examination of the brain tissue for purposes of contesting the mother's will, which the mother had made three years prior to her death. Because the courts recognize the sanctity of the grave, they will not disturb the grave absent good cause. The court and the legislature have intimated that such good causes may include criminal investigations, see, e.g., *People v. Hoyt*, 210 A.D.2d 786, 620 N.Y.S.2d 520 (N.Y.A.D. 3 Dept. 1994); N.Y. PUB. HEALTH LAW §42.10(4) (McKinney, 1996) McKinney; authorizations by a medical examiner, the sale of land in which bodies have been interred, and the removal of bodies to other locations, see, e.g., *Weinstein v. Mintz*, 148 Misc. 2d 820, 526 N.Y.S.2d 917 (N.Y. Sup. 1990). Here, the order was denied for lack of public necessity or a compelling private interest. The Surrogate Court of New York also concluded that there was not sufficient medical evidence that Alzheimer's disease could be diagnosed after the body had been interred for more than five years. The court stated: "The law, then, will not reach into the grave in search of 'the facts' except in the rarest of cases, and not even then unless it is clearly necessary and there is reasonable probability that such a violation of the sepulchre will establish what is sought." *Camilli*, 244 N.J. Super. at 713 (quoting *In re Sheffield Farms Co.*, 22 N.J. 548, 556, 126 A.2d 886 [1956]). Therefore, if it can be established with certainty that Alzheimer's may be diagnosed by autopsy for "*X*" number of years after interment, the dicta in the *Camilli* case opens the door for innumerable probate contests.

202. See CONFUSED MINDS, sup. note 201 (ch. 1), at 2, 9. See also LOSING A MILLION MINDS, sup. note 195 (ch. 1). In one Boston, Massachusetts, study of noninstitutionalized people over the age of 65, 91 percent of those with latter stages of dementia were found to have Alzheimer's disease. See Denis A. Evans, H. Harris Funkenstein, Marilyn S. Albert, Paul A. Scherr, Nancy R. Cook, Marilyn J. Chown, Liesi E. Herbert, Charles H. Hennekens and James D. Taylor, *Prevalence of Alzheimer's Disease in a Community Population of Older Persons; Higher Than Previously Reported*, 262 JAMA 2551, 2556 (1989) [hereinafter Evans et al.] (1989). See also CONFUSED MINDS, sup. note 201 (ch. 1), at 9; *Alzheimer's Rise*, sup. note 193 (ch. 1), at 118; Jim Ipoco, Don L. Boroughs, David Lawday, Kenneth T. Walsh, William F. Allman and Michael Stachell, "Scary New Facts About Alzheimer's," *U.S. News & World Report*, November 20, 1989, at 13. The norm, however, is 66 percent. LOSING A MILLION MINDS, sup. note 189 (ch. 1), at 12. Researchers concluded that 10.3 of all people over age 65 have Alzheimer's disease—3 percent were age 65-74, 18.7 percent were age 75-84, and 47.2 percent were over age 85. See Evans et al., sup. note 202 (ch. 1) at 253-254. These figures show that Alzheimer's may be twice as prevalent as previously suspected. *Alzheimer's Rise*, sup. note 193 (ch. 1), at 118. "[T]he public health impact of Alzheimer's disease will increase with the continuing growth of the oldest population groups in the United States . . . and emphasize the need to define potentially modifiable causal factors." Id. Continuing research, however, has proven positive. See Paul Recer, "Early-Onset Alzheimer's Gene Is Isolated," *Philadelphia Inquirer*, August 18, 1995, at A2.

203. See CONFUSED MINDS, sup. note 201 (ch. 1), at 2.

204. See id.

205. "[U]ntil we have an effective treatment for Alzheimer's disease, the best strategy is to assist actively patients, families, and caregivers with long-term management of the problems associated with this disease." Eric B. Larson, *Alzheimer's Disease in the Community*, 262 JAMA 2591, 2592 (1989).

206. LOSING A MILLION MINDS, sup. note 189 (ch. 1), at 6.

207. See Spencer Rich, "Research Effort on Diseases of the Aging Boosted by Congress," *The Washington Post*, November 28, 1990, at A21.

208. See id.
209. See id.
210. Presently, a suspected Alzheimer's sufferer must complete a multitude of tests before diagnosis can be established. Research in therapeutic testing would allow accurate diagnosis long before symptoms of the disease become noticeable. Accurate therapeutic testing could increase diagnostic effectiveness, thereby saving money. With successful drug research that would delay the onset of the disease, early diagnosis would allow the patient to live a longer normal life. See id.
211. "With the skyrocketing cost of health care for the elderly and the rapidly growing number of older Americans, this legislation is expected to stave off financial ruin of both our public health system and family pocketbooks." Id. (quoting from the Senate labor committee report on the bill proposed by Congress). "[E]very dollar put into Alzheimer's and similar research on aging is a 'blue chip investment.'" Id. (quoting Senator Thomas Harkin, of Iowa, who sponsored the bill).
212. See Robert Boyd, "GOP Leaders Alarmed by Cuts in Research," *Philadelphia Inquirer*, July 31, 1995, at A2.
213. Id.
214. Id.
215. LOSING A MILLION MINDS, sup. note 189 (ch. 1), at 20.
216. Id. at 11.
217. Id. at 20.
218. Id. at 21.
219. "In-home services may include home health care, personal care, chore services, and homemaker services to the client's house, apartment, or other residence." Id. at 37.
220. "Nursing homes are health care facilities that provide 24-hour care, nursing, and personal services in an institutional setting." Id. Studies have suggested that the use of nursing homes and other forms of services is more often than not due to the caretakers inability to properly perform their role as such than the condition of the patient. See id. at 20-21. Every year approximately 216,000 nursing home patients are hospitalized unnecessarily which costs more than $92 million. See *More Than 200,000 Nursing Home Patients Hospitalized Needlessly*, 45 GERIATRICS 15, 15-16 (February 1990). More than half of the hospital admissions from nursing homes are avoidable. See id.

> Given the increasing numbers of elderly and the escalating cost of health care, we in the United States must at some point decide if we can afford to sustain long-term care as a profit-making industry. If the money that is paid to the nursing home industry could be redirected to purchase additional professional services, the quality of care would surely improve.

Id. at 16 (quoting Dr. Kayser-Jones, University of California, San Francisco, professor of nursing and medical anthropology). The Department of

Rehabilitative Services in Illinois has established a program to specifically prevent the unnecessary institutionalization of Alzheimer's patients. See ILL. ANN. STAT. ch. 23 ¶ 3434, § 3(g) (Smith-Hurd 1988 & Supp. 1990).

221. "Board and care facilities are nonmedical residential care facilities that provide room and board and variable degrees of protective supervision and personal care. These range in size from foster care units with a few residents to large domiciliary facilities that house several hundred people." LOSING A MILLION MINDS, sup. note 189 (ch. 1), at 37.

222. "Hospitals are facilities for medical care of those temporarily residing in them. The primary services available are diagnosis and treatment, but hospitals also often serve as foci for rehabilitation, case management. counseling, [and] family support. They may also be affiliated with nursing homes, day care centers, home health agencies, or other settings and services." Id.

223. "State mental hospitals are generally large state-funded institutions that provide acute and long-term psychiatric care primarily for mentally ill people, but also for some patients with dementia—especially those with behavioral symptoms that are difficult to manage." Id.

224. "Hospices are facilities for the care of terminally ill people. The emphasis in hospices is on alleviating symptoms and providing personal support, rather than cure and rehabilitation." Id.

225. "Adult day care centers are day treatment facilities, some of which provide intensive medical, physical, or occupational therapy. Others provide primarily social activities and personal services for several hours during the day." Id.

226. "Community mental health services are psychiatric and psychological treatment facilities that provide a variety of mental health services for people with acute and chronic mental illnesses. Most services are provided on an outpatient basis." Id.

227. "Outpatient facilities and clinics are medical settings for diagnosis and treatment of diseases. They may also become involved in delivering other services such as case management and counseling." Id.

228. "Senior centers are facilities intended for use by older Americans. Day care, recreational activities, family support, case management, and mental health services are available at some but not all senior centers." Id.

229. See id. at 21.

230. See id.

231. See id.

232. See id.

233. See id.

234. CONFUSED MINDS, sup. note 201 (ch. 1), at 2-3.

235. See id. at 3-4.

236. "A recurring theme in the history of each family's problems is the difficulty experienced in finding both medical and social resources for the diagnosis, management, and, particularly, the care of the patient whose mind and

body are failing." Id. at 4 (quoting the Alzheimer's Association). This criteria is what is referred to as the "linking system." See generally Id. (discussing problems associated with the linking system and their effect on policy decisions concerning services).

237. See id.

238. Armond D. Budish, *Helping Clients Face the LTC Threat; Long-Term Care*, 91 BEST'S REV. 68 (November 1990).

239. See Cleonice Tavani, *Report on a Seminar on Financing and Service Delivery Issues in Caring for the Medically Underserved*, 106 PUB. HEALTH REP. 19, 22 (January/February 1991).

240. See Abigail Trafford, "Access to Health Care: Is It a Basic American Right?," *The Washington Post*, February 5, 1991, Health, at 6, col. 2 [hereinafter, "Access to Health Care"].

241. See Anthony Schmitz, *Health Assurance*, 5 HEALTH 39, 40 (January-February 1991); Tavani, sup. note 214 (ch. 1), at 22.

242. See Spencer Rich, "'MediPlan': Coverage for Rest of U.S.," *The Washington Post*, January 28, 1991, at A9, col. 6.

243. See Malcolm Gladwell, "Uninsured Get Less Care: Patients' Finances Found to Limit Treatment," *The Washington Post*, January 16, 1991, at A20, col. 2 [hereinafter "Uninsured Get Less Care"].

244. See id. The American Hospital Association has reported that in 1989, hospitals lost $8.9 billion on uncompensated care and $4.3 billion on the 22 percent of hospital bills that Medicaid does not cover. See "Bentsen Warns White House Against New Medicare Cuts," *The Washington Post*, January 29, 1991, at A17, col. 1 [hereinafter "Bentsen Warns White House"]. In 1989, $212 million in hospital bills went unpaid in the District of Columbia alone. See Neil Henderson, "D.C. Health Fund Proposed For Uninsured City Residents," *The Washington Post*, April 17, 1991, at D6, col. 1.

245. Trafford, sup. note 240 (ch. 1), at 6.

246. See id.

247. See id.

248. See Jack Hadley, Earl P. Steinberg and Judith Feder, *Comparison of Uninsured and Privately Insured Hospital Patients: Conditions on Admission, Resource Use and Outcome*, 265 JAMA 374, 378 (January 16, 1991). See generally Sundwall & Tavani, *The Role of Public Health in Providing Primary Care for the Medically Underserved*, 106 PUB. HEALTH REP. 2, 2-5 (January/February 1991) (calling for an expansion of the role of public health providers for both long-term and primary care); Abigail Burgh Crane, *HRSA's Collaborative Efforts with National Organizations to Expand Primary Care for the Medically Underserved*, 106 PUB. HEALTH REP. 10, 10-14 (January/February 1991).

249. See "Uninsured Get Less Care," sup. note 243 (ch. 1). Uninsured patients are 1.2 to 3.2 times more likely to die in the hospital than those patients who are supported by private insurance. See id.

250. BARRY R. FURROW, THOMAS L. GREANEY, SANDRA H. JOHNSON, TIMOTHY JOST & ROBERT L. SCHWARTZ, HEALTH LAW, at 563 (Vol. 2, 1995) [hereinafter, HEALTH LAW].

251. See Sally Squires, "State-Sponsored Health Plans Attract Uninsured," *The Washington Post*, March 26, 1991, at Z5, col 3.

252. The California plan will be partly funded by the state's tobacco surtax and will cover hospitalization and prescription drugs. Although the plan does not cover elderly who are already eligible for medicare, participants continue to grow. See id.

253. *Brock v. Guaranty Trust Life Insurance Co.*, 175 Ga.App. 273, 333 S.E.2d 158 (1985).

254. See Llana Ruber, "Long-Term Care Policies Improving, *Business Journal—Phoenix & V. Sun,* November 24, 1995, at 26.

255. See id.

256. See LOSING A MILLION MINDS, sup. note 189 (ch. 1), at 20.

257. See Jan M. Rosen, "Planning for Elderly Health Care: Experts Recommend Private Insurance to Help Handle Costs," *The New York Times*, April 15, 1991, at C4.

258. The average income of persons over the age of 65 is $12,000, while the average annual cost of nursing home care is $23,000. See "Economic, Medical Costs of Alzheimer's Disease on the Rise," 45 GERIATRICS 15, 15 (March 1990).

259. See id.

260. See *Pennsylvania Perspective*, sup. note 165 (ch. 1), at 8.

261. See id.

262. See Frank Swoboda, "Health Care Costs Climb 21.6% in '90," *The Washington Post*, January 29, 1991, at D1, col. 2.

263. LOSING A MILLION MINDS, sup. note 189 (ch. 1), at 11.

264. This figure has risen 46.3 percent since 1988. See Swoboda, sup. note 262 (ch. 1), at D1. In 1989, the average medical cost per employee was $2,600; in 1990 it was $3,161. Id. Some companies have had claims as high as $2 million for one employee. Id.

265. See, e.g., text accompanying notes 293-295 (ch. 1).

266. "Controlling medical expenses through traditional health plans has become a losing proposition." Swoboda, sup. note 262 (ch. 1), at D1 (quoting John Erb, director of a survey on nationwide benefits by Foster Higgins & Co.).

267. "Slower Rise in Medical Costs," *Philadelphia Inquirer*, August 14, 1995, at F1 [hereinafter "Slower Rise"].

268. Abigail Trafford, "Medicare and Medicaid; Time to Rethink Society's Needs," *The Washington Post*, January 15, 1991, at 26 [hereinafter "Time to Rethink"]. "What the . . . plan[s] allow[] is protection for individuals who are able to recover, who are hospitalized with acute but curable illnesses. On the other hand, senior citizens who suffer from chronic and long-term incurable illnesses are left to fend for themselves." *Pennsylvania Perspective*, sup. note 165 (ch. 1), at 3.

269. 42 U.S.C. § 1395 (1982 & Supp. IV 1986).
270. See David Blumenthal, Mark Schlesinger, Pamela Brown Drumheller, and The Harvard Medicare Project, *The Future of Medicare*, 314 N. ENG. J. MED. 722, 722 (1986)[hereinafter Blumenthal et al.].
271. Id.
272. See John Holahan and Margaret B. Sulvetta, *Assessing Medicare Reimbursement Options For Skilled Nursing Facility Care*, 10 HEALTH CARE FIN. REV. 13, 13 (1989).
273. See Trafford, sup. note 240 (ch. 1), at 6.
274. See Blumenthal et al., sup. note 270 (ch. 1), at 722-723.
275. Despite this reduction, the Office of Management and Budget approved the release of $75 million to compensate service providers and beneficiaries. There is still $26.3 million in administrative costs outstanding, however. See *Bentsen Warns White House*, sup. note 244 (ch. 1), at A17.
276. Trafford, sup. note 240 (ch. 1), at 6 (quoting Gail R. Wilensky, administrator of the Health Care Financing Administration).
277. See Ira Mothner, *Medicare, Medigap and Medicaid*, 10 AM. HEALTH 67, 67 (1991).
278. "Health Care Costs, Future Medicare Costs Linked to Cures for Aging Disorders," *Daily Report for Executives*, May 3, 1990, at A8.
279. See id.
280. See *Pennsylvania Perspective*, sup. note 165 (ch. 1), at 2. Studies show that 80 percent of Medicare beneficiaries are under the impression that their long-term health care needs will be covered by Medicare and other private insurance. In reality, less than one tenth of one percent will be adequately protected. Id.
281. See id. at 3.
282. See Spencer Rich, "Medicare Trust Funds' Outlook Bleak," *The Washington Post*, April 2, 1991, at A19, col. 1.
283. Id. (quoting Deborah Steelman, head of the Social Security Advisory Council).
284. See sup. text accompanying notes 16-23 (ch. 1).
285. Id.
286. See Thomas E. Getzen, *Longlife Insurance: A Prototype for Funding Long-Term Care*, 10 HEALTH CARE FIN. REV. 47, 47 (1988).
287. See Budish, sup. note 213 (ch. 1), at 68. "In . . . Pennsylvania, for some considerable time, if you weren't lucky enough to be schizophrenic, but instead had Alzheimer's disease, you would not be entitled to any community mental health services; if you were schizophrenic, you would." Robert N. Butler, Diane Meier, John J. Regan, Robert Wolf, and Elias Cohen, *Physicians and Their Elderly Patients' Legal Rights, Part I: Medicare, Medicaid, Elder Abuse*, 44 GERIATRICS 57, 58 (1989) (Panel discussion) [hereinafter Butler et al.].
288. Budish, sup. note 238 (ch. 1), at 68.
289. See id.

290. The spousal impoverishment rules requires nursing home residents and their spouses to retain only half of their life savings up to $62,580 and still qualify for coverage under Medicaid. Unmarried nursing home residents may retain about $2,000, however this figure varies by state. See id.

291. See Butler, *Dealing with the Real Catastrophe*, 45 GERIATRICS 13, 13 (March 1990).

292. John J. Kang, *Perpetuating Market Misallocations in Health Care Through Employer Health Insurance Mandates*, 12 AM. J. TAX POL'Y 513, 546 (1995).

293. See Deborah Shalowitz, "Group Long-Term Care Insurance; Programs Gaining Flexibility as Employers and Workers Show More Interest in Benefit," *Business Insurance*, April 1, 1991, at 23.

294. Id.

295. Id.

296. Id.

297. See Barry, sup. note 59 (ch. 1), at D1.

298. See generally Susan J. Hemp and Cheryl Rae Nyberg, *Elder Law: A Guide to Key Resources*, 3 ELDERL. J. 1 (1995). This research guide identifies and describes 163 books, periodicals, reference tools, databases, electronic discussion groups, organizations, and U.S. government agencies useful to the elder law practitioner and the legal researcher. Appendices include a state-by-state list of state aging agencies, bar association committees and sections, law school courses and clinics, and publications; acronyms; and subject headings and index terms used in library catalogs, periodical indexes, and related sources.

299. See generally UNITED STATES ACCOUNTING OFFICE, MEDICAID EST. PLAN., GAO/HRD 93-29R, for a review of 403 Medicaid applications for nursing home benefits in Massachusetts, where more than half of the applicants had already converted available assets into exempt assets or had transferred assets to another person within the period of time allowed prior to their application.

300. See, e.g., Fein, sup. note 12 (ch. 1), at 39; Jane Bryant Quinn, "Do Only the Suckers Pay?," *Newsweek*, December 18, 1989.

301. 42 U.S.C. 1395d(a)(2)(A) (1988 & Supp. IV. 1993).

302. Id.

303. See generally Krauskopf, sup. note 11 (ch. 1), at 435-436.

304. Gladwell, sup. note 243 (ch. 1).

305. See 140 CONG. REC. S5834 (1994)(statement of Senator Cohen, including this average cost while introducing S. 2122, The Public-Private Long-Term Care Partnership Act of 1994).

306. See Burwell, sup. note 12 (ch. 1), at 374 (quoting statements from Sheldon Goldberg, President of the American Association of Homes for Aging); Id. at 403-404 (quoting Steven Chies on behalf of the American Health Care Association, to this effect).

307. Gladwell, sup. note 243 (ch. 1).

308. Peterson, sup. note 26 (ch. 1), at 124.
309. Id. at 123-124.
310. Id. at 124.
311. See Lamm and Bluemke, sup. note 47 (ch. 1), at 20.
312. See id.
313. See, e.g., Erick J. Bohlman, *Financing Strategies: Long-Term Care for the Elderly*, 2 ELDERL.J. 167,187 (1994) (discussing the ethical duties owed to the elderly; a Fordham Law School symposium), *Special Issue Ethical Issue in Representing Older Clients*, 62 FORD. L. REV. 961 (1994).
314. *Compassion in Dying v. State of Washington*, 79 F.3d 790 (9th Cir. 1996), rehearing denied, 85 F.3d 1440 (1996); Tamar Lewin, "Ruling Sharpens Debate on 'Right to Die'," *The New York Times*, March 8, 1996, at A8.
315. *Compassion in Dying*, 79 F.3d 790, at 801.
316. Id. at 816.
317. Id. There are six related state interests: (1) the state's general interest in preserving life; (2) the state's more specific interest in preventing suicide, (3) the state's interest in avoiding the involvement of third parties and in precluding the use of arbitrary, unfair, or undue influence; (4) the state's interest in protecting family members and loved ones; (5) the state's interest in protecting the integrity of the medical profession; and (6) the state's interest in avoiding adverse consequences that might ensue if the statutory provision at issue is declared unconstitutional.
318. Id. at 838.
319. *Quill v. Vacco*, 80 F.3d 716 (1996).
320. Id. at 728.
321. Id. at 731.
322. *Compassion in Dying*, 79 F.3d at 838 (1996).
323. Oregon's Death With Dignity Act makes it a felony to coerce, influence or contract for a request for aid-in-dying. See 13 OR. REV. STAT. §127.890 (1995), which provides, in pertinent part, as follows:

> 1. A person who without authorization of the patient willfully alters or forges a request for medication or conceals or destroys a rescission of that request with the intent or effect of causing the patient's death shall be guilty of a Class A felony.
>
> 2. A person who coerces or exerts undue influence on a patient to request medication for the purpose of ending the patient's life, or to destroy a rescission of such a request, shall be guilty of a Class A felony.

See also, 13 OR. REV. STAT. §127.995 (1995), which provides, in pertinent part, as follows:

> 1. It shall be a Class A felony for a person without authorization of the principal to willfully alter, forge, conceal or destroy an instrument, the reinstatement or revocation of an instrument or any other evidence or document reflecting the principal's desires and interests, with the intent and effect of causing a withholding or withdrawal of

life-sustaining procedures or of artificially administered nutrition and hydration which hastens the death of the principal.

2. Except as provided in subsection (1) of this section, it shall be a Class A misdemeanor for a person without authorization of the principal to willfully alter, forge, conceal, or destroy an instrument, the reinstatement or revocation of an instrument, or any other evidence or document reflecting the principal's desires and interests with the intent or effect of affecting a health care decision.

324. A report from Cornell University projects that baby-boomers stand to inherit trillions of dollars from their now aged parents. See Tracy Thompson, "The Changing Face of Philanthropy; Thrifty Members of WWII Generation Are Bequeathing Their Fortunes," *The Washington Post*, March 31, 1996, §A, at 1. However, the representatives of the National Center for Financial Education proclaim: "Not so." This is because as the elderly demographic continues to live longer, they spend more of their savings, particularly on long-term health care and on expensive technology designed to prolong life. See Gannett News Service, "Baby-Boomer Windfall Only A Dream?," March 25, 1995, at 9.

325. *Lee v. State*, 891 F. Supp. 1421 (D.Or. 1995).

326. Lee, sup. note 79 (ch. 1).

327. See id.

328. See id.

329. See Lamm and Bluemke, sup. note 47 (ch. 1), at 20.

330. Id.

331. In 1963, there were approximately 1,100 managed-care service providers. However, by the year 1994, there were approximately 14,000 managed-care service providers for 6 million recipients. Expenditures in 1993 exceeded $21 billion for managed care, of which Medicare accounted for 33 percent. Still, this was four times less expensive than the cost of remaining in the hospital. Pam Slater, "Home Health Boom," *Sacramento Bee*, March 21, 1994, at C3.

Chapter 2

1. *Schweiker v. Gray Panthers*, 453 U.S. 34, 43 (1981).
2. *Friedman v. Berger*, 547 F.2d 724, 727 (2d Cir. [N.Y.] 1976), cert. denied, 430 U.S. 984, 97 S. Ct. 1681 (1977).
3. Id. at 727, n.7.
4. See COMMITTEE ON ENERGY AND COMMERCE, 103D CONG., 1ST SESS., *Medicaid Source Book: Background Data and Analysis (A 1993 Update)*, (Comm. Print 103-A). Less than one percent of those persons entering nursing homes have long-term insurance. Id. at 59-60.
5. In New York City, Medicaid annually provides nearly $1 billion for long-term care of the elderly with "much of it going to middle- and upper-middle class senior citizens in nursing homes who become eligible by transferring their assets to their children." "Mayor and Pataki," sup. note 9 (ch. 1), at 1.
6. Paul R. Willing, *Financing Long-Term Care in America Poses a Major Challenge to Society*, FED. OF AM. HEALTH SYS. REV., at 47 (January/February 1988).
7. The New Jersey Supreme Court refers to the identity of the husband in *L.M. v. State, Div. of Medical Assistance of Health Services*, 140 N.Y. 480, 659 A.2d 450 (N.J. 1995), only as L.M.
8. The Medicaid Gap is that range of income that is too high for Medicaid eligibility but too low to afford nursing home services. See *L.M. v. State Div. of Medical Assistance & Health Services*, 140 N.J. at 481, 659 A.2d at 450 (citing Jill Quadagno, Madonna Harrington Meyer, and J. Blake Turner, *Falling Into the Medicaid Gap: The Hidden Long-Term Care Dilemma*, 31 GERONTOLOGIST 521, 521 (1991)).
9. See Chris Conway, "N.J. High Court Allows Divorce For Medicaid," *Philadelphia Inquirer*, June 8, 1995, at A1.
10. The Whitman administration in New Jersey is contemplating a proposal to allow persons who do not qualify for Medicaid to receive benefits once they spend all but $433.00 of their monthly income on their health care. See id. at A24.
11. The reform anticipated by the Court is the plan to allow qualifying trusts for Medicaid Gap members, which will revert back to the state upon death in the amount funded by the state during the period of long term care. See *L.M. v. State Division of Medical Assistance and Health Services*, note 7 (ch. 2), 659 A.2d at 454.
12. See *Lewis v. Hegstrom*, 767 F.2d 1371 (9th Cir. (Or.) 1985). See also *Hearing Before the Subcommittee on Health and Environment of the House Committee on Energy and Commerce*, 103d Cong. 1st Sess. 337 (1993) [hereinafter *Health and Environment*] (statement of Brian Burwell, Division Manager for Systemetrics/Medstat Systems during hearings in Medicare and Medicaid Budget Reconciliation).
13. Omnibus Reconciliation Act of 1980, Pub. L. No. 96-611, 94 Stat. § 5, 94 Stat. 3567, codified at 42 U.S.C. §§ 1382b(c) and 1396 a(j).

14. See 20 C.F.R. § 416.1210 (1994).
15. See 20 C.F.R. § 416.1210 (1994).
16. Omnibus Budget Reconciliation Act of 1980, Pub. L. No. 96-611, § 94 Stat. 3566 (amending § 1917 (c)(2)(B) of Title XIX regarding the rules of transfer of the applicant's home).
17. 1982 Amendments: Committee Reports and Supplementary Material, Department of Health and Human Services New Release, Medicare and Medicaid Guide, New Developments (CCH) 24, 559 (1982).
18. Medicare Catastrophic Coverage Act of 1988, Pub L. No. 100-360, 100th Cong., 2d Sess., 102 Stat. 754 (1988).
19. Medicare Catastrophic Coverage Act of 1988, Pub. L. No. 100-360, 100th Cong., 2d Sess., 102 Stat. at 761 (1988)(amending 42 U.S.C. § 1396p(c)).
20. Omnibus Budget Reconciliation Act of 1989, Pub. L. No. 101-239, 101st Cong., 1st Sess., 103 Stat. 2270 (1989).
21. Omnibus Budget Reconciliation Act of 1989, Pub. L. No. 101-239, 101st Cong., 1st Sess., 103 Stat. 2271 (1989).
22. Omnibus Budget Reconciliation Act of 1993, Pub. L. No. 103-66, 103rd Cong., 1st Sess., 107 Stat. 622; see also Sanford J. Schlesinger and Barbara J. Scheiner, *OBRA '93 Makes Sweeping Changes in Medicaid Rules*, 21 EST. PLAN. 74 (1994).
23. 42 U.S.C. § 1396p(c)(3)-(5).
24. 42 U.S.C. § 1396p(c)(1).
25. 42 U.S.C. § 1396p(c)(2)(B)(i)-(iii).
26. 42 U.S.C. § 1396p(d). For a history of trust treatment prior to 1993, see David P. Callahan, *The Use of Trusts in Estate Planning for the Elderly or Incapacitated Client*, 209 PLI/Est. 101 (February 6-7, 1992).
27. 42 U.S.C. § 1396p(c)(1)(A),(E).
28. 42 U.S.C. § 1396p(b).
29. Jane Bryant Quinn, "Paring the Loopholes That Let The Well-Off Into Medicaid," *The Washington Post*, October 3, 1993, at H3. See also Sanford J. Schlesinger and Barbara J. Scheiner, sup. note 22 (ch. 2).
30. Fein, sup. note 12 (ch. 1), at 39.
31. See generally John J. Regan, *Tax, Estate & Financial Planning for the Elderly*, §10.19 (Matthew Bender & Co. 1996).
32. John J. Kang, *Perpetuating Market Misallocations in Health Care Through Employer Health Insurance Mandates*, 12 AM. J. TAX POL'Y 513, 546 (1995).
33. Jane Bryant Quinn, "New Law Lets Medicaid Tap Middle-Class Seniors' Estates," *The Washington Post*, October 10, 1993, at H3.
34. *Medicare and Medicaid Budget Reconciliation: Hearings Before the Subcommittee on Health and the Environment of the House Committee on Energy and Commerce*, 103d Cong., 1st Sess. 348 (1993). The American Public Welfare Association reports that in 1992, the year before OBRA'93, 25 states and the District of Columbia maintained an estate recovery program. See American Public Welfare Association, *Estate Recovery Survey*

Results (1992). Unlike California, few of the programs are successful. See GENERAL ACCOUNTING OFFICE, MEDICAID: RECOVERIES FROM NURSING HOME RESIDENT'S ESTATES COULD OFFSET PROGRAM COSTS, GAO/HRD-89-56 (March 1989); OFFICE OF THE INSPECTOR GENERAL, MEDICAID ESTATE RECOVERIES, HHS OAI-09-86-0078 (June 1988).

35. See Quinn, sup. note 33 (ch. 2), at H3.
36. See Commonwealth of Massachusetts, SPECIAL COMMISSION ON MEDICAID ESTATE RECOVERY: REPORT AND PROPOSED LEGISLATION (November 1991) [hereinafter COMMONWEALTH OF MASSACHUSETTS]. See generally Bove, sup. note 12 (ch. 1). In fiscal year 1993, when the Medicaid budget totaled $3.2 billion, Massachusetts recovered $8.6 million from 535 cases with a ten-person staff. Id.
37. See Bonita Brodt, "No Quick, Easy Cure for Medicaid Program," *Chicago Tribune*, July 14, 1994, at 1.
38. Tennessee passed TennCare, a program to address the costs of Medicaid. See Paula Wade, "For Sundquist, Trip Won't Be All Uphill," *Commercial Appeal*, November 27, 1994, at 5B.
39. See Social Security Act of 1972, Pub. L. No. 92-603, 86 Stat. 1329 (1972) at §209(b) [codified at 42 U.S.C. § 1396a(f)]. See also *Savage v. Toan*, 795 F.2d 643 (8th Cir. 1986). The states are: Connecticut, Hawaii, Illinois, Indiana, Minnesota, Missouri, New Hampshire, North Carolina, North Dakota, Ohio, Oklahoma and Virginia. For an article suggesting that 209(b) invites arbitrariness, see note, *Spending Down for Medicaid Eligibility in Section 209(b) States: Should the Procedure Be Changed?*, 1 ELDERLAW J. 199 (1993).
40. See, e.g., Burwell, sup. note 12 (ch. 1). In Florida, the Streimer Rule states that the action of one co-owner can not be considered in determining the Medicaid eligibility of another; in Wisconsin a withdrawal from a joint bank account is a prohibited transfer, as is true in Michigan, Arizona, and Virginia.
41. See *State ex. rel. Dept. of Human Services*, 890 P.2d 1342 (Okla. 1995) (ruling on 42 U.S.C. § 1396p(d)(3)(B)(i)(I)).
42. See Kenneth M. Coughlin, *Here Come the Trustbusters: States Move to Restrict Medicaid Planning*, ELDERL. REP. 1 (November 1992) (Connecticut sought a 60-month period).
43. See Regan, sup. note 31 (ch. 2), §10.19, at 10-140-46 (describing plans in New York, Connecticut, and California).
44. See 42 U.S.C. § 1396p(b)(1)(C)(i) (1988 & Supp. V. 1993) (allowing for an estate recovery program to seek adjustment of recovery from an estate in the case of an individual who has received benefits under a long-term care insurance policy).
45. 42 U.S.C. §1396p(b)(1)(C)(ii) (1988 & Supp. V. 1993).
46. See Feldesman and Canning, *Long-Term Care Insurance Helps Preserve an Estate*, 20 EST. PLAN. 76 (1993).
47. Connecticut, Indiana, and California have an arrangement known as "dollar-for-dollar" protection. See Mahoney and Wetle, *Public-Private Partnerships: The*

Connecticut Model for Financing Long-Term Care, 40 J. AM. GERIATRICS SOC'Y 1026 (1992) (explaining Connecticut's partnership for long-term care).
48. See Quinn, sup. note 33 (ch. 2), at H3.
49. See, e.g., Kenneth M. Coughlin, *Ohio Flirts with License Revocation*, ELDERL. REP. at 2 (November 1992). But see *Helvering v. Gregory*, 69 F.2d 809, 810 (2d Cir. 1934), aff'd 293 U.S. 465 (1935) (wherein Judge Learned Hand wrote: "Anyone may so arrange his affairs that his taxes shall be as low as possible; he is not bound to choose that pattern which will best pay the Treasury; there is not even a patriotic duty to increase one's taxes.").
50. See generally Steven H. Hobbs and Fay Wilson Hobbs, *Proceeding of the Conference on Ethical Issues in Representing the Older Client*, 62 FORD- HAM L. REV. 1411 (1994).
51. Gladwell, sup. note 10 (ch. 1), at A10, col. 2.
52. Id.
53. See Ken Foskett, "Block Grants Could Shortchange Georgia," *Atlanta Constitution*, September 10, 1995, at C4. See also *Catherine L. Fisk, The Last Article About the Language of ERISA Preemption? A Case Study of the Failure of Textualism*, 33 HARV. J. ON LEGIS. 35 (1996) (arguing for a more practical approach toward ERISA preemption and suggesting that this is the future of the law as the courts work toward a balance between state and federal regulation); Devon P. Groves, *ERISA Waivers and State Health Care Reform*, 28 COLUM. J. L. & SOC. PROBS. 609 (1995) (arguing for greater freedom for states from federal ERISA control).
54. *New State Ice v. Liebmann*, 285 U.S. 262, 311 (1932) (Brandeis, J., dissent- ing). See also James E. Halloway, *"Cooperative Federalism" to Preserve the States' Role in Formulating Health Care Policy*, 16 CAMPBELL L. REV. 405 (1994) (arguing for greater federalism in the health care agenda); Michael S. Sparer, *Federal Menus and State Programs: An Intergovernmen- tal Health Care Partnership for the 1990s*, 21 N.Y.U. REV. L. & SOC. CHANGE 323 (1994/95) (advocating a higher degree of partnership between the federal government and the states than that envisioned by more traditional federalism); Fernando R. Laguarda, *Federalism Myth: States as Laboratories of Health Care Reform*, 82 GEO. L. J. 159 (1993) (arguing that modern interest groups prevent states from serving as proper laboratories of federalism).
55. Angelo A. Sito III, *State Government: The Laboratory for National Health Care Reform*, 19 SETON HALL LEGIS. J. 322, 372 (1994). For the unique federal role ERISA plays in regulating insurance plans, see generally Kevin Caster, *The Future of Self-Funded Health Plans*, 79 IOWA L. REV. 413 (1994); Eliot L. Engel, *Health Care Reform and ERISA*, 68 ST. JOHN'S L. REV. 343 (1994).
56. See Thomas C. Fox, Joel M. Hamme and Lynn Sargent Berner, *Long Term Care and the Steady Trend Toward Federalization of the Medicaid Program: Past and Future*, National Health Lawyers Association, Health Law Practice

Guide (Clark, Boardman, Callaghan) (1995) [hereinafter Fox, Hamme, and Berner].

57. See 42 USC 1396(a)(13)(e).
58. The Boren Amendment required rates that are reasonable and adequate to meet the costs which must be incurred by efficiently and economically operated facilities in order to provide care and services in conformity with applicable state and federal laws, regulations and quality and safety standards. See 42 USC 1396(a)(13)(A).
59. See Fox, Hamme, and Berner, sup. note 56 (ch. 2), at 33-37.
60. See id. at 33-38.
61. See *Wilder v. Virginia Hospital Association*, 496 U.S. 498 (1990).
62. See Fox, Hamme, and Berner, sup. note 56 (ch. 2), at 33-40.
63. Republican National Committee, RESTORING THE DREAM: THE BOLD NEW PLAN BY HOUSE REPUBLICANS, at 27 (S. Moore 1995).
64. Id. at 227.
65. Ellen O'Brien, "Retire? Never!," *Philadelphia Inquirer*, July 25, 1995, at G1.
66. Id.
67. Id.
68. GREEN BOOK, sup. note 4 (ch. 1), at 807.
69. Id.
70. Id. at 795.
71. See Judith Havemann, "Much at Stake for States, Patients in Little-Noted Plans for Medicaid," *The Washington Post*, May 30, 1995, at A11.
72. Id.
73. Polman, sup. note 14 (ch. 1), at E2.
74. Tom Joe and Julie Farber, "Shortsighted Medicaid Fix: The States Will Be Left Holding the Bag," *The Washington Post*, July 6, 1995, at A21 [hereinafter "Medicaid Fix"].
75. See Mary Hurtig, "The Dangers in Changing Medicaid," *Philadelphia Inquirer*, July 15, 1995, at A7.
76. See Tom Joe and Julie Farber, "Most Fail to Realize That Majority of Medicaid Goes to Old and Infirm," *Greensboro News & Record*, July 10, 1995, at A6; Hurtig, sup. note 475 (ch. 2), at A7.
77. In Pennsylvania, Medicaid pays for 30 percent of the total costs for services for people with mental illnesses. These services include clinic visits, prescription drugs, case management, and hospitalization. An even greater 53 percent of institutional care and 33 percent of community care is expended for mentally retarded Pennsylvanians. See Hurtig, sup. note 75 (ch. 2), at A7.
78. Between 1988 and 1993, the elderly and disabled population grew by 32 percent from 6.6 million to 8.7 million Medicaid beneficiaries. See "Medicaid Fix," sup. note 74 (ch. 2), at 21. Medicaid expenditures for this growing group within the same time frame has increased by 96 percent.
79. By the year 2018, there is estimated to be 6.2 million people who will be age 85 or older. This is a 72 percent increase from the 3.6 million people who

were 85 or older in 1993. Further, as a result of medical developments in the acute, neonatal, and prenatal fields, as well as the "coming of age," so to speak, of the baby-boomer generation, more of these elderly will be capable of living with disabilities. See "Medicaid Fix," note 74 (ch. 2), at A21. Despite increased restrictions on Medicaid eligibility, the Congressional Budget Office predicts that the number of persons eligible for Medicaid will increase annually by 12 percent. See Judith Havemann, "Drive for Block Grants is Running into a Wall," *The Washington Post*, July 8, 1995, at A4. Not only will the elderly population eligible for Medicaid increase, but by living longer with their disabilities, this demographic will remain eligible for Medicaid longer. Presently, the average length of time on Medicaid in Missouri is 27 years. See id.

80. See id.
81. Joe and Farber estimate that the $180 billion reduction proposed in Missouri will require the ousting of 4 million otherwise eligible Medicaid recipients. If proportioned, approximately 400,000 elderly, 600,000 disabled and 3 million families would become ineligible. See "Medicaid Fix," sup. note 74 (ch. 2), at A21.
82. Hurtig, sup. note 75 (ch. 2), at A7.
83. See Harold Pollack and James Tobin, "Welfare Reform Needs More Carrots," *Philadelphia Inquirer*, Aug 14, 1995, at A9.
84. See Havermann, sup. note 79 (ch. 2), at A4 (including Congressional Budget Office graph demonstrating disparities in federal spending on Medicaid for Connecticut, Florida, Virginia, Maryland, and the District of Columbia).
85. Id.
86. Id.
87. Id.
88. Id.

Chapter 3

1. For an excellent overview of Medicaid eligibility rules, see Barbara J. Collins, *Medicaid*, 239 PLI/Est 55 (1995).
2. Resources include: Family Caregiver Alliance, 425 Bush Street, Suite 500, San Francisco, California 94108 (415/434-3388); National Academy of Elder Law Attorneys, 1604 N. Country Club Road, Tucson, Arizona 85716.
3. VIRGINIA MORRIS, HOW TO CARE FOR AGING PARENTS 263 (1996).
4. During 1992, $4.5 billion dollars was spent on home health care under Medicaid. GREEN BOOK, sup. note 4 (ch. 1), at 807.
5. Id. at 791.
6. Id. at 789.
7. 42 U.S.C. § 1396p (1988 & Supp. V. 1993) (Amended 1993).
8. See *The Medical Component of Retirement Planning*, § 3509.10 Medicaid Planning, Commerce Clearing House, Inc. (1993).
9. See generally Stanley A. Pelli, *Planning for the Older Client: Medicaid & Living Trusts*, Pennsylvania Bar Institute, EST. PLAN., ch. 7 (1994); Regan, sup. note 31 (ch. 2), at §10.19.
10. New York allows for you to transfer all your assets, go into a nursing home, and apply for Medicaid all in one day. See The Medical Component of Retirement Planning, sup. note 8 (ch. 3), at §3511 (1993).
11. Id.
12. 45 C.F.R. § 233.20(a)(3)(D)(1994). See also *Couch v. Director*, 795 S.W.2d 91 (Mo.Ct.App. 1990); *Tidrow v. Director*, 688 S.W.2d 9 (Mo.Ct.App. 1985).
13. 45 C.F.R. § 233.20 (a)(3)(D)(1994). See also *Couch v. Director*, 795 S.W.2d 91 (Mo.Ct.App 1990); *Tidrow v. Director*, 688 S.W.2d 9 (Mo.Ct.App. 1985).
14. See 20 C.F.R. § 416.1210 (1994).
15. See generally, Colleen M. Grogan, *Hope in Federalism? What Can the States Do and What Are They Likely To Do?*, 20 J. HEALTH POL. POL'Y & L. 477 (1995).
16. Omnibus Budget Reconciliation Act of 1993, Pub. L. No. 103-66, 103rd Cong., 1st Sess., 107 Stat. 622 (1993).
17. 42 U.S.C. § 1396p(c)(1).
18. See, e.g., Schlesinger and Scheiner, sup. note 22 (ch. 2), at 75.
19. 42 U.S.C. § 1396p(c))2)(B)(i)-(iii).
20. 42 U.S.C. § 1396p(e)(1) (1988 & Supp. V. 1993).
21. 42 U.S.C. § 1396p(c)(1)(A), (E)(i)(I) (1988 & Supp. V. 1993).
22. 42 U.S.C. § 1396p(c)(3) (1988 & Supp. V. 1993). Note that states had different rules for this among themselves and the effect of OBRA'93 was to create uniformity.
23. See generally, Krauskopf, sup. note 11 (ch. 1), at § 11.41.
24. There is a rebuttable presumption that assets transferred within the thirty-six month period are considered as seeking Medicaid eligibility. HCFA Pub. No.

45-3 (State Medicaid Manual) § 3250.3. The important distinction is that the individual transferring the assets must believe that he or she is receiving fair market value. 42 U.S.C. § 1396p(c)(2)(B)(i).

25. 42 U.S.C. § 1396p(c)(2)(B)(ii).

26. 42 U.S.C. §1396p(c)(2)(A)(i) (1988 & Supp. V 1993).

27. 42 U.S.C. §1396p(c)(2)(A)(i)(1988 & Supp. V 1993).

28. Any transfers to or from the applicant's spouse still are not considered uncompensated transfers so long as they are for the sole benefit of the spouse. 42 U.S.C. § 1396p(c)(2)(B)(i)-(ii).

29. 42 U.S.C. § 1396p(c)(D)(2) (1988 & Supp. V 1993). See Roger A. McEowen, *Estate Planning for Farm and Ranch Families Facing Long-Term Health Care*, 73 NEB. L. REV. 104 (1994).

30. Pub. L. No. 99-272, § 6202, 99th Cong., 1st Sess. (1985)(codified at 42 U.S.C. 1396a(k) (1988)) (repealed by §§ 13611-13612 of the Omnibus Budget Reconciliation Act of 1993, Pub. L. No. 103-66, 107 Stat. 312 (1993) (codified at 42 U.S.C. § 1396p).

31. See Regan, sup. note 31 (ch. 2), at § 10.13(1) (1994).

32. See id.; Peter J. Strauss, *To Have and Have Not: Trusts After 'Tutino'*, N.Y.L.J., July 24, 1990, at 3.

33. See Strauss, sup. note 32 (ch. 3), at 3.

34. See id. But see *Vanderbilt Credit Corp. v. Chase Manhattan Bank*, 100 A.D.2d 544, 473 N.Y.S.2d 142 (N.Y. App. Div. 1984) (restricting the creation of trusts in order to protect assets from creditors such as health care providers).

35. Butler et al., sup. note 287 (ch. 1), at 61 (quoting Elias Cohen, attorney and vice-president, Community Services Institute, Inc., located in Pennsylvania).

36. Strauss, sup. note 32 (ch. 3), at 6. This drawback may be superseded somewhat, however, by the spousal resource allowance of $62,580, which is statutorily granted under the Medicare Catastrophic Coverage Act § 303(f).

37. See 42 U.S.C. § 1396p(d)(3)(A) & (B) (1988 & Supp. V 1993).

38. 42 U.S.C. § 1396p(d)(3)(A)(i).

39. 42 U.S.C. § 1396p(d)(3)(A)(ii).

40. See 45 C.F.R. § 811 (1993).

41. See 42 U.S.C. § 1396p(c)(1)(B)(i) (1988 & Supp. V 1993).

42. 42 U.S.C. § 1396p(d)(3)(B)(i) (1988 & Supp. V 1993). Availability is the operative word, not actuality of receipt. 42 U.S.C. § 1396p(d)(3)(B)(i). See *also* Elizabeth C. Kolshorn, *The Effect of the Federal Availability Principle on State AFDC Asset-Transfer Rules*, 89 COLUM. L. REV. 580 (1989); *Couch v. Director*, 795 S.W.2d 9 (Mo.Ct.App. 1990); *Tidrow v. Director*, 688 S.W.2d 9 (Mo.Ct.App. 1985).

43. 42 U.S.C. § 1396p(d)(3)(B)(i)(I).

44. See 42 U.S.C. § 1396p(d)(A)(iii) (1988 & Supp. V 1993) and 42 U.S.C. § 1396p(d)(3)(b)(2) (1988 & Supp. V 1993). Additional transferred assets are all those that are paid to or earned by an irrevocable trust that specifically prohibits distribution to the applicant. 42 U.S.C. § 1396p(d)(3)(B)(ii) (1988

& Supp. V 1993). These are subject to the 60 month look back period. 42 U.S.C. § 1396p(c)(1)(B)(i).

45. 42 U.S.C. § 1396p(c)(1)(B)(i).
46. Peter J. Strauss, *Medicaid Revisions Contained in the 1993 Budget Act*, NEW YORK LAW JOURNAL, September 30, 1993, at 31 (comparing drafting of the provisions on revocable and irrevocable trusts as "clearly the product of midnight drafting done by the four horseman [*sic*] of the apocalypse").
47. See, e.g., *Link v. Town of Smithtown*, 616 N.Y.S.2d 171 (N.Y. App. Div. 1994); *Estate of Wallace v. Director, Missouri State Div. of Fam. Serv.*, 628 S.W.2d 388 (Mo.Ct.App. 1982); *Zeoli v. Connecticut Dept. of Soc. Serv.*, 425 A.2d 533 (Conn. 1979).
48. See Brian Burwell, *SysteMetrics: State Responses to Medicaid Estate Planning*, 17 (1993).
49. See generally, Clifton Kruse, "Discretionary Trusts: Insulating Discretionary Trust Assets for Elders and Incapacitated Persons from Consideration by Medicaid and Other Public Support Providers" (presented at the 3rd Annual Symposium on Elder Law, National Academy of Elder Law Attorneys, Orlando, Florida, May 1991).
50. See Schlesinger and Scheiner, sup. note 22 (ch. 2), 75.
51. See Ronald R. Volkmer, *Impact of Various Trusts on Medicaid*, 22, EST. PLAN. 315 (September/October 1995).
52. 424 N.W.2d 144 (N.D. 1988).
53. 527 N.W.2d 226 (N.D. 1994).
54. See, e.g., *Missouri Div. of Fam. Serv. v. Wilson*, 849 S.W.2d 104 (Mo.App. 1991).
55. 42 U.S.C. § 1396p(d)(4)(A); see *Moretti*, 606 N.Y.S.2d 543 (N.Y.App.Div. 1993) (exempting a supplemental needs trust created for a 15-year-old by the court with the parent as a conservator). But see *Frerks v. Shalala*, 848 F.Supp. 340 (E.D.N.Y. 1994). As to older state holdings finding supplemental needs trusts exempt, see *Matter of Ginsberg*, 52 N.Y.2d 1006 (1981). See *also Garbow*, 591 N.Y.S.2d 754 (N.Y. App. Div. 1992); *State v. Coyle*, 171 A.D.2d 288 (N.Y.App.Div., 1991).
56. See 42 U.S.C. § 1396p(d)(4)(A) (1988 & Supp. V 1993).
57. 42 U.S.C. § 1396p(d)(4)(A) (1988 & Supp. V 1993).
58. 33 Cal. App.4th 161, 38 Cal. Rptr.2d 917 (Cal.Ct.App. 1995).
59. See Harry S. Margolis, *Income-Only Trusts Resuscitated Under HCFA Interpretation of OBRA-93*, ELDERL. REP. 1 (Feb. 1994).
60. Id. at 1-3.
61. See *Estate of Rosenberg v. Dep't of Pub. Welfare*, 165 Pa. Comm. 9, 644 A.2d 215, 216 (1994).
62. 746 F.Supp. 19 (Colo. 1990).
63. See 42 U.S.C. § 1396p(f)(4)(c); 42 C.F.R. § 435.722(a); 42 C.F.R. § 435.1005.
64. *Miller v. Ibarra*, 746 F. Supp. 21-22 (Colo. 1990).

65. 42 U.S.C. § 1396p(d)(4)(B)(i).
66. 42 U.S.C. § 1396p(d)(4)(B)(i).
67. See Ark. Code Ann. §28-69-102 (Michie Supp. 1995).
68. 319 Ark. 782, 894 S.W.2d 584 (1995).
69. See Ronald R. Volkmer, *When Will Trust Preclude Eligibility for Medicaid*, 22 EST. PLAN. 316 (September/October 1995).
70. 635 N.E.2d 853 (Ill. 1994).
71. 42 U.S.C. § 1396p(d)(5).
72. See generally McEowen, sup. note 29 (ch. 3).
73. 42 U.S.C. § 1396p(c)(1)(E) (1988 & Supp. V. 1993).
74. 42 U.S.C. § 1396p(c)(1)(E) (1988 & Supp. V. 1993).
75. See 42 U.S.C. § 1396p(c)(1)(E) (1988 & Supp. V 1993).
76. 42 U.S.C. § 1396p(c)(1)(E) (I)-(II) (1988 & Supp. V. 1993).
77. 42 U.S.C. § 1396p(c)(1)(C)(ii) (1988 & Supp. V. 1993).
78. See sup. text accompanying notes 33-38 (ch. 2), inf. text accompanying notes 1-9 (ch. 3).
79. See Medicare Catastrophic Coverage Act of 1988, Pub. L. No. 100-360, 100th Cong., 2d Sess., 102 Stat. 754 (1988); Jeanne Fineberg and Roger Schwartz, *Implementation of the Medicaid Provisions of the Medicare Catastrophic Coverage Act*, 23 CLEARINGHOUSE REV. 370, 373-75 (1989).
80. Omnibus Budget Reconciliation Act of 1989, Pub. L. No. 101-239, 101st Cong., 1st Sess., 103 Stat. 2271 (1989).
81. See 42 U.S.C. § 1396p(c)(2)(B)(i)-(ii) (1988 & Supp. V. 1993).
82. Id. Similar transfers can be made to blind or disabled children, or for the benefit of disabled persons over sixty-five years of age. Id. at (iii). See generally Strauss, sup. note 32 (ch. 3), at 7.
83. See 42 U.S.C. § 1396(c)(2)(B)(iv)(1988 & Supp. V 1993).
84. See generally Regan, sup. note 31 (ch. 2) at §10.19.
85. 416 Mass. 629, 624 N.E.2d 110 (1993).

Chapter 4

1. 42 U.S.C. § 1396p(b) (1988 & Supp. V. 1993).
2. Tax Equity and Fiscal Responsibility Act of 1982, § 132(b), Pub. L. No. 97-248, 96 Stat. 370-371 (1982).
3. See American Public Welfare Association, ESTATE RECOVERY SURVEY RESULTS (1992).
4. Office of the Inspector General, *Medicaid Estate Recoveries*, HHS OAI-09-86-00078 (June 1988); GAO, *Medicaid: Recoveries from Nursing Home Residents' Estates Could Offset Program Costs*, GAO/HRD-89=56 (March 1989).
5. 42 U.S.C. § 1396p(b)(1)(B) (1988 & Supp. V 1993).
6. 42 U.S.C. § 1396p(b)(4)(A) (1988 & Supp. V 1993); 42 U.S.C. § 1396p(b)(4)(B) (1988 & Supp. V. 1993).
7. 42 U.S.C. § 1396p(b)(1)(C)(i) (1988 & Supp. V. 1993).
8. 42 U.S.C. § 1396p(b)(1)(C)(i) (1988 & Supp. V. 1993).
9. See generally COMMONWEALTH OF MASSACHUSETTS, sup. note 36 (ch. 2).
10. Exodus 20:12 (New American Bible).
11. See Roscoe Pound, *Individual Interests in the Domestic Relations*, 14 MICH. L. REV. 177, 185 (1916) ("the principles of reciprocal duties of support on the part of the ascendent and descendants . . . is universally recognized by the Roman Law world").
12. Jacobus tenBroek, *California's Dual System of Family Law: It's Origin, Development, and Present Status, Part I*, 16 STAN. L. REV. 257, 283 (1964)(quoting 43 Eliz. 1, c. 2, § VI (1601): "The parents, grandparents, and children of "everie poore olde blind lame and impotente person, or other poore person not able to worke, beinge of a sufficient abilitie, shall at their owne Chardges relieve and maintain everie suche poore person, in that manner and according to that rate, as by the Justices of the Peace of that Countie where suche sufficient persons dwell, or the greater number of them, at their generall Quarter Sessions shal be assessed; upon paine that everie one of them shall forfeite twenty shillings for everie monthe which they shall faiile therein.").
13. See, e.g., *Swoap v. Superior Court of Sacramento County*, 10 Cal.3d 490, 11 Cal. Rptr. 136, 516 P.2d 840 (1973) (discussing the history of the California Civil Code); *Savoy v. Savoy*, 433 Pa. Super. 549, 533, 641 A.2d 596, 599 (1994) ("The duty of parental support is created by statute, for '[a]t common law an adult child has no duty or obligation to contribute to support of his parents.'").
14. Usually the parent has transferred property to the child as the consideration for future support. Some states have codified this maintenance procedure. See, e.g., N.D. Cent. Code § 14-09-10 (1991 & Supp. 1995).
15. See *Savoy*, 641 A.2d at 599; *in re Gerald*, 36 Cal.3d 1, 678 P.2d 917, 210 Cal. Rptr. 342 (1984); *Mallatt v. Luihn*, 206 Or. 678, 294 P.2d 871 (1956); *Maricopa*

County v. Douglas, 69 Ariz. 35, 208 P.2d 646 (1949); *State v. Lindstrom*, 68 Idaho 226, 191 P.2d 1009 (1948); *State v. Griffith*, 130 Colo. 312, 275 P.2d 945 (1954); *Worcester Co. v. Quinn*, 304 Mass. 276, 23 N.E.2d 463 (1939); *Morris County Welfare Board v. Gilligan*, 130 N.J.L. 83, 31 A.2d 805 (1943).

16. See Ann Britton, *America's Best Kept Secret: An Adult Child's Duty to Support Aged Parents*, 26 CAL. W. L. REV. 351 (1990).

17. California has all three types of support statutes: CAL. FAM. CODE §§ 4400-05 (West 1994 & Supp. 1996), CAL. WELF. & INST. CODE § 18511 (West 1991), and CAL. PENAL CODE § 270c (West 1988 & Supp. 1996) The Virginia Code is a hybrid by providing for reimbursement to an aid-giving authority by a responsible relative and also providing for a criminal penalty for failure to obey a support order. See VA. CODE ANN. § 20-88 (Michie 1995). Pennsylvania incorporates a duty to provide for indigent relatives, regardless of whether or not they are a public charge. See 62 PA. CONS. STAT. ANN. § 1973(a) (1980 & Supp. 1995).

18. See, e.g., *Noble v. Edberg*, 252 Iowa 135, 106 N.W.2d 102 (1960); *Radich v. Kruly*, 226 Cal. App. 2d 683, 38 Cal. Rptr. 340 (1964); *Gardner v. Hines*, 68 N.E.2d 397 (Ohio 1946).

19. See, e.g., N.H. REV. STAT. ANN. § 546-A:5 (1990):
    When determining the amount due for support the court shall consider all relevant factors including but not limited to: (a) the standard of living and situation of the parties; (b) the relative wealth and income of the parties; (c) the ability of the obligor to earn; (d) the ability of the obligee to earn; (e) the need of the obligee; (f) the age of the parties; (g) the responsibility of the obligor for the support of others.
    DEL. CODE ANN. tit. 13 § 505 (1991):
    The duties of support . . . shall be performed according to the following order of priority: (1) duty to support one's own minor child, (2) duty to support a spouse; (3) duty to support a woman pregnant with child conceived out of wedlock; (4) duty to support a stepchild or the child conceived out of wedlock; (5) duty to support a poor person . . . .).

20. See, e.g., Idaho Code §32-1002 (1983 & Supp. 1995); La. Civ. Code Ann. Art. 229 (West 1993 & Supp. 1996); Montana Code Ann. §40-6-301 (1995); S.D. Codified Laws §25-7-27 (Michie 1996). In South Dakota, a supporting child has a right of contribution from his or her nonsupporting siblings for the medical care of their dependent parent. See S.D. Codified Laws §25-7-27 (Michie 1996).

21. See *Review of Selected 1975 California Legislation*, 7 PAC. L. J. 237, 419-21 (1976).

22. Oregon has a good record of enforcing its reciprocal support laws. See Britton, sup. note 16 (ch. 4), at 361.

23. See Timothy Egan, "Old, Ailing and Finally a Burden Abandoned," *The New York Times*, March 26, 1992, at A1.

24. Id.

25. HCFA–Pub. 45–3 § 3812.

26. See George F. Indest, III, *Legal Aspects of HCFA's Decision to Allow Recovery from Children for Medicaid Benefits Delivered to Their Parents Through State Financial Responsibility Statutes: A Case of Bad Rule Making Through Failure to Comply with the Administrative Procedure Act*, 15 S.U.L.REV. 225, 266-227, (1988).

Chapter 5

1. By the year 2008, the ratio of working Americans to retired Americans will decrease by 40 percent, from 5:1 to 3:1. THE CONCORD COALITION, THE ZERO DEFICIT PLAN: A PLAN FOR ELIMINATING THE FEDERAL BUDGET DEFICIT BY THE YEAR 2002, at 28.
2. Id. at 28.
3. "Each child born in America today inherits a charge of $180,000 in lifetime taxes just to pay the interest on the federal debt." REPUBLICAN NATIONAL COMMITTEE, RESTORING THE DREAM: THE BOLD NEW PLAN BY HOUSE REPUBLICANS, at 13 (1995). The Heritage Foundation reports that in 1948, a typical family of four paid only 2 percent of their income in taxes. Today, the same family of four pays approximately 24 percent of its income. Similarly, the value of the personal exemption has decreased from 42 percent to 11 percent of a families' income. Id. at 23.
4. Id.
5. CONCORD COALITION, sup. note 1 (ch. 5), at 30.
6. Id. Social Security is the largest of all federal entitlement programs. Alone, it will cost $481 billion, or 22 percent of the entire federal budget, by the year 2002. By the same year, Medicare will be the second largest entitlement program, costing more than $300 billion.
7. Id.
8. Id. at 31.
9. See Eric Pianin, "Hill Leaders Agree on Seven Year Budget," *The Washington Post*, June 23, 1995, at A1. The plan will consist of $270 billion of savings in Medicare and $180 billion of savings in Medicaid, which will be incorporated in the block-grant programs.
10. Dan Morgan, "Medicaid Costs Balloon into Fiscal 'Time Bomb'," *The Washington Post*, January 30, 1994, at A18 (chart).
11. Congressional Research Service, *Medicaid Source Book: Background Data and Analysis*, 83-84 (1993).
12. See Kenneth R. Wing, *The Impact of Reagan Era Politics on the Federal Medicaid Program*, 33 CATH. U. L. REV. 1 (1983).
13. Id. at 7.
14. See Eleanor D. Kinney, *Current Issues in Insurance Law: Rule and Policy Making for the Medicaid Program: A Challenge to Federalism*, 51 OHIO ST. L. J. 855, 857 (1990) (citing K. Erdman and S. Wolfe, POOR HEALTH CARE FOR POOR AMERICANS: A RANKING OF STATE MEDICAID PROGRAMS, Pub. Citizens Health Res. Group, 1988).
15. See generally W. John Thomas, *The Oregon Medicaid Proposal: Ethical Paralysis, Tragic Democracy, and the Fate of a Utilitarian Health Care Program*, 72 OR. L. REV. 47 (Spring 1993).
16. General Accounting Office, *Budget Issues, 1991 Budget Estimates: What Went Wrong?*, 57 (January 1992) [hereinafter *Budget Issues*].

17. Id. at 57-58.
18. See Dan Morgan, "Small Provision Turns into Golden Goose: States Used Subsidy to Balance Budget," *The Washington Post*, January 31, 1994, at A8. See also *Budget Issues*, sup. note 16 (ch. 5), at 60-61.
19. See Morgan, sup. note 18 (ch. 5), at A8.
20. General Accounting Office, *Medicaid, A Program Highly Vulnerable to Fraud*, GAO/T-HEHS-94-106, February 25, 1994, 1994 WL 2476452 (testimony of Leslie G. Aronovitz, Associate Director for Health Financing Issues, before the Subcommittee on Human Resources and Intergovernmental Relations, House Committee on Government Operations).
21. Id. Providers are often in short supply and the program administrators do not want to discourage participation by imposing controls that would be unduly burdensome.
22. Id.
23. See Robert A. Rosenblatt, "Hospital Medicare Fraud Alleged," *The Washington Post*, August 17, 1995, at A18.
24. General Accounting Office, *Health Care: Actions to Terminate Problem Hospitals from Medicare Are Inadequate*, GA0/HR0-91-95, December 1, 1991, WL 2659285.
25. General Accounting Office, *Health Care Reform 4* (December 1992).
26. See Health Security Act H.R. 3600/S. 1757. See also *The White House, Health Security: Preliminary Plan Summary* (1993).
27. See Sandra G. Boodman, "One in Five Americans Is Covered by an HMO," *The Washington Post*, June 13, 1995, at 5. HMOs cover 51.5 million Americans and one in five Americans receive care from 574 different HMOs. The organizations result in part from the increase in health care costs and they are more economical because they restrict access to specialty care and retain a "gatekeeper" to watch over costs. Id.
28. See Paul Cotton, *Clinton Tinkers with Health System Status Quo: Critics Seek to Pick Apart Managed Competition*, 269 JAMA 1299-1230 (1993).
29. Chris Mondies, "Governors' Fears Over U.S. Cutbacks Dominate Sessions," *Philadelphia Inquirer*, July 30, 1995, at A3.
30. Edwin Chen, "A Familiar Tactic on Medicare," *Philadelphia Inquirer*, July 30, 1995, at C3.
31. Id.
32. Nancy Benac, "President, GOP Trade Charges Over Medicare," *Philadelphia Inquirer*, July 30, 1995, at A2.
33. See Janet Hook, "The Times Poll: GOP Medicare Proposals Win Broad Support," *The Los Angeles Times*, September 21, 1995, at 1. Of the people over 65 years of age, 54 percent favored the premium increase; 62 percent of those under age 65 favored the increase. A surprising 81 percent of those surveyed who earned income over $60,000 supported the premium hike, while those earning under $20,000 favored it 50 to 41 percent. See id.
34. See id. Of those 60 percent, 64 percent of the HMO supporters were under age 65.

35. See id.
36. See generally CONTRACT WITH AMERICA: THE BOLD PLAN BY REP. NEWT GINGRICH, REP. DICK ARMEY, AND THE HOUSE REPUBLICANS TO CHANGE THE NATION (Ed Gillespie and Bob Schellhas, eds., 1994) [hereinafter CONTRACT WITH AMERICA].
37. These include, for example, welfare spending cutbacks and tax cuts and credits for families. See CONTRACT WITH AMERICA, sup. note 36 (ch. 5), at 65-90.
38. See, e.g., Susan Frelich Appleton, *Standards for Constitutional Review of Privacy-Invading Welfare Reforms: Distinguishing the Abortion-Funding Cases and Redeeming the Undue-Burden Test*, 49 VAND. L. REV. 1, 49 (1996) (asserting that AFDC program cutbacks threaten the welfare of children and racial integrity); Association of the Bar of the City of New York, *Report and Recommendation of the Association of the Bar of the City of New York "The Personal Responsibility Act of 1995"*, 17 WOMEN's RTS. L. REP. 93, 101 (Winter 1995) (asserting that AFDC alternatives endanger millions of American children); Laura T. Kessler, *PPI, Patriarch, and the Schizophrenic View of Women: A Feminist Analysis of Welfare Reform in Maryland*, 6 MD. J. CONTEMP. LEGAL ISSUES 317, 322 (1995) (suggesting that the AFDC program perpetuates the patriarchal notion of the proper role of women in society); Barbara Bennet Woodhouse, *Home Visiting and Family Values: The Powers of Conversation, Touching and Soap*, 143 U. PA. L. REV. 253, 263 (1994) (suggesting that ineffective income support policies, like the AFDC program, detract from America's spirit of self-reliance); Marion Buckley, *Eliminating the Per-Child Allotment in the AFDC Program*, 13 LAW & INEQ. J. 169, 201 (1994) (suggesting the potential for harm to America's children).
39. LISBETH B. SCHORR WITH DANIEL SCHORR, WITHIN OUR REACH: BREAKING THE CYCLE OF DISADVANTAGE at 283 (1988).
40. Id. at 281.
41. Id. at 267.
42. See HEALTH LAW, sup. note 250 (ch. 1), at 576-577.
43. See Judith Havemann and Eric Pianin, "Medicaid Plan Divides House, Senate GOP; Governors Also at Odds," *The Washington Post*, September 13, 1995, at A6, col. 1.
44. See HEALTH LAW, sup. note 250 (ch. 1), at 577.
45. See 29 U.S.C.A. §1144(a) (1996). For an excellent discussion of the practical implications of ERISA, see Jesselyn Alicia Brown, *Erisa and State Health Care Reform: Roadblock or Scapegoat?*, 13 YALE L. & POL'Y REV. 339 (1995) (discussing ERISA preemption and *New York State Conference of Blue Cross & Blue Shield Plans v. Travelers Ins. Co.*, 115 S. Ct. 1671 [1995]).
46. See HEALTH LAW, sup. note 250 (ch. 1), at 577-578.
47. 115 S. Ct. 1671 (1995).

48. See Catherine L. Fisk, sup. note 53 (ch. 2) at 35 (arguing that the Court has abandoned textualism and adopted a more pragmatic approach to a working relationship between the federal and state objectives).

49. See sup. text accompanying notes 467-483 (Oregon) and 548-654 (Tennessee) (ch. 5).

50. See HEALTH LAW, sup. note 250 (ch. 1), at 578.

51. Id.

52. Id. (citing GAO, *Access to Health Insurance: State Efforts to Assist Small Businesses* (1992); Mark A. Hall, *Reforming the Health Insurance Market for Small Businesses*, 326 N. ENG. J. MED. 565 (1992)).

53. See sup. text accompanying notes 222-230 (Illinois), 249-250 (Indiana), 342 (Mississippi), and 373 (Nevada) (ch. 5).

54. See HEALTH LAW, sup. note 250 (ch. 1), at 578.

55. Bare bones policies offered to small group participants proved unsuccessful in 11 of 16 states that implemented bare bones reform. 1994 proved equally unsuccessful for small group reform because of an increase in premiums due to community rating, which prohibits insurers from considering claim histories of specific groups. New York's implementation of community rating led to a decline in coverage in its first year. Id. at 579.

56. Id.

57. See 42 U.S.C.A. §1396a(a)(13)(A) and 1396r-4 (1988 and Supp. V. 1993).

58. See sup. text accompanying notes 193-219 (ch. 5).

59. See sup. text accompanying notes 467-483 (ch. 5).

60. See sup. text accompanying notes 695-705 (ch. 5).

61. See sup. text accompanying notes 548-654 (ch. 5).

62. See HEALTH LAW, sup. note 250 (ch. 1), at 582.

63. Id.

64. Id. at 583.

65. Id.

66. Id.

67. See HAW. REV. STAT. (ch. 393) (1985 & Supp. 1992).

68. See HEALTH LAW, sup. note 250 (ch. 1), at 580.

69. See HAW. REV. STAT. ch. 431N.

70. See MASS. GEN. LAWS ANN. ch. 118F (West 1993 & Supp. 1996).

71. See HEALTH LAW, sup. note 250 (ch. 1), at 580-581.

72. See FLA. STAT. ANN. § 408.70 (West 1996). Florida has been very active in seeking legislative solutions to its health care dilemma. See, e.g., Sandra Greenblatt and Michael Cherniga, "Florida as Health Care Bellwether: The State's New Laws Foreshadow U.S. Trends," 5 HEALTHSPAN 8 (1992).

73. MINN. STAT. ANN. §§ 62N, 62P, 256.-9351 et seq. (West 1996).

74. See WASH. REV. CODE ANN. § 70.47 (West 1996).

75. See 1993 Wash. Laws Ch. 492.

76. See HEALTH LAW, sup. note 250 (ch. 1), at 582.

77. Id.

78. Id.

79. See MD. ANN. CODE of 1957, Art. 48A, §§ 698-713.
80. See HEALTH LAW, sup. note 250 (Ch. 1), at 583.
81. See Deborah L. Rogal and W. David Helms, *State Models: An Overview*, HEALTH AFFAIRS, at 27-88 (Summer 1993).
82. Id. at 27.
83. Havemann and Pianin, sup. note 43 (ch. 5).
84. Id.
85. See Russell Hubbard, *Blue Cross Seeks Exemption from Patient Choice Law*, BIRMINGHAM BUS. J., September 4, 1995, at 6.
86. Said one attorney for Blue Cross: "It's a turf battle . . . Doctors are finding themselves smaller fish in a bigger pond. This is a response to being managed and no one likes to be managed." Id.
87. Id.
88. See Anita Sharpe, "Healthsouth to Buy Division of NovaCare," *Wall Street Journal*, February 7, 1995, §B, at 5, col. 3; Alvin Benn, "Health-Care Companies Form Alliance," *Montgomery Advertiser*, August 3, 1994, at §B, at 2.
89. See Tim Bradner, *Legislature Considers Two Health Care Reform Proposals*, ALASKA J. OF COMMERCE, March 14, 1994, §1, at 1.
90. See Cathy Brown, "Health Care Crisis on Hold," *Alaska Business Monthly*, June 1, 1995, at 22.
91. Id.
92. See Bradner, sup. note 89 (ch. 5), at 1.
93. See Brown, sup. note 90 (ch. 5), at 22.
94. Id. See also Tim Bradner, *Hospitals Work to Contain Costs*, ALASKA J. OF COMMERCE, July 25, 1994, at A9.
95. See Brown, sup. note 90 (ch. 5) at 22. See also, Will Swagel, "Pay Less, Feel Better: Self-Funding of Health Benefits," *Alaska Business Monthly*, June 1, 1994, at 20.
96. See Swagel, sup. note 95, at 20.
97. Id.
98. Id.
99. See 42 U.S.C. § 1396a(a)(10) (1988 & Supp. V 1993); 42 C.F.R. Part 435, Subpart B, Mandatory Coverage of the Medically Needy, (§§ 435.100-435. 170) (1993).
100. States such as Maryland, Minnesota, Nebraska, North and South Dakota, and Mississippi, which have delivery limitations due to their rural configurations, may not easily adapt to such a managed-care plan. See inf. note 366 (ch. 5).
101. See Sarah Neville, "Arizona's Managed Care System Offers Lessons for Rest of U.S.," *The Washington Post*, September 25, 1995, §A, at 4.
102. Id. (quoting health care analyst Nelda McCall).
103. In its first year of implementation, Arizona's plan netted a loss of $3.7 million. Upon acquisition of control by the state, it has consistently averaged savings of 7 percent. Id.

104. Id.
105. Id. (quoting Joseph Anderson, former deputy director of the Arizona medicaid program and current president and chief executive of Arizona Physician IPA, one of the largest health care plans in the state).
106. Id.
107. See "The Segal Company Announces Over $300 Million in Savings from Arizona Managed Care Innovations," *PR Newswire*, September 28, 1995.
108. See Martin Van Der Werf, "Legislature Is asked to Save a Life, Will Vote on Letting Tax Cover Transplant," *Arizona Republic*, September 27, 1995, at B1; Pat Flannery, "Indigent Patients Get Shot of Hope, Lawmakers Likely to OK Transplants," *Phoenix Gazette*, September 27, 1995, at B1.
109. See Flannery, sup. note 108 (ch. 5), at B1.
110. Id.
111. See Van Der Werf, sup. note 108 (ch. 5), at B1.
112. See John Hofheimer, "UAMS Unveils One-Stop Eldercare," *Arkansas Business*, July 24, 1995, §2 at 4. But cf. *Typical American Voter*, sup. note 148 (ch. 1).
113. See Joan I. Duffy, "Dalton Has Health Plan Suggestions," *Commercial Appeal*, February 23, 1995, at 9A.
114. Id.
115. See Jim Harris, "Hospitals Make the Move Toward Alliance in '94," *Arkansas Business*, January 2, 1995, §1, at 21.
116. Id.
117. See Joan I. Duffy, "Bill Would Raise Tax on Soda to 5 Cents to Fund Medicaid," *Commercial Appeal*, March 7, 1995, at 1A.
118. Id.
119. See "The Medicaid Mess, GOP Reforms Would Give States Flexibility," *San Diego Union-Tribune*, September 28, 1995, at 6-8.
120. Id.
121. See Jack Cheevers, "Private Hospitals Seek Voice in Reform," *Los Angeles Times*, September 27, 1995, at B1.
122. See Michael A. Hiltzik, "Activists Hail HMO Reforms Sent to Wilson," *Los Angeles Times*, September 19, 1995, at A1. The bill requires aggressive follow-up on complaints filed by HMO members, the establishment of a toll-free hotline to receive complaints, and more frequent inspection of HMO facilities from at least every five years to three years, with public disclosure of regulatory failures.
123. These include bills such as one requiring health insurers to pay for minimum hospital stays of 48 hours after childbirth. Id.
124. See Barbara Marsh, "San Diego in Lead of Health Care Revolution," *Los Angeles Times*, August 31, 1995, at A14.
125. Id.
126. Id.
127. Id.
128. Id.

129. See Dana Wilkie, "County Fiscal Health in Peril," *San Diego Union-Tribune*, August 31, 1995, at B1.
130. Id.
131. See Caron Schwartz Ellis, "Health-Care Reforms Make CliniCom Systems a Huge Money-Maker," *Boulder County Business Report*, June 1, 1995, §1, at 7.
132. Id.
133. See David Iler, "Bill Aims to Limit Liability for Uncompensated Care," *Denver Business Journal*, February 24, 1995, at C11.
134. Id.
135. See L. Wayne Hicks, "Canadian-Style Health Care May Hit Ballot," *Denver Business Journal*, January 20, 1995, A9.
136. Id.
137. See Jackie Fitzpatrick, "The State Tackles Health Care Reform," *The New York Times*, October 9, 1994, §13CN, at 1, col. 4.
138. See Hilary Stout, "Despite Health Bill Failure, Oxford Sees HMO Growth—OXHP," *Dow Jones News Service,* October 4, 1994.
139. Id.
140. See Stephen Higgins, "Hospital Mergers in State Foreseen," *New Haven Register*, May 24, 1994, at D2.
141. Id.
142. Id.
143. See Coughlin, sup. note 42 (ch. 2). Ohio also sought such a waiver. Id.
144. See Regan, sup. note 31 (ch. 2), at §10.30.
145. See Mahoney and Wetle, sup. note 385, at 1026.
146. See Kimberly Quillen, "State Commission Refocuses in Wake of National HC Reform," *Delaware Business Review*, March 13, 1995, at 10.
147. Id.
148. Id.
149. Id.
150. See "Health Care Commission Announces New Initiatives," *Delaware Business Review*, March 6, 1995, §1, at 2.
151. See Amy Goldstein, "Health Care: Still Seeking a Cure," *The Washington Post*, September 28, 1994, at A1.
152. Id.
153. See Rene Sanchez, "Tax Would Drive Many D.C. Doctors Away, Ray Told," *The Washington Post*, May 16, 1991, at C3. Approximately 100,000 District of Columbia residents are without health insurance. Id. See also Vincent McCraw, "Stark Says D.C. Health Plan Can Be a National Model," *The Washington Times*, May 16, 1991, §B, at B3.
154. Sanchez, sup. note 153 (ch. 5), at C3.
155. Id.
156. *Pennsylvania Perspective*, sup. note 165 (ch. 1), at 3.
157. See id. at 26.

158. See Amy Goldstein, "DC Health Spending Exceeds Other Cities'; New Report Also Details Inadequate Care," *The Washington Post*, March 8, 1995, at A1.
159. Id.
160. Other cities' expenditures per capita include: Austin—$281; Denver—$274; Indianapolis—$216; Metro-Nashville—$159. Id.
161. Id.
162. Other cities' hospital employee per 10,000 residents ratio include: New York—72; Boston—50; Indianapolis—43; Denver—41; Austin—39; and Metro-Nashville—15. Id.
163. Id.
164. See "Health Reform and the District," *The Washington Post*, August 18, 1994, at A20 [hereinafter "Health Reform and the District"]; Amy Goldstein, "Georgetown Hospital Lays Off 230 Workers; Move Is a Sign of Troubled Times for Medical Facilities in D.C.," *The Washington Post*, January 11, 1995, at A1.
165. See "Health Reform and the District," sup. note 164 (ch. 5), at A20.
166. See Goldstein, sup. note 158 (ch. 5), at A10, col. 5.
167. See "Health Reform and the District," sup. note 64 (ch. 5) at A20.
168. See Goldstein, sup. note 58 (ch. 5), at A10, col. 4.
169. See "President for National Center for Policy Analysis Available to Discuss Medical Savings Accounts," *PR Newswire*, September 14, 1995.
170. Id. (quoting Milton Friedman).
171. See Spencer Lucas, "Local Company Markets Medical Savings Accounts," *Memphis Business Journal*, August 7, 1995, §1, at 7.
172. Id.
173. Id.
174. See Mike Griffin, "Special Session Delayed Again," *Orlando Sentinel*, September 10, 1995, at G5.
175. See Peter Mitchell, "Chiles Appears Alone Pushing Insurance Plan," *The Wall Street Journal*, August 23, 1995, at F1 (Florida Journal).
176. Id.
177. See Glenn Singer, "Chiles Postpones Health-Care Reform Special Session," *Orlando Sentinel*, September 8, 1995, at D1; Mitchell, sup. note 175 (ch. 5).
178. Singer, sup. note 177 (ch. 5), at D1.
179. Mitchell, sup. note 175 (ch. 5).
180. See Foskett, sup. note 53 (ch. 2), at 4C.
181. See Charles Walston, "The Winds of Change: Around the Nation How Georgia Stacks Up," *Atlanta Constitution*, January 8, 1995, at 8C.
182. See Foskett, sup. note 53 (ch. 2), at 4C.
183. The states that stand to lose the most in Medicaid funds by 2002 are as follows: West Virginia—$3.3 billion (24.2 percent increase in loss from projected spending); Florida—$9.6 billion (23.8 percent); Georgia—$6 billion (23.4 percent); North Carolina—6.7 billion (23.3 percent); Mon-

tana—$.77 billion (22.5 percent); Mexico—$1.3 billion (22.3 percent); Arkansas—$2.4 billion (22.1 percent); Virginia—$2.8 billion (21.8 percent); Alaska—$.43 billion (21.4 percent); Kentucky—$3.8 billion (20.9 percent). Id.

184. Id.
185. Id.
186. Id. (quoting Representative Nan Orrock [D-Atlanta]).
187. Id.
188. See "Medication Safety Legislation Awaits Action By House; Law Will Ensure That Patients Get 'Just What the Doctor Ordered'," *PR Newswire*, March 7, 1995.
189. See "Massive Legal Action Filed Today Against Top Drug Makers and Mail-Order Drug Houses," *PR Newswire*, October 17, 1994. In total, there were more than 1700 suits filed against larger manufacturers. Federal law suits were filed in Connecticut, Florida, Georgia, Idaho, Illinois, Kansas, Kentucky, Louisiana, North Carolina, Ohio, Oklahoma, Pennsylvania, South Carolina, Tennessee, and Texas. Id.
190. Id.
191. Id.
192. Id.
193. See *Hawaii Prepaid Health Care Act*, HAW. REV. STAT. § 393 (1988); Daniel M. Fox, *Hawaii: A Leader, Not a Model*, 14 HEALTH CARE 312 (1995); Laguarda, sup. note 54 (ch. 2), at 179.
194. See *Hawaii Prepaid Health Care Act*, HAW. REV. STAT. § 393. See generally General Accounting Office, *Health Care in Hawaii: Implications for National Reform 1* (March 1994).
195. See Rogal and Helms, sup. note 81 (ch. 5), at 27.
196. Congressional Research Service, *Medicaid Source Book: Background Data and Analysis*, at 77 (1993).
197. See John K. Iglehart, *Health Policy Report, Health Care Reform, the States*, 330 NEW ENG. J. MED. 75 (1994).
198. Id.
199. See Laguarda, sup. note 54 (ch. 2), at 182.
200. Id.
201. Id. at 183.
202. Id. at 181. See also Daniel M. Fox and Daniel C. Schaffer, *Health Policy and Erisa: Interest Groups and Semi-Preemption*, 14 J. HEALTH POL'Y & LAW 239, 247 (1989).
203. Between 3.75 percent and 7 percent of the population is uninsured. General Accounting Office, *Health Care in Hawaii: Implications for National Reform 2* (1994).
204. Id. at 2-3.
205. Id. at 6.
206. "Both business and labor interests have consistently opposed further exemptions to ERISA [because] state innovation will increase costs and

'prevent employers from providing uniform benefits to their employers on a nationwide basis.'" Id. at 183-185.

207. See "AMA Meets in Hawaii; Examines State's Unique Health Care System," *Business Wire*, December 5, 1994, [hereinafter, "AMA Meets in Hawaii"]. Hawaii is also top on the list in terms of over-all health and is leading the world in the physician-to-population ratio. See Deane Neubauer, *State Model: Hawaii, a Pioneer in Health System Reform*, HEALTH AFFAIRS, 12 (Summer 1993).

208. Neubauer, sup. note 207 (ch. 5), at 31.

209.   Although the national trend is to continue a networking of providers, which provide a full range of services for a community as a way of controlling costs...there is a strong demand for a free-choice plan in which people will be able to choose their providers. . . . The challenge for free-choice is not HMOs. The challenge is controlling health care costs.

Steve Jefferson, "Like Mainland, Reform Is Name of the Game for Hawaiian Health Care Providers, Insurers," *Pacific Business News (Hawaii)*, July 18, 1994, at 2 (quoting Fred Fortin, vice president of communications at HMSA).

210. Id.

211. See "AMA Meets in Hawaii," sup. note 207 (ch. 5) (quoting Lonnie R. Bristow, MD, president-elect of the American Medical Association). Much of the savings comes from control of excessive services. For example, only 5.8 percent of Hawaii residents per year have surgery, compared to the national average of 9.2 percent. See Jefferson, sup. note 209 (ch. 5).

212. About 96 percent of Hawaiians have health insurance. See Adam Clymer, "Hawaii is a Health Care Lab as Employers Buy Insurance," *The New York Times*, May 6, 1994, at A1, col. 5; Edwin Chen, "Hawaii's Health Plan Offers Lessons for Future Medicine: An Employer Mandate Achieves Coverage for 96% of the State's Workers. But Other Efforts Still Must Help Those Who Fall Through the Cracks," *The Los Angeles Times*, July 8, 1994, at A18, col. 1.

213. See "AMA Meets in Hawaii," sup. note 207 (ch. 5).

214. See Jay McWilliams, "Painful Cuts May Inspire Positive Change," *Pacific Business News*, September 4, 1995, at 21.

215. Id.

216. See, e.g., *New York State Conference of Blue Cross & Blue Shield Plans v. Travelers Insurance Company*, 115 S. Ct. 1671 (1995). See generally, Walter E. Schuler, *The ERISA Pre-Emption Narrows: Analysis of New York State Conference of Blue Cross & Blue Shield Plans v. Travelers Insurance Company and Its Impact on State Regulation of Health Care*, 40 ST. LOUIS U. L. J. 783 (Summer 1996); Rebecca S. Fellman-Caldwell, *New York State Conference of Blue Cross & Blue Shield Plans v. Travelers Insurance Co.: The Supreme Court Clarifies ERISA Preemption*, 45 CATH. U. L. REV. 1309 (Summer 1996); Nicole Weisenborn, *ERISA Pre-*

emption and Its Effect on State Health Reform, 5 KAN. J.L. & PUB. POL'Y 147 (Fall 1995); Michael G. Pfefferkorn, Comment, *Federal Preemption of State Mandated Health Insurance Programs Under ERISA–The Hawaii Prepaid Health Care Act in Perspective*, 8 ST. LOUIS. U. PUB. L. REV. 339 (1989); Jolee Ann Hancock, Comment, *Diseased Federalism: State Health Care Laws Fall Prey to ERISA Preemption*, 25 CUMB. L. REV. 383 (1994-1995).

217. See Kit Smith, "Suit Challenges State on Health Care," *Honolulu Advertiser*, July 18, 1995, at C1. An exclusion requires a one-year waiting period before prior conditions are covered. An exclusive plan was previously thought of as a trade-off for other benefits, such as eye-care or prescription plans. Id.

218. Id.

219. See Steve Jefferson, "Warning Sounded for Reform," *Pacific Business News*, March 27, 1995, at 1.

220. See Larry Gardner, "Idaho Job Loss Calculated in Health Care Proposals," *Idaho Business Review*, May 31, 1993.

221. Id. (quoting Pete Skamser, state director of the National Federation of Independent Business/Idaho).

222. See Jean Latz Griffin, "Krause Happy Her Health-Care Bill Now Alive and Well in the Senate," *Chicago Tribune*, April 13, 1995, at 2.

223. Preexisting conditions can range anywhere from AIDS to hypertension to short-term conditions such as pregnancy. See Marianne Taylor, "Lawmakers Target 'Job Lock' Plans Would Make Workers' Health Coverage 'Portable'," *Chicago Tribune*, May 29, 1995, at 1.

224. See Griffin, sup. note 222 (ch. 5), at 2.

225. See Taylor, sup. note 223 (ch. 5), at 1. Similar bills are also supported by the Health Insurance Association of America and the National Federation of Independent Business. Id.

226. Id.

227. Id. at 1 (quoting Sally Bullen, vice president at Kemper National Insurance Companies).

228. See "Blue Cross Blue Shield Association Supports Thomas Bill on Health Insurance Portability," *PR Newswire*, May 12, 1995.

229. See id.

230. See Taylor, sup. note 223 (ch. 5) at 1.

231. See Maurice Possley, "State's Choices Hike Costs of Medicaid Surgeries," *Chicago Tribune*, March 31, 1994. These centers were originally established in 1974 in Illinois to perform abortions. Id.

232. Id.

233. For example, between June 1993 and June 1994, costs for 169 hernia operations performed at outpatient centers averaged costs of $609; 57 similar operations conducted at inpatient hospitals ran the state an average bill of $7,027. The average facility fee of 134 arthroscopic knee operations conducted in outpatient facilities was $643; for 17 inpatient operations of

the same nature—average fees cost the state $6,792. An average outpatient facility fee for a dilation and curettage procedure costs Medicaid $642, while an inpatient procedure averages $4,212. Id.

234. Id.
235. See Maurice Possley, "Medicaid Controls Missing the Mark, Study Says," *Chicago Tribune*, March 9, 1995, at 7. The bill for the disabled, alone, reached $2.2 billion, which is an increase of more than 200 percent since 1984. AIDS patients accounted for $44 million in 1993 hospital bills. Id.
236. Id.
237. Id.
238. See Gwen Rodenberger, "Doctors Debate Medical Savings Accounts," *Lafayette Business Digest*, July 24, 1995, at 3.
239. Id.
240. See Phil Kuntz, "Golden Rule Insurance Takes Lead in Advocating MSAs as Way of Controlling Health-Care Costs," *The Wall Street Journal*, May 15, 1995, at A24.
241. Id.
242. See Jan O. Spalding, "Capitation Turns Heads, Even in Michiana," *South Bend Tribune Business Weekly*, April 5, 1995, §1, at 1 (quoting John Kolbas, director of the health care group at Crowe Chizek).
243. A.J. Schneider, "Insurance Portability Key Issue for State Legislators," *Indianapolis Business Journal*, January 9, 1995, §1, at 29.
244. Id.
245. See Spalding, sup. note 242 (ch. 5), at 1.
246. Id.
247. Id.
248. Id.
249. See Schneider, sup. note 243 (ch. 5), at 29 (discussing a proposed Bill before the Indiana General Assembly by Sen. Patricia L. Miller).
250. Id.
251. See Frank Swoboda, "For Iowa Retirees, a Promise Goes on the Chopping Block; Meatpacker's Axing of Health Care Benefits Spawns a Court Ruling that 'Lifetime' Means Only the Life of a Contract," *The Washington Post*, March 5, 1995, at H7.
252. See Tammy Williamson, "Taking Health Benefits for Granted a Thing of the Past," *Business Record (Des Moines, IA)*, August 22, 1994, §1 at 1.
253. The cost of health care for retired workers in Iowa rose by almost 8 percent in 1993, when each worker's benefits cost approximately $2,700. Id.
254. See Jackie King, "Iowa Health System Signs on to Health-Care Offering," *Business Record (Des Moines, IA)*, June 20, 1994, §1, at 13.
255. See Tony Cox, "Legislature Stumbles on Health Care Reform," *Wichita Business Journal*, April 29, 1994, §1, at 1.
256. Id.
257. Id.
258. Id.

259. This plan was proposed by Secretary of the Kansas Department of Health and Environment, Robert Harder, but was rejected. Id.

260. This proposal was offered by Representative Susan Wagle (D-Wichita), but was rejected. Id.

261. See Jim Sullinger, "Bipartisan Group Works for Health Care Reform," *Kansas City Star*, February 10, 1994 at C4.

262. See generally Julia Field Costich and Mike Helton, *The Kentucky Health Reform Act*, 22 N. KY. L. REV. 381 (1995).

263. See Gil Lawson, "State to Use Managed Care for Medicaid; Money-Saving Move Will Affect 500,000," *Courier-Journal (Louisville, KY)*, October 12, 1995, at 1A.

264. Id.

265. Id.

266. Id.

267. See Gil Lawson, "Kentucky Advised Not to Drop Health Plan; State Employees, Teachers Could Face Higher Premiums," *Courier-Journal (Louisville, KY)*, October 13, 1995, at 3B.

268. Id.

269. See Kelly King Alexander, "Legislature Considers 'Other' Health Care Issues," *Greater Baton Rouge Business Report*, June 13, 1995, at 45.

270. In 1995, there were more than a dozen employer mandate bills, all of which were opposed by small businesses. The bills required group insurers to cover divorcees and several specific illnesses., like Tourettes Syndrome, chemotherapy, cancer treatments, infertility treatments, and bone marrow transplantation. Id.

271. HB318 guarantees women's enrollment in a managed-care plan and assures two self-referred visits to a gynecologist each year. Id.

272. This bill prohibits judges from sealing information on hazardous products in lawsuits against manufacturers for damages. Id.

273. This Act proposes to allow advanced practice nurses to write certain prescriptions, as is done in 46 other states. The bill also mandates that advanced nurses earn a Master's degree after January 1, 1996. Id.

274. The bill referred to as "the women's right to know" bill proposes that a woman be informed of the consequences and alternatives to abortion within 24 hours of an abortive procedure is expected to be passed. The House also passed a bill granting more authority to judges, including mandating mental health counseling and parental involvement, regarding requests by minors to obtain abortions. Id.

275. This bill makes it a crime to help someone commit suicide, and has been termed, "the anti-Kevorkian bill." Id.

276. See Kelly King Alexander, "Medicaid Crisis, Reform Spur HMO Growth," *Greater Baton Rouge Business Report*, February 21, 1995, at 48.

277. Id.

278. Id.

279. California has the highest HMO enrollment at 35 percent. Id.

280. Id.
281. See Kelly King Alexander, "RNs Squeezed by Oversupply, Health Care Reform," *Greater Baton Rouge Business Report,* June 13, 1995, at 45. In Louisiana, 1993 marked the highest enrollment of nurses—13,242. This was a 22 percent increase from 1992 and 145 percent increase over the previous decade. Nine percent of nurses in Louisiana are men. Fourteen percent of Louisiana nurses come from ethnic backgrounds; 11 percent are black. In 1994, 16 percent of nurses were under age 30; 65 percent were between 30 and 49-years-old. Sixty-seven percent of nurses worked in hospitals in 1994. Nationally, nursing enrollment reached its highest level in 1992—257,983—only 4.3 of those employed were men. Ten percent of nurses come from ethnic backgrounds; 4 percent are black. In 1992, 11 percent of nurses were under 30 years old; 60 percent were between 30 and 49 years old. The average age was 43 years old. Sixty-six percent of nurses work in hospitals; 70 percent are employed full-time. Id.
282. Id. (quoting Marie Kelley, chief nursing officer at Our Lady of the Lake Regional Medical Center).
283. See Randy Wilson, "Despite a Flood of Bills, The Legislature Puts Off the Major Issues," *Maine Times,* April 22, 1994, at 12.
284. Id.
285. See Phyllis Austin, "The Managed Care Bandwagon," *Maine Times,* August 31, 1995, at 6.
286. Id.
287. Id.
288. Id. (quoting Bangor attorney, Greg Brodek).
289. Id.
290. For discussion of the effects of hospital restructuring on patient care, see Phyllis Austin, "If the Nurses Get Cut, Who Draws the Blood," *Maine Times,* May 5, 1995, at 10.
291. Id.
292. Id. (quoting Greg Brodek).
293. Id. (quoting Bruce Reuben, Maine Hospital Association president).
294. See Gerard Anderson, Patrick Chaulk and Elizabeth Fowler, *State Model: Maryland—A Regulatory Approach to Health System Reform,* HEALTH AFFAIRS, 40 (Summer 1993) [hereinafter, *State Model: Maryland].*
295. Many states, such as Maryland, have diverse populations. Eight states lack a city with a population greater than 360,000; five of those eight have no cities with more than 180,000 people. Id. at 46-47.
296. The need for health care reform in Maryland was evident in 1993, at which time the preamble to Maryland's health care reform—now codified at Md. Code Ann. § 19-102—listed twenty-six reasons why health reform in the state was necessary. The twenty-six reasons included the following:

(1) Hospital rate setting in Maryland has worked to slow the increase in hospital costs. (2) Maryland has a comprehensive database on hospital costs and services but no comparable information on costs and services

rendered by other health care providers. (3) The thirty-two state-mandated benefits apply only to 20 percent of the population. Self-insured organizations are governed by federal Employee Retirement Income Security Act (ERISA) requirements and are therefore not subject to state insurance regulations. (4) Many Maryland businesses continue to experience increases in health insurance premiums of 15 to 20 percent each year. These employers, along with many of the uninsured, are willing to purchase health care coverage but cannot afford the premiums. (5) Over 15 percent of Maryland state residents under age sixty-five do not have health insurance. (6) Providers, payers, and planners must undertake cooperative efforts to develop appropriate guidelines for the practice of efficient medicine.

See *State Model: Maryland*, sup. note 294 (ch. 5), at 41.

297. See id, at 40.
298. Id.
299. Id.
300. Id. at 42.
301. Id.
302. Id. at 43.
303. Id.
304. Id.
305. Id. at 44.
306. Id.
307. Id.
308. Mass. Health Security Act of 1988, Gen. L., ch. 118F; ch. 151a, 14g. The premise under the Act is that, by paying the state a tax of $1,680 per worker per year, small businesses can opt out of coverage, yet still ensure that the state fully covers the employee and his or her entire family for a full year. See William A. Glaser, *Universal Health Insurance That Really Works: Foreign Lessons for the United States*, 18 J. HEALTH POL., POL'Y & L. 695, 697-698 (Fall, 1993).
309. General Accounting Office, *Access to Health Care: States Respond to Growing Crisis*, 38 (1992).
310. Id. at 33-34.
311. Id. at 34-35.
312. See generally Bove, sup. note 12 (ch.1).
313. See COMMONWEALTH OF MASSACHUSETTS, sup. note 36 (ch. 2).
314. See Greg Kerstetter, "Hospitals Moving to Managed Care," *Daily Hampshire Gazette*, February 6, 1995, at 30.
315. See Jay Fitzgerald, "Alliance Fever in Health Care Shows No Letup," *Boston Business Journal*, December 30, 1994, at 6.
316. Id.
317. Id.; Cathryn J. Prince, "Lack of Capital Causing Biotechs to Brew Up Financial Alternatives," *Boston Business Journal*, December 30, 1994, at 9.

318. See Fitzgerald, sup. note 315 (ch. 5), at 6 (quoting Ellen Lutch Trager, a health care consultant with the Boston law firm of Brown and Rudnick).

319. See Chris Rizk, "New Life for Health Insurance Reform," *Detroiter*, October 1, 1995, at 28.

320. Id. (quoting Dennis McCafferty, cochairman of the Greater Detroit Chamber of Commerce Health and Human Resources Committee).

321. Id.

322. Id.

323. Id.

324. See Frank Webster, "Principles of Community-Based Health Reform," *Greater Lansing Business Monthly*, October 1, 1995, at 6; Steve Raphael, "National Health Reform Reborn Via Local Efforts," *Crains Detroit Business*, June 12, 1995, at 5.

325. See Lois Servaas, "Results Oriented Health Care Gains Steam," *Grand Rapids Business Journal*, September 25, 1995, at A8.

326. See Webster, sup. note 324 (ch. 5), at 6.

327. See Steve Raphael, "Patient, Heal Thyself," *Crains Detroit Business*, May 29, 1995, at 8.

328. Webster, sup. note 324 (ch. 5), at 6.

329. See Howard M. Leichter, *State Model: Minnesota—The Trip From Acrimony to Accommodation*, HEALTH AFFAIRS 48 (Summer 1993).

330. Id.

331. Id. at 48.

332. Id.

333. Id. at 49-50.

334. Id. at 50.

335. Id.

336. Id.

337. Id. at 50-51.

338. See Shep Montgomery, "Insurance Department Grapples with Health Care Reform," *Mississippi Business Journal*, October 2, 1995, at 20.

339. Id.

340. See Nita Chilton McCann, "Health Care Expert Predicts Managed Care Could Arrive in 1997," *Mississippi Business Journal*, April 10, 1995, at 8.

341. Id. (quoting Phil Macon, health care advisor for Mississippi CPA firm, May & Co.).

342. See Montgomery, sup. note 338 (ch. 5), at 20.

343. See Michael R. Dunaway, "Medicaid Changes: Reform or Ruin?," *St. Louis Post*, May 12, 1995, at 21C.

344. Id.

345. Id.

346. See Bonar Menninger, "Proposed Medicare Cuts Would Bleed Hospitals," *Kansas City Business Journal*, September 29, 1995, at 3.

347. Id.

348. Id.

349. See Toni Cardarella, "Healthcaregate: Restricting Access to Medical Specialists Has Become a Main Means of Cutting Health Care Costs," *Ingram's*, February 1, 1995, at 32.
350. Id.
351. See Pat Bellinghausen, "No Overhaul in Health Care, Says Bradley," *Billings (Montana) Gazette*, November 14, 1994, [hereinafter "No Overhaul"], at A1.
352. Id.
353. See Dana Priest, "Montana Skepticism Epidemic; Talk of Health Reform Gets Pulses Racing," *The Washington Post*, June 7, 1994, at A1.
354. See Mea Andrews, "Health Rules May Prove Tricky," *Missoulian (Montana)*, August 5, 1994, at B1.
355. See Bellinghausen, sup. note 351 (ch. 5), at A1.
356. See Pat Bellinghausen, "Hospitals 'Going Back to Basics' Consultant Says," *Billings Gazette*, September 22, 1995, at A1.
357. Id.
358. Id.
359. In 1994, for the first time in six years in Montana, Medicare patients accounted for a larger share of all patient days in the hospital, yet Medicare billed its patients for $195.6 million more than it reimbursed Montana hospitals for the services. Medicaid also received a discount in 1994 of $46.5 million. Id.
360. Id. (quoting Montana Hospital Association President, Jim Ahrens).
361. See Martha Stoddard, "Group Health Premiums See Smallest Growth in Years," *Lincoln (Nebraska) Evening Journal*, April 14, 1995, at 20.
362. Firms with 500 employees or more reduced costs on an average of 1.9 percent while businesses with between 10 and 499 employees saw an increase of 6.5 percent. Id.
363. Id. (quoting Steve Albin, employee benefit consultant).
364. See Pat Dinslage, "St. Francis, GI Physicians Join Forces," *Grand Island Independent*, April 2, 1995, §B, at 1.
365. Id.
366. Nationally, nearly 20 million Americans—1 in 12—live in rural areas where primary care doctors are scarce. There are 141 counties in the nation which employ no doctors at all. See, e.g., Marie Puente, "Rural Towns Desperate for Doctors; Exodus to Cities Could Worsen with Health Care Reform, *USA Today*, May 14, 1993.
367. See Adrian Havas, "Containing Health Care Costs Spurred by Vigilance," *Las Vegas Business Press*, January 23, 1995, at 11.
368. Id.
369. Id.
370. Nevada hospitals were historically ranked first in the nation for costs per day but are now ranked ninth, with rates at approximately $1,000 per day, due to increased regulation. Nevada's largest Hospital still averages a $736 profit per admission. Still, Nevada hospitals, like most other hospitals in

the Western states, have one of the shortest stay rates in the nation—averaging less than six days, while the rest of the nation averages between seven and nine days. Newer hospitals and more efficient technology may account for this difference. Id.

371. Id.
372. Id.
373. See Adrian Havas, "Medical Access Plan: Will It Pass?," *Las Vegas Business Press*, December 12, 1994.
374. Id.
375. See Bob Sanders, "Medical Community Anticipates Cutback Blow," *New Hampshire Business Review*, June 9, 1995, at 1.
376. Id.
377. Id.
378. Id.
379. See Holly Babin, "A Small Hospital Confronts Health Care Reform," *Business New Hampshire Magazine*, December 1, 1994, at 29.
380. See Bob Sanders, "Merger Mania Hits Health Care," *New Hampshire Business Review*, July 22, 1994, at 25.
381. See Paul Gentile, "Managed Care's Arrival Fosters Change," *New Jersey Business*, August 1, 1995, at 40.
382. See Kevin G. Volpp and Bruce Siegel, "State Model: New Jersey-Long-Term Experience with All-Payer State Rate Setting," HEALTH AFFAIRS 12, at 59 (Summer 1993).
383. Id.
384. Id.
385. Id. at 60.
386. Id. at 61.
387. Id. at 62.
388. Id. at 63.
389. This figure is still only 14 percent of New Jersey's population. The leading state—California—insures 36 percent of its populous through HMOs. In 1993, New Jersey had 149 hospital admissions per 1,000 residents; California had 108. One-thousand New Jersey residents spent 1,358 days in the hospital; Californians only 757. New Jersey spends $3,317 per capita on health care; California, only $2,997. See Gentile, sup. note 381 (ch. 5), at 40.
390. Id.
391. See Joseph F. Sullivan, "For New Jersey Welfare Recipients, a Rule to Join HMOs," *The New York Times*, June 9, 1995, at B7.
392. See Gentile, sup. note 381 (ch. 5), at 40.
393. See Christopher Biddle, "1994 Health Benefits: Growth of Managed Care in New Jersey 1993-1994," *New Jersey Business*, April 1, 1995, at 30.
394. Id.
395. Id.
396. Id.

397. See Gentile, sup. note 381 (ch. 5), at 40.

398. See Biddle, sup. note 393 (ch. 5), at 30.

399. See Gentile, sup. note 381 (ch. 5), at 40.

400. See N.J. STAT. ANN. § 26:24-18.51 et. seq. (West 1996).

401. See Gentile, sup. note 381 (ch. 5), at 40. See also Gary Carter, "Hospitals Join Together for Stronger Healthcare System," *New Jersey Business*, March 1, 1995, at 28.

402. See Carter, sup. note 401 (ch. 5), at 28.

403. See Gentile, sup. note 381 (ch. 5), at 40.

404. Id.

405. See "Enrollment in NJ's Individual Health Coverage Program Increased 21 Percent During First Quarter 1995," *Business Wire*, July 11, 1995.

406. Id.

407. See Volpp and Siegel, sup. note 382 (ch. 5), at 65.

408. Id.

409. See Ed Ivey, "The Corridor: Health Care Challenge," *New Mexico Business Journal*, April 1, 1994.

410. Id.

411. See Arlene Cinelli Odenwald, "Hospitals, HMOs, Patients: Surviving the Crisis," *New Mexico Business Journal*, May 1, 1993.

412. See Joy Waldron, "Health Care Reform: Wading Through the Maze," *New Mexico Business Journal*, August 1, 1994.

413. Id.

414. Id.

415. Id.

416. Id.

417. Id.

418. See "New York Flubs Medicaid Reform," *Newsday*, September 24, 1995, at A39.

419. Id.

420. Id.

421. See Ethan de Seife, "Hospitals Searching for Allies to Cut Costs, Improve Services," *Westchester County Business Journal*, July 31, 1995, at 1.

422. See Annemarie Franczyk, "Pataki's Chief Health Aide Promotes Reform Proposal," *Business First-Buffalo*, May 22, 1995, §A, at 7. Some of the proposals include reducing the certificate of need limitation for new equipment and major capital additions from two years to four months, with an estimated savings of up to $9.8 million; creating more flexible standards for therapy and certified nursing aide staffs, saving an approximated $19.5 million; eliminating duplicative hospital surveillance efforts, saving $2.75 million; mandating managed-care systems for all Medicaid recipients and to mandate the inclusion of all disabled and elderly enrollees by 1997; and continuing a 13 percent surcharge on all commercially insured and HMO employee benefit plan hospital bills, thereby raising $200 million. Id.

423. See Josh Kurtz, "Firms Define Managed Care Standards," *Crains New York Business*, June 19, 1995, at 39.
424. See Jeffrey L. Reynolds, "Rights Bill Is an Rx for HMO Flaws," *Newsday*, June 8, 1995, at 43.
425. A 1994 General Accounting Office report, however, reveals that the government spent 28 percent more on Medicare patients enrolled in an HMO than it did on traditional Medicare patient coverage. Id.
426. Some states include in their definition of "long-term care" qualified services provided in the home. For example, Pennsylvania defines long-term care as:

> those services designed to provide diagnostic, therapeutic, rehabilitative, supportive or maintenance services for individuals who have chronic functional impairments in a variety of institutional and non-institutional care settings, including the home.

See 71 PA. CONS. STAT. ANN. § 581-582 (1990).
427. Reynolds, sup. note 424 (ch. 5), at 43.
428. Id.
429. Id.
430. See Paul M. Barrett and Ron Winslow, "Justices Allow States' Overhaul of Health Care," *The Wall Street Journal*, April 27, 1995, §B, at 1, col. 6.
431. See id. (quoting Richard Ruda, Attorney for the National Governors Association).
432. See Kathleen Coleman, "Sans Reform, Health Care Still Faces Revolution," *Business Journal of Charlotte (North Carolina)*, January 2, 1995, at 15.
433. Id.
434. Id.
435. Id. (quoting Ted Carpenter, President of Kaiser Foundation Health Plan of North Carolina).
436. Id.
437. See Heather Harrold, "Doctor Claims HMO Misled Him," *Triangle Business Journal*, June 9, 1995, at 1 (describing consistent losses for PruCare of Prudential Health Care Plan, Inc., which posted losses of $9 million in its first three months of operation).
438. If you can keep up with the results/outcomes, if you can follow patients and show that you're providing care that's cost effective on the front end, that your patients don't have relapses and such, then when you go to industry or a managed-care company to sell your services, you're going to be the winner.

Coleman, sup. note 432 (ch. 5), at 15 (quoting health care consultant, Will Latham).
439. Id.
440. See Sue Ellyn Scaletta, "Rural America Manages Health Care Without Competition," *Grand Forks Herald (North Dakota)*, May 4, 1993, WL3143689.
441. Id.
442. Id.

443. Almost 23 percent of Americans live in rural areas but, according to the Journal of the American Medical Association, in 1991, only 12.6 percent of physicians were servicing these Americans. Id.
444. Id.
445. Thirteen HMOs already service Medicaid recipients on a voluntary basis and are expected to fare well when bidding for new enrollees when Ohio-Care takes off the ground. See Sara Selis, "HMOs, Hospitals Weigh Advantages of OhioCare," *Business First-Columbus*, March 27, 1995, at 8.
446. Id.
447. Id.
448. Id.
449. See Gigi Verna, "Medicaid to Impact Hospitals," *Greater Cincinnati Business Record*, Jan. 23, 1995, at 4.
450. See Rodney Washington, "Local Employers Prefer State, Private Health Reform," *Business First-Columbus*, March 6, 1995. A survey by the management consulting firm of Godwins, Brooke & Dickenson reveals that 64 percent of participating employers favor a greater state government role in health care reform. Fifty-eight percent felt Republicans were more apt to achieve favorable reform. Thirty-percent reported cost savings under a managed-care system. Id.
451. See Dan Monk, "Big Names Come Out vs. Bills," *Cincinnati Business Courier*, October 2, 1995, at 3.
452. Id.
453. See Lisa Beeler, "Home Health Care: Local Firms Report Solid Growth," *Business Journal of Five-County Region (Youngstown, Ohio)*, November 15, 1994, §2, at 1.
454. Id.
455. Id.
456. Id.
457. Id.
458. Id. (quoting Judy Schumaker, coordinator of field management development for First Ohio Home Health, Boardman). Between 1987 and 1993, the average cost of living increased by 27 percent; costs for physician services increased by 48.5 percent and hospital costs rose by 73.4 percent, while home health care costs increased by only 17 percent. Id.
459. Id.
460. Id.
461. See Dan Rutherford, "Local Pharmacy Takes on Big Guys," *Muskogee Daily Phoenix & Times Democrat*, August 8, 1994.
462. See Scott Wenger, "IRAs Are Seen as Model for Health Care," *The Wall Street Journal*, October 23, 1992, at 5A.
463. Id.
464. Id.
465. See "Forum Addresses Medical Savings Accounts as a Health Care Reform Alternative," *PR Newswire*, July 12, 1995.

466. Wenger, sup. note 462 (ch. 5), at 5A (quoting John Goodman, president of the National Center for Policy Analysis, in Dallas).

467. See OR. REV. STAT. § 424.036 et seq. (1989). See generally Thomas, sup. note 15 (ch. 5), at 47; Eric Lamond Robinson, "The Oregon Basic Health Services Act: A Model for State Reform?," 45 VAND. L. REV. 977 (1992).

468. General Accounting Office, *Access to Health Care: States Respond to Growing Crisis*, GAO/HRD-92-70, at 39, November 1, 1992, 1992 WL 2640862 [hereinafter *States Respond*].

469. See generally GEORGE P. SMITH, II, BIOETHICS AND THE LAW: MEDICAL, SOCIO-LEGAL AND PHILOSOPHICAL DISCUSSIONS FOR A BRAVE NEW WORLD, at 39 (1993).

470. Harvey D. Klevit, Alan C. Bates, Tina Castanares, Paul Kirk, Paige R. Sipes-Metzler and Richard Wopat, *Prioritization of Health Care Services: A Progress Report by the Oregon Health Services Commission*, 151 ARCH. INTERN. MED. 912-916 (May, 1991).

471. Laguarda, sup. note 52 (ch. 2), at 186.

472. Id.

473. See Daniel M. Fox and Howard M. Leichter, *State Model: Oregon—The Ups and Downs of Oregon's Rationing Plan*, 12 HEALTH AFFAIRS, 66 (Summer 1993).

474. See *States Respond*, sup. note 468 (ch. 5), at 41.

475. See General Accounting Office, *Medicaid: Oregon's Managed Care Program and Implications for Expansion* (Report to the Chairman, Subcommittee on Health and Environment, Committee on Energy and Commerce, House of Representatives) 2-3 (1992).

476. H. Gilbert Welch and Eric B. Larson, *The Oregon Decision to Curtail Funding for Organ Transplantation*, 319 NEW ENG. J. MED. 189-190 (1988).

477. See Fox and Leichter, sup. note 473 (ch. 5), at 66.

478. See Thomas, sup. note 15 (ch. 5), at 54.

479. Id.

480. Id.

481. For an explanation of the political criticism of the original version of the Oregon plan on the basis that it discriminated against the disabled population under the Americans with Disabilities Act by qualifying the value of life, see Fox and Leichter, sup. note 473 (ch. 5), at 67-69.

482. Id. at 70.

483. Id. at 53.

484. See AGING AMERICA, sup. note 193 (ch. 1), at 18.

485. See *Pennsylvania Perspective*, sup. note 165 (ch. 1), at 16.

486. The seven other states beside Pennsylvania were California, Florida, Illinois, Michigan, New York, Ohio, and Texas. See AGING AMERICA, sup. note 193 (ch. 1), at 18.

487. Id.

488. The twelve other states beside Pennsylvania were Arkansas, Connecticut, Florida, Iowa, Kansas, Maine, Massachusetts, Missouri, Nebraska, New Jersey, New York, North Dakota, Oregon, Rhode Island, South Dakota, West Virginia, and Wisconsin. Id.
489. Id. at 19.
490. Id.
491. See Elizabeth Cummings, "Medicaid Costs Cripple State Budget," *Central Pennsylvania Business Journal*, June 23, 1995, at 1.
492. Id. at 21.
493. Id. at 22. The other states receiving a high percentage of elderly Florida migrants were Michigan, New York and Ohio. Id.
494. Id.
495. The cost of nursing homes for Pennsylvania's Medicaid patients increased by 10 percent in 1995—double that of the national health care inflation. This increase is mostly due to the expense of caring for sicker nursing home patients, who are prematurely discharged from the hospital as a result of pressure from managed care insurers to employ shorter hospital stays. Id.
496. Id.
497. Id.
498. Overall, Pennsylvania expends approximately 16 percent of its budget on Medicaid expenses. Reliance on Medicaid for long-term care is continuing—even increasing; only about 3 to 4 percent of the population has long-term care insurance.
499. See *Pennsylvania Perspective*, sup. note 165 (ch. 1), at 25.
500. See "Federal Judge Upholds Limit on Fees for Treating Elderly, " *Philadelphia Inquirer*, February 2, 1991, at 2-B, col. 6 [hereinafter "Federal Judge"]. See also *Massachusetts Med. Soc'y v. Dukakis*, 815 F.2d 790 (1st Cir.) (upholding a Massachusetts law requiring physicians to accept the Medicare price structure), cert. denied, 108 S. Ct. 229 (1987).
501. See "Federal Judge," sup. note 500 (ch. 5), at 2B.
502. Id.
503. Id. Despite the financial savings for the elderly and judicial support of the statute, the Pennsylvania Medical Society, which represents more than 19,000 doctors in Pennsylvania, claims that the statute is unconstitutional and plans to appeal the decision. Id. Such statutes have found support in sixteen states, including: California, Colorado, Florida, Indiana, Iowa, Maine, Maryland, Minnesota, Mississippi, New Jersey, New York, Ohio, Pennsylvania, Rhode Island, South Carolina, and Wyoming. See Ross, *The Effect of Mandatory Medicare Assignment on Health Care*, 10 J. LEGAL MED. 529, 530 n.9 (1989).
504. See Marian Uhlman, "Pa. Wants Drug Aid for Elderly," *Philadelphia Inquirer*, March 3, 1991, at D1, col. 5. This may be due to the high populous of elderly in Pennsylvania caused by heavy countermigration. See sup. notes 491-493 (ch. 5) and accompanying text.

505. Id. at 1.
506. See *Pennsylvania Perspective*, sup. note 165 (ch. 1), at 6-7.
507. "Unsuited Prescriptions Harm Elderly, GAO Says," *Philadelphia Inquirer*, August 9, 1995, at A7.
508. Id.
509. See Uhlman, sup. note 504, at 1. Notwithstanding the potential savings from the new legislation, the Department of Aging faced a $50 million budget cut after 1991. Id.
510. Id. Of the $3.5 billion that was returned to the Medicaid programs in the 50 states between 1991 and 1996, Medicaid in Pennsylvania received approximately $172 million, $40 million of which was in the first year.
511. Id.
512. Id. (quoting Tom Snedden, director of the PACE program).
513. Id. (quoting Jeffrey L. Trewhitt, spokesman for the Pharmaceutical Manufacturers Association).
514. The average cost of bringing a new drug to the market (a process that may take up to twelve years) is $231 million. Pharmaceutical companies advocate the cost-effectiveness of this process by arguing that developments in medicines reduce the otherwise high costs of surgery, which is sometimes the only other alternative. Id. at 2.
515. Id. at 1-2.
516. Id. at 1.
517. Id. at 2.
518. Pamela Sampson, "Pa. Advocate for Elderly Has a Growing Clientele," *Philadelphia Inquirer*, August 13, 1995, at B7.
519. Id.
520. Associated Press, "Medicaid to Put All in HMOs," *Philadelphia Inquirer*, August 9, 1995, at B2.
521. Id.
522. Gold, sup. note 16 (ch. 1), at N2.
523. See Elizabeth Cummings, "More Changes Forecast for Health Care Industry," *Central Pennsylvania Business Journal*, January 6, 1995, at 4.
524. See Jane-Ellen Robinet, Health Care's Hectic Pace to Accelerate in Coming Year, *Pittsburgh Business Times & Journal*, December 26, 1994, at 15.
525. Gold, sup. note 16 (ch. 1), at N2.
526. Id. at N1.
527. Id. at N2.
528. Benac, sup. note 146 (ch. 1), at A2.
529. Chen, sup. note 30 (ch. 5), at C3.
530. See John E. Mulligan, "Area Legislators Hew to Party Line," *Providence Journal-Bulletin*, October 20, 1995, at 8A; Felice J. Freyer, "Democrats Bash GOP on Medicare," *Providence Journal-Bulletin*, August 29, 1995, at 1B.
531. See Mulligan, sup. note 530 (ch. 5), at 8A.
532. Id.

533. See Freyer, sup. note 530 (ch. 5), at 1B.
534. See Elliot Krieger, "The Changing Safety Net Search for Security Wary of Medicare Repair," *Providence Journal Bulletin*, October 9, 1995, at A1.
535. Id.
536. Id.
537. See Leslie Broberg, "For Hospitals, It Was a Year of Mergers, Restructuring," *Providence Business News*, December 26, 1994, at 12.
538. It is estimated that the reductions in Medicare and Medicaid will bring about a loss of up to 7,500 jobs for the 10 percent of the Rhode Island work force (some 47,000 people) employed in the health care industry. See Krieger, sup. note 534 (ch. 5).
539. Id. See also, Peter Phipps, "Cleveland: Health Care the Way It Can Be in R.I.," *Providence Sunday Journal*, July 30, 1995, at 1F.
540. See Phipps, sup. note 539 (ch. 5), at 1F; Felice Freyer, "Group to Blaze New Trail in Health Care," *Providence Journal-Bulletin*, July 13, 1995, at 1B.
541. See Phipps, sup. note 539 (ch. 5), at 1F.
542. See Freyer, sup. note 540 (ch. 5), at 1B.
543. Id.
544. See Amy Corley, "Hospitals Catch on to Merger Trend," *Florence Morning News (South Carolina)*, December 22, 1993, WL3048454.
545. See Judy H. Longshaw and Al Dozier, "Governor Targets Medicaid Reform," *Sacramento Bee*, December 19, 1993 at D9.
546. Id.
547. Id.
548. Id.
549. Id.
550. Nationally, small business accounts for approximately one-half of all uninsured Americans. See Michael Selz, "Health Program for Small Firms Is No Panacea," *The Wall Street Journal*, June 29, 1993, at B1, col. 6.
551. See Longshaw and Dozier, sup. note 545 (ch. 5), at D9.
552. Id.
553. See Richard Wolf, "In S. Dakota, Problem Is Plain: Too Few Doctors," *USA Today*, February 18, 1994, at 7A.
554. Id.
555. Id.
556. See Robert L. Rose, "Chilly Sunset: Firms' Attempts to Cut Health Benefits Break Calm of Retirement," *The Wall Street Journal*, February 24, 1993 at A1, col. 1.
557. See, e.g., "Illinois Blue Cross to Merge with Iowa, South Dakota Groups," *Chicago Tribune*, May 26, 1993 at A2. The Merged Blue Cross plan in South Dakota, which is part of the fourth largest Blue Cross and Blue Shield plan in the nation, serves more than 2.4 million people. Id.
558. See Eric Harrison and Edith Stanley, "Alternative to Medicaid Leaves Many Dissatisfied," *Los Angeles Times*, November 20, 1995, at A1, col. 5.

559. Id.
560. David Brown, "Deluged by Medicaid, States Open Wider Umbrellas Series: Tennessee's Economy of Care: TennCare's First Three Years," *The Washington Post*, June 9, 1996, at A1 [hereinafter "Deluged by Medicaid"]. See also David Brown, "Inviting Uninsured to Become Part of Medical 'System' Series: Tennessee's Economy of Care: TennCare's First Three Years," *The Washington Post*, June 9, 1996, at A6.
561. Id.
562. Id.
563. Id.
564. Id.
565. Id.
566. A more recent study states that, now, 75 percent of the same class say that their care is the same or has improved. Id. See also, Richard Locker, "Survey: TennCare Enrollee Approval Up in '95," *Commercial Appeal*, November 5, 1995, at 1B.
567. The largest of the participating plans, Blue Cross and Blue Shield, which covered half of the enrollees, recorded losses of almost $9 million in 1994 and anticipated $35 million in losses in 1995. See Harrison and Stanley, sup. note 558 (ch. 5), at A15, col. 2.
568. Premiums now run on a sliding scale, ranging from $3.50 per month for those with income under $3,684 annually, to $207 per month, for those with annual incomes over $59,000. A $3.5 million safety net fund will pay for those who cannot afford premiums, like the disabled or mentally ill. See Paula Wade, "TennCare to Increase Premiums Next Year," *Commercial Appeal*, October 25, 1995.
569. "Deluged by Medicaid," sup. note 560 (ch. 5), at A1.
570. See Harrison and Stanley, sup. note 558 (ch. 5) (quoting Charlotte Collins, chief legal counsel of the Regional Medical Center, Tennessee's largest public hospital).
571. See Locker, sup. note 566 (ch. 5), at 1B.
572. See Jon Hamilton, "Oregon Finds 'Happy' Contrast to TennCare," *Commercial Appeal*, January 29, 1995, at 1A.
573. Id. See also Jon Hamilton "TennCare: Ready for a Check-Up," *Business Journal Upper East Tennessee and Southwest Virginia*, January 1, 1996, at §1, at 28 [hereinafter "TennCare Check-Up"].
574. See Hamilton, sup. note 572 (ch. 5), at 1A; "TennCare Check-Up," sup. note 573 (ch. 5), at 28.
575. See Hamilton, sup. note 572 (ch. 5), at 1A (commenting on statement by Dr. James Todd, executive vice president of the American Medical Association).
576. See James W. Brosnan, "National Official Cites TennCare as Example of Managed-Care Woes," *Commercial Appeal*, June 7, 1995, at 4A (referring to statement by Larry Gage, president of the National Association of Public Hospitals).

577. See Bill Snyder, "Recovering Addicts Slam TennCare," *Nashville Banner*, December 15, 1995, at A1.
578. Id.
579. Id.
580. Id.
581. Id.
582. Id.
583. Id.
584. See Hamilton, sup. note 572 (ch. 5), at 1A. Pharmacists were also affected in April 1995, when the pharmacy network capped its monthly reimbursement to pharmacists at $75 per month for medicines for long-term care patients. See Sarah A. Derks, "Druggists, Long-Term Care Patients Get TennCare Surprise," *Commercial Appeal*, March 6, 1995, at 1A. Consequently, many pharmacists abandoned the program. Id.
585. See "TennCare Check-Up," sup. note 573 (ch. 5), at 28. Most complaints stem from limited physician access and inadequate reimbursements—physicians receive only about $.25 on the dollar for their services. Id.
586. See Hamilton, sup. note 572 (ch. 5), at 1A.
587. *TennCare Check-Up*, sup. note 573 (ch. 5), at 28 (quoting Dr. Paul Stanton, dean of the James H. Quillen College of Medicine at East Tennessee State University).
588. See Bill Snyder, "TennCare Stats 'Impressive,' But Experts Cautious," Nashville Banner, February 6, 1996, at B1; "Achievement for TennCare," *Nashville Banner*, February 13, 1996, at A6.
589. Id.
590. Id.
591. Id. See also, Carol Jouzaitis, "Medicaid Is No Issue in Tennessee—It's Dead," *Chicago Tribune*, February 8, 1996, at 3.
592. See "State, Patients May Pay More in TennCare," *Commercial Appeal*, July 1, 1995, at 2B.
593. Id.
594. Id.
595. Premiums for the 124,000 non-Medicaid eligible patients below the poverty line, who, before, had received TennCare at no cost, would see increases in premiums of between $3.50 and $10.00. See Paula Wade, "Hospitals, Citizens, Poor: Who Pays to Fix TennCare?," *Commercial Appeal*, July 17, 1995, at 1A.
596. Id. (quoting Bob Corker, State Finance Commissioner).
597. Id.
598. Id.
599. Id. (quoting Rusty Seibert, TennCare Director).
600. TennCare's Consumer Advocacy Program reported that, in 1994, nearly half of its 2,721 cases were the result of administrative problems with the TennCare Bureau itself, such as processing applications, correcting premium errors and assigning managed care organizations. See Richard

Locker, "46% of TennCare Gripes Linked to State Oversight Agency," *Commercial Appeal*, June 6, 1995, at 1B. Another 35 percent were problems with providers and managed care organizations, such as a lack of specialists, defining "medically necessary" and determining what drugs the organizations will pay for. Id. Another 17 percent were with the TennCare participants, such as misfiled enrollment forms and dissatisfaction with providers. Id.

601. See James W. Brosnan, "Tenn. May Be Protected in Medicaid Gap," *Commercial Appeal*, March 24, 1995, at 4B.

602. Id.

603. See Bill Snyder, "Texas Firm Wins $28M TennCare Data Contract," *Nashville Banner*, September 8, 1995, at A13.

604. See James W. Brosnan, "Gov. Asks Funding Flexibility to Refine Tenn-Care," *Commercial Appeal*, June 9, 1995, at 1B.

605. See Richard Lawson, "State of the Health-Care Industry: Managing Managed Care," *Business Journal Upper East Tennessee and South West Virginia*, January 1, 1996, at 24. See also, Mary Powers, "THA Seeks TennCare Refinement," *Commercial Appeal*, September 7, 1995, at 7B; James W. Brosnan, "Sundquist Makes Concession OK'ing Medicaid Reform," *Commercial Appeal*, September 20, 1995, at 1A.

606. In 1995, there were three major hospital mergers in Tennessee. See Tim Sewell, "Health Care Industry Will Continue to Undergo Changes in '96," *Memphis Business Journal*, January 1, 1996, at 10. Cyril F. Chang, professor of economics at the Fogelman College of Business and Economics at the University of Memphis explains the effect of the growth of managed care by stating: "All of the major players in health care are trying to make changes that will put them in a stronger competitive position." Id.

607. See Lawson, sup. note 605 (ch. 5), at 24.

608. Id. Some feel that although Tenncare was designed to serve rural areas better because it allows managed care organizations to set up delivery systems in smaller communities, it has not yet been completely successful in rural Tennessee. See Ryan Underwood, "Big Medicine Going Small Town," *Tennessean*, January 28, 1996, at 1B. The TennCare program has attempted to alleviate the overabundance of specialized physicians by offering stipends to medical school students who agree to practice in rural areas. Id.

609. See Brosnan, sup. note 605 (ch. 5), at 1A.

610. Id.

611. Id.

612. Id.

613. Id.

614. See, e.g., Tammie Smith, "Meharry Doctoring Image," *Tennessean*, February 11, 1996, at 1A.

615. The number of nursing homes has increased from 264 to 321 and the number of beds has gone from 28,000 to 38,000. See Shirley Downing,

"Medicaid Cuts Could Stunt Growth Trend of Tenn. Nursing Homes," *Commercial Appeal*, October 16, 1995, at 1A.

616. Id.
617. Some reasons for the expanding nursing home market in Tennessee include the following:
    — Lower interest rates, available mortgage, and bond money
    — Attempts to meet anticipated nursing home needs of an aging population
    — The trend toward managed health care—which requires shorter stays in the hospital—and which has encouraged development of transitional care beds in hospitals and nursing homes
    — A state law that allows a home to add ten beds a year outside of the certificate of need process
    — Continued high occupancy at nursing homes statewide, ranging in most counties from 95 to 98 percent

    Id.
618. Id.
619. See "Nursing Home Costs Could Fall on the Kids," *Nashville Banner*, December 18, 1995, at A3.
620. Id.
621. Id.
622. See Bill Lewis, "Long Term Care Committee to Study Nursing Homes," *Memphis Business Journal*, December 25, 1995, at 8.
623. Id.
624. Id.
625. See Sewell, sup. note 606 (ch. 5), at 10 (quoting Bob Gordon of Baptist Memorial Health Care System).
626. Id.
627. Id.
628. See Tammie Smith, "TennCare Providers Can't Deny Needed Treatments," *Tennessean*, January 5, 1996, at 1A.
629. See "Transplant Surgery for Girl to Proceed," *Commercial Appeal*, January 10, 1996, at 2B [hereinafter "Transplant Surgery"].
630. See Smith, sup. note 628 (ch. 5), at 1A.
631. See "Insurers Must Cover Girl's Transplants," *Commercial Appeal*, January 5, 1996, at 2B; Smith, sup. note 628 (ch. 5), at 1A.
632. See Smith, sup. note 628 (ch. 5), at 1A.
633. Id.
634. Id.
635. Id.
636. Id.
637. See "Transplant Surgery," sup. note 629 (ch. 5), at 2B.
638. See Tammie Smith, "New Cancer Therapy OK'd by TennCare," *Tennessean*, January 24, 1996, at 1B [hereinafter "New Cancer"]; Alisa LaPolt

and Bill Snyder, "TennCare Decision Gets Kudos from Cancer Patients, Legislators," *Nashville Banner*, January 24, 1996, at B5.

639. See "New Cancer," sup. note 638 (ch5).

640. Id.

641. Id.; LaPolt and Snyder, sup. note 638 (ch. 5), at B5.

642. See "Solid Move by TennCare," *Tennessean*, January 26, 1996, at 12A.

643. The drugs are administered in conjunction with the anti-aids drug, AZT. See Bill Snyder, "TennCare Mulls Cost of 2 AIDS Drugs," *Nashville Banner*, January 26, 1996, at B1 [hereinafter "TennCare Mulls Cost"]. Paula Wade, "State May Offer AIDS Drugs," *Commercial Appeal*, February 6, 1996, at 1B. For a more comprehensive discussion of the AIDS epidemic and health care reform, see William A. Bradford, Jr. and Michele A. Zavos, "The AIDS Epidemic and Health Care Reform," 27 J. MARSHALL L. REV. 279 (1994).

644. See "TennCare Mulls Cost," sup. note 643 (ch. 5), at B1; Tammie Smith, "HIV Drugs Could Stress TennCare," *Tennessean*, February 6, 1996, at 1A [hereinafter "HIV Drugs"].

645. "HIV Drugs," sup. note 644 (ch. 5), at 1A.

646. Id.

647. See Bill Snyder, "Tenncare Stats 'Impressive,' But Experts Cautious," *Nashville Banner*, February 6, 1996, at B1.

648. See "TennCare Mulls Cost," sup. note 643 (ch. 5), at B1; "HIV Drugs," sup. note 644 (ch. 5), at 1A.

649. See "TennCare Mulls Cost," sup. note 643 (ch. 5), at B1.

650. See "HIV Drugs," sup. note 644 (ch. 5), at 1A.

651. Paula Wade, "TennCare Can't Make In-State Residency a Qualifier," *Commercial Appeal*, February 13, 1996, at 1A (quoting Rusty Siebert).

652. Id.

653. Id.

654. State officials are planning to establish standard policies to study the long-term health savings of new drugs and treatments to determine whether the procedures will eventually save the state money by reducing subsequent medical costs. See Paula Wade, "TennCare Drugs to be Reviewed," *Commercial Appeal*, February 14, 1996, at 6A.

655. See Laura Johannes, "TEXAS JOURNAL: Insurers Raise Business Rates As Law Looms," *Dow Jones News Service–Wall Street Journal Stories*, August 23, 1995, at 6A.

656. Id.

657. See Laura Johannes, "Insurance Reform Nears for Small Firms," *The Wall Street Journal*, September 28, 1994, at T1 (Texas Journal) [hereinafter "Reform Nears"].

658. Id. (quoting Thomas Porter, vice president of American National Insurance Co.).

659. The law provides that insurers must provide coverage to all small employers "without regard to claim experience, health status or medical history."

Still, the Texas Department of Insurance determined that this language did not prohibit raising premium prices on employers with sick workers and not demographically similar employers with healthy employees. Id.

660. Id.

661. See Laura Johannes, "Political Tide May Swamp Parts of Small-Firm Health-Care Law," *The Wall Street Journal*, November 16, 1994, at T4 (Texas Journal).

662. As of September 1995, at least 15 states employed guaranteed issue provisions for small businesses: California, Florida, Hawaii, Kentucky, Maine, Maryland, Massachusetts, Minnesota, New Hampshire, New Jersey, New York, Ohio, Texas, Vermont, and Washington. See "Reform Nears," sup. note 657 (ch. 5). As of January 1995, at least 21 states employed guaranteed issue provisions for qualified state-designed small employer plans: Alaska, Arizona, Colorado, Connecticut, Delaware, Idaho, Iowa, Kansas, Missouri, Montana, Nebraska, North Carolina, North Dakota, Oklahoma, Oregon, Rhode Island, South Carolina, Tennessee, Virginia, Wisconsin, and Wyoming. Id.

663. Id.

664. Family Medical Savings and Investment Act of 1995, H.R. 1818, 104th Cong., 1st Sess., (June 13, 1995). For a discussion of how Medical Savings Accounts, like those proposed by H.R. 1818, are implemented, see Brian Lopina, "Medical Savings Accounts: Free Market Magic," *Buffalo News*, March 29, 1996, at C3. For a discussion of the applicability and effect of Medical Savings Accounts to the health care program in Jersey City, New Jersey—the first governmental entity to offer Medical Savings Accounts to its employees, see Bret Schundler, *Revamping Civil Service*, Cong. Testimony (Fed. Doc. Clear. House), December 13, 1995, 1995 WL13415434 (testimony of Jersey City Mayor, Bret Schundler, before the U.S. House of Representatives Subcommittee on Civil Service, Committee on Government Reform and Oversight). Bret Schundler testified in favor of H.R. 1818 before the House Ways and Means Subcommittee on Health.

665. See "Archer Bill Proposes NCPAS Medical Savings Account Ideas," *PR Newswire*, June 13, 1995.

666. See Mike Griffin, "Special Session Delayed Again: The Postponements Appear to Be Tied to Delays in the U.S. Senate's Block-Grant Debate," *Orlando Sentinal*, September 10, 1995, at G5; "MSAs for Medicaid, Medicare May Be Around Corner," *Inside Health Care Reform*, June 1, 1995.

667. See Robb Hicken, "Utah Health Firms Manage to Cure High Costs," *Daily Herald (Provo, Utah)*, May 7, 1994, §A, at 3.

668. Id.

669. Id. (quoting Steve Kohlert, senior vice president for Intermountain Healthcare).

670. Id.

671. See Janet Hart, "IHC Hoping Reforms Don't Ruin Health Care," *Daily Herald (Provo, Utah)*, March 13, 1994, §H, at 26.

672. Id. (quoting Steve Kohlert).
673. See Howard M. Leichter, *State Model: Vermont—Health Care Reform in Vermont: A Work in Progress,* 12, HEALTH AFFAIRS (Summer 1993).
674. Id. at 80.
675. Id. at 72.
676. Id.
677. Id. at 73.
678. Id.
679. Id.
680. Id. at 74.
681. See Goldstein, sup. note 151 (ch. 5), at A1.
682. Id.
683. Id.
684. See Peter Baker, "VA's Free-Market Remedy for Health Care Has Detractors," *The Washington Post,* June 1, 1994, at D1.
685. See Amy Goldstein and Dana Priest, "States Trying to Ferret Fiscal Impact Data Out of Clinton Health Plan," *The Washington Post,* January 29, 1994, at A8.
686. See Goldstein, sup. note 151 (ch. 5), at A1.
687. See Baker, sup. note 684 (ch. 5), at D1.
688. See Goldstein, sup. note 151 (ch. 5), at A1.
689. "While Virginia has studied the issue quite a bit and undertaken a few important initiatives, it is not known as one of the leaders and would have to play a certain amount of catch-up." Baker, sup. note 684 (ch. 5), at D1 (quoting Debra J. Lipson, Associate Director of the Alpha Center, a non-profit health policy organization).
690. Id.; Peter Heerwagen, "Local Health Care Providers Network in Face of Reform," *North Valley Business Journal,* March 1, 1994, §1, at 9 [hereinafter Heerwagen "Network"]; Peter Heerwagen, "The Future for Hospitals Is the Outpatient," *North Valley Business Journal,* March 1, 1994, at 12 [hereinafter Heerwagen "Future"].
691. See Heerwagen "Network," sup. note 690 (ch. 5).
692. See id. (quoting David Goff, president of Winchester Medical Center).
693. For a discussion of how medical schools encouraging students to broaden their education by experiencing rural health care, see Robert M. D'Alessandri, "Medicine's Challenge Is Health, Not Illness," *Newsday,* November 29, 1993, at 39.
694. See Baker, sup. note 684 (ch. 5), at D1.
695. See Robert A. Crittenden, *State Model: Washington—Managed Competition and Premium Caps in Washington State,* 12, HEALTH AFFAIRS 82 (Summer 1993).
696. Id. at 83.
697. Id. at 83-84.
698. Id. at 84.
699. Id.

700. Id. at 85.
701. Id. at 84.
702. Id. at 85.
703. Id. at 86.
704. Id.
705. In 1992, Washington attempted to promote a comprehensive plan that legitimately avoided the restrictions of ERISA. However, "[i]n 1993 it was simpler and more effective politically to act in violation of ERISA and to work on changing ERISA to allow Washington and other states to innovate in ways they see fit." Id. at 88.
706. West Virginia led the nation in 1994 in the percentage of its state national product spent on health care—17.5 percent. See Associated Press, "Wyo. Health Care System in Good Shape Study Says, But 15% in State Lacked Medical Insurance in '93, Placing It 35th in the Nation," *Rocky Mountain News*, December 20, 1994, at 12A [hereinafter "Wyo. Health Care"].
707. See Scott McCaffrey, "Lagging Behind in Health Care, W. Va. Welcomes Change," *Morning Journal (Martinsburg, West Virginia)*, September 23, 1993.
708. See William Doolittle, "City Hospital Celebrates Beginning of a New Era," *Morning Journal (Martinsburg, West Virginia)*, May 8, 1994, §A, at 1.
709. See McCaffrey, sup. note 707 (ch. 5).
710. See Doolittle, sup. note 708 (ch. 5).
711. "Every year the equivalent of the entire Medicaid budget is spent on tobacco-related illness in West Virginia." See Jack Bailey, "Physician: Universal Access No Closer in W.Va.," *State Journal (Charleston, West Virginia)*, May 1, 1993, §1, at 8 (quoting Dr. James Comerci, West Virginia Medical Association).
712. See Abbey L. Zink, "Poll: 86 Percent Covered by Company Health Care Plan," *State Journal (Charleston, West Virginia)*, October 1, 1992, §1, at A.
713. Id.
714. See McCaffrey, sup. note 707 (ch. 5).
715. West Virginia is the second most rural state in the nation and is the leader in unemployment. See Doolittle, sup. note 708 (ch. 5).
716. See Abbey L. Zink, "St. Mary's Hospital Ready to Meet Challenges of Health-Care Reform," *State Journal (Huntington, West Virginia)*, August 1, 1993, §2 at 11.
717. See Laura Merisalo, "A Grass-Roots Health Reform Effort," *Business Journal-Milwaukee*, June 10, 1995, at A1.
718. Id. (quoting Bonnie Gaver, committee member of the Oconomowoc Area Health Care Network).
719. See Julie Sneider, "Health Costs Fight Not Over," *Business Journal-Milwaukee*, March 11, 1995, at 1.
720. Id.
721. See John Diedrich, "Health Care Reform 'On The Rocks'," *Kenosha News (Wisconsin)*, March 7, 1995, at A3.

722. See Steve Prestegard, "The Big Two: A Look at the Fox River Valley's Two Dominant Health Systems," *Marketplace Magazine*, January 31, 1995, at 36.
723. Id.
724. See Michael Muckian and Jean Muckian, "Hospital, Heal Thyself," *Corporate Report Wisconsin*, January 1, 1995, at 20 (quoting Robert Taylor, President of the Wisconsin Hospital Association).
725. Id.
726. Nationally, between 1982 and 1992, inpatient admissions dropped 15.1 percent, from 36.3 million to 30.8 million; Wisconsin's inpatients admissions dropped 24.2 percent, from 765,000 to 580,000 during the same time period. Nationally, the drop in number of days spent inpatient was 24.5 percent, while Wisconsin's decrease was 38.9 percent. Id.
727. Nationally, outpatient visits went from 248.1 million to 348.5 million—a 40 percent increase—between 1982 and 1992. Wisconsin experienced a 59.7 percent increase in outpatient visits over the same time, from 4.4 million to nearly 7 million. Id.
728. Id.
729. See "Wyo. Health Care," sup. note 706 (ch. 5), at 12A.
730. Id.
731. In 1994, Wyoming spent 8.7 percent of its gross state product on health care. Only Alaska spent less—6 percent. The national average is 13 percent. Id.
732. Id.
733. See Joseph C. Morreale, *The Medicare Catastrophic Coverage Act of 1988: Issues of Equity in a Policy Reversal*, 7 J. CONTEMP. HEALTH L. & POL'Y 1301 (1990), which stipulates that any acute-care expenditures, totalling more than 10 percent of the elderly household income, would be covered by the federal government. All elderly who are below 150% of the federal poverty line would be eligible. Flat premiums would be charged to this group but paid for by the respective state governments. Though this would increase state expenditures, the federalization of elderly poor Medicaid expenditures would reduce state expenditures to a greater extent. Id.
734. Id. For an article recommending personal responsibility, coupled with managed open-market competition instead of a government monopoly, see Woodrow E. Eno, *Private Market-Based Health Reform Is the Answer*, 3-FALL KAN. J. L. & PUB. POL'Y 35 (1993).
735. Id. A recent bill introduced to congress on February 7, 1991, proposed to amend the 1986 Internal Revenue Code "to allow a deduction from gross income for home care and adult day and respite care expenses of individual taxpayers with respect to a dependent of the taxpayer who suffer from Alzheimer's disease or related organic brain disorder." See Daily Rep. Exec., February 11, 1991, at F-2. The Bill is H.R. 931, 102nd Cong., 1st Sess. (1991). Congress did enact legislation treating long term health insurance the same as accident and health plans for tax purposes.

736. See sup. text accompanying note 467-483 (ch. 5).

737. Speech and interview with Dr. Daniel Callahan, Director of the Hastings Center, Briarcliff Manor, NY, The Brendan F. Brown Lecture, Catholic University of America, Columbus School of Law, Washington, DC (March 27, 1991) (lecture titled "What Is Our Claim Upon Health Care Resources?").

738. See Schmitz, sup. note 241 (ch. 1), at 47.

739. Id. at 47.

740. See Callahan, *Meeting Needs and Rationing Care*, 16 L. MED. & HEALTH CARE 261, 266 (1988). For a discussion of governmental limits on the allocation of Medicare resources, see Kinney, *Setting Limits: A Realistic Assignment for the Medicare Program?*, 33 ST. LOUIS U.L.J. 631 (1989).

741. Nathanson, *Symposium: Health Care for an Aging Society*, 26 HOUS. L. REV. 777, 780-781 (1989).

742. See Schmitz, sup. note 241 (ch. 1), at 41 (quoting John Golenski, a bioethicist who designed the Oregon plan).

743. Robert G. Frank, Michael J. Sullivan, and Patrick H. DeLeon, *Health Care Reform in the States*, 49 AMERICAN PSYCHOLOGIST 855, 857 (1994).

744. *Pennsylvania Perspective*, sup. note 165 (ch. 4), at 20 (statement by E. Joyce Gould).

745. See James Kuhnhenn, "Today's Bills May Guide Tomorrow's Adults," *Kansas City Star*, August 13, 1995, at A23 (quoting Charles Murray).

746. See Rogal and Helms, sup. note 81 (ch. 5), at 30.

747. Michael S. Sparer, *Federal Menus and State Programs: An Intergovernmental Health Care Partnership for the 1990s*, 21 N.Y.U. REV. L. & SOC. CHANGE 323 (1994/95).

748. See HEALTH LAW, sup. note 250 (ch. 1), at 584.

Chapter 6

1. See David S. Broder, "It's Now the GOP's Turn to Learn That August is the Cruelest Month in Washington," *Philadelphia Inquirer*, August 14, 1995, at A8.
2. PAUL T. MENZEL, MEDICAL COSTS, MORAL CHOICES: A PHILOSO-PHY OF HEALTH CARE ECONOMICS IN AMERICA, at 3-4 (1983).
3. See BRUCE NUSSBAUM, GOOD INTENTIONS: HOW BIG BUSINESS AND THE MEDICAL ESTABLISHMENT ARE CORRUPTING THE FIGHT AGAINST AIDS, (1990).
4. GEORGE P. SMITH, II, THE NEW BIOLOGY: LAW, ETHICS, AND BIO-TECHNOLOGY, at viii (1989).
5. See HEALTH LAW, sup. note 250 (ch. 1), at 565.
6. See Hilary Stout, "Average U.S. Family Is Spending 11.7% of Income on Health Care, Study Finds," *The Wall Street Journal*, December 11, 1991, at A2.
7. See HEALTH LAW, sup. note 250 (ch. 1), at 565.
8. Id. at 566.
9. JOHN RUSKIN, MUNERVA PULVERIS: SIX ESSAYS ON THE ELE-MENTS OF POLITICAL ECONOMY, 1-26 (1891) (Brantwood edition, First Greenwood Reprinting, 1969).
10. NICCOLÓ MACHIAVELLI, THE PRINCE 149 (1532) (W.K. Marriott, trans.), New York: E.P. Dutton and Co., 1908.
11. See HEALTH LAW, sup. note 250 (ch. 1), at 572.
12. Id. at 573-575.
13. Id. at 575-576.
14. See Stout, sup. note 6 (ch. 6), at A2. Corporate spending on health care totaled $237.6 billion in 1991, up from $74 billion in 1980. This figure will more than double by the year 2000, reaching as high as $511 billion. Id.
15. See HEALTH LAW, sup. note 250 (ch. 5), at 576.
16. See Stout, sup. note 6 (ch. 6), at A2.
17. See Laurie McGinley, "Medicare Proposals Raise Questions and Anxiety," *The Wall Street Journal*, May 9, 1995, at B1.
18. See Laura Merisalo, "An Answer to Managed Care's Call, with Comforts of Home," *Business Journal (Milwaukee)*, February 11, 1995, at A12.
19. ERNEST ECKHOLM, ED., SOLVING AMERICA'S HEALTH-CARE CRISIS 301 (1993). See generally Lisa Disch, *Publicity-Stunt Participation and Sound Bite Polemics: The Health Care Debate 1993-94*, 21 J. HEALTH POL. POL'Y & L. 3 (1996); Theda Skocpol, *The Rise and Resounding Demise of the Clinton Plan*, 14 HEALTH AFFAIRS 66 (Spring, 1995).
20. Mollyann Brodie, *Americans' Political Participation in the 1993-94 National Health Care Reform Debate*, 21 HEALTH POL. POL'Y & L. 99, 122 (1996); Margaret Weir, *Institutional and Political Obstacles to Reform*, 14 HEALTH AFFAIRS 102 (Spring, 1995); Allen Schick, How a Bill Did Not Become a Law, in INTENSIVE CARE: HOW CONGRESS SHAPES

HEALTH POLICY, 227-272 (Thomas E. Mann and Norman J. Ornstein, eds.),

21. See, e.g., Judith Feder and Larry Levitt, *Steps Toward Universal Coverage*, 14 HEALH AFFAIRS 140 (1995).

22. See Arlene Cinelli Odenwald, "Hospitals, HMOs, Patients: Surviving the Crisis," *New Mexico Business Journal*, May 1, 1993, at 6.

23. Mothner, sup. note 162 (ch. 1), at 64-65.

24. See *Pennsylvania Perspective*, sup. note 165 (ch. 1), at 15.

25. See Schmitz, sup. note 241 (ch. 1), at 39-40.

26. Id. at 40-41, 44.

27. Barbara J. Collins, *Medicaid*, 17 J. HEALTH POL. POL'Y & L. 403 (1995).

28. See Harold Pollack and James Tobin, "Welfare Reform Needs More Carrots," *Philadelphia Inquirer*, August 14, 1995, at A9, col. 1.

29. See Health Insurance Portability and Accountability Act of 1996, Pub. L. 104-191, August 21, 1996, 110 STAT. 1936.

30. See Hilary Stout, "People Lacking Health Benefits Increased in '92," *The Wall Street Journal*, December 15, 1993.

31. Id.

32. Id.

33. Id. (quoting Rosi Sweeney, Vice President of social, economic and policy analysis at the American Academy of Family Physicians).

34. See Health Insurance Portability and Accountability Act of 1996, Pub. L. 104-191, August 21, 1996, 110 STAT, 1936, § 7702B(a)(1).

35. Janey Novak, "Old Age Security," *Forbes*, June 19, 1995, at 220.

36. Id.

37. Id.

38. Id. at 220 and 222. "California, New York, Connecticut, and Indiana allow you to protect some or all of your assets and still go on Medicaid if you buy and exhaust a certain amount of long-term care insurance."

39. LAWRENCE A. FROLIK AND RICHARD L. KAPLAN, ELDER LAW IN A NUTSHELL, at 127 (West 1995).

40. Id. at 135-138.

41. For example, New York has a state long-term care security program. The state requires that policies provide at least $100-a-day nursing home benefits with a three-year coverage period and $50 a day for home care with a six-year coverage period. An important factor is that a purchaser of insurance may retain an unlimited amount of assets and still qualify for Medicaid if he or she has an approved plan. Thus, there is an incentive for insurance in New York. See Regan, sup. note 31 (ch. 2) at § 10.19.

42. Frolik and Kaplan, sup. note 39 (ch. 6), at 138.

43. Id. at 138-139.

44. 42 U.S.C. § 1396p(b)(1)(C)(i) (1988 & Supp. V 1993).

45. Mahoney, "The Connecticut Partnership for LTC," *Generations*, at 71-72 (Spring 1990).

46. They were granted waivers under previous Medicaid rules and continue to enjoy waivers from OBRA'93. See 42 U.S.C. § 1396p(b)(1)(C)(ii) (1988 & Supp. V 1993).

47. See Richard Price, Congressional Research Service, N. 93-302 EPW, *Medicaid: Long-Term Care and the Elderly*, 39 (1993)("Private long-term care insurance is generally considered to the most promising private sector option for providing the elderly additional protection for long-term care expenses."). But see United States Gen. Accounting Office, *Long-Term Care Insurance: Proposals to Link Private Insurance and Medicaid Need Close Scrutiny*, GAO/HRD-90-154 (September 1990).

48. Less than one percent of persons entering into nursing homes are covered under long-term insurance policies. See generally, COMMITTEE ON ENERGY AND COMMERCE, 103D CONG., 1ST SESS. MEDICAID SOURCE BOOK: BACKGROUND DATA AND ANALYSIS, 59-60 (COMM. PRINT 1993).

49. See generally Willing, sup. note 6 (ch. 2).

50. See generally Walter Feldsman and Joann Canning, *Long-Term Care Insurance Helps Preserve an Estate*, 20 EST. PLAN. 76 (1993) (offering a complete analysis of the New York plan of approved insurance coverage).

51. Novak, sup. note 35 (ch. 6), at 220.

52. "Rubin Says Social Security Will Be Sound Beyond 2050," *Philadelphia Inquirer*, August 14, 1995, at B5, col. 4.

53. See Price, sup. note 47 (ch. 6), at 39.

54. See generally Hobbs and Hobbs, sup. note 50 (ch. 2), at 1411.

55. REPUBLICAN NATIONAL COMMITTEE, RESTORING THE DREAM: THE BOLD NEW PLAN BY HOUSE REPUBLICANS, at 41-42 (1995).

56. Id. at 206.

57. Id. at 211. More than $7 billion is spent simply for the travel expenses of bureaucratic Washington.

58. Id. at 208.

59. Id.

60. Id.

61. See generally ROBERT F. KEETON AND ALAN I. WILDISS, INSURANCE LAW: A GUIDE TO FUNDAMENTAL PRINCIPLES, LEGAL DOCTRINES, AND COMMERCIAL PRACTICES, (West 1988).

62. See, e.g., *Hearing Before the Subcommittee on Oversight and Investigation of the House Committee on Energy and Commerce*, 101st Cong., 1st Sess., 197 (1993) (statement of Ronald D. Hagan, AMEX Life Assurance Company); *Medicare and Medicaid Budget Reconciliation: Hearings Before the Subcommittee on Energy and Commerce*, 103d Cong., 1st Sess., 376 (1993) (statement of Sheldon Goldberg, representing the American Association of Homes for the Aging).

63. LEON TROTSKY, DIARY IN EXILE 106 (1935: Elena Zarudnaya, trans., Harvard University Press, 1958).

64. This is suggested in, JOHN R. WOLFE, THE COMING HEALTH CRISIS: WHO WILL PAY FOR CARE FOR THE AGED IN THE TWENTY-FIRST CENTURY? 134-138 (University of Chicago Press, 1993).

Index

University of New Mexico Hospital,
139
Urban Institute, welfare benefits, 8
Utah
health care reform, 165-166
Medicaid funds distribution, 64

Value purchasing, 20
Vermont, health care reform,
166-168
Vermont Health Care Act
of 1992, 166,167-168
Vermont Health Care Authority, 166
Vermont Health Insurance Plan, 167
Virginia
adopts TennCare plan, 160
health care reform, 168-169
Medicaid funds distribution, 64
Virginia Hospital Association
v. Wilder, 58
Voter registration, elderly
Americans, 25
Voting patterns
elderly, 24-25
women, 18-19,24
young adults, 24

Washington
health care reforms, 96,169-170
Health Plan, 97
lacks Medicaid waiver, 97
Washington Health Services Act
of 1993, 169
Washington Post, The
AIDS payments, 21
on HMOs, 16
on TennCare, 154-155

Wedding ring, Medicaid exempt
asset, 67
Welfare, spending on, 190
Welfare benefits
immigrant, 8
native born, 8
"Welfare magnets," 63
Welfare reform, punitive nature of, 4
West Virginia
health care expenditures, 170
health care reform, 170-171
impact of Medicaid block grants,
62
Whitman, Christine Todd, New
Jersey, 136
Wilder v. Virginia Hospital
Association, 58
Wilson, Peter, on immigration
reform, 7
Wisconsin
health care reform, 171-172
Medicaid estate recovery system,
54
Within Our Reach: Breaking the
Cycle of Disadvantage, 93
Women
disparity in medical care, 22
and Pennsylvania's abortion
control law, 22
voting patterns, 18-19,24. *See also*
Females
"Workshops of democracy," 57
Wyoming, health care reform, 172

Young adults, voting patterns of, 24
Young v. Dept. of Public Welfare, 83
Younger issues, 25
Young-old, nursing care spending, 44

Order Your Own Copy of
This Important Book for Your Personal Library!

LONG-TERM CARE
Federal, State, and Private Options for the Future

_____ in hardbound at $49.95 (ISBN: 0-7890-0173-X)

_____ in softbound at $24.95 (ISBN: 0-7890-0261-2)

COST OF BOOKS _____

OUTSIDE USA/CANADA/
MEXICO: ADD 20% _____

POSTAGE & HANDLING _____
*(US: $3.00 for first book & $1.25
for each additional book)
Outside US: $4.75 for first book
& $1.75 for each additional book)*

SUBTOTAL _____

IN CANADA: ADD 7% GST _____

STATE TAX _____
*(NY, OH & MN residents, please
add appropriate local sales tax)*

FINAL TOTAL _____
*(If paying in Canadian funds,
convert using the current
exchange rate. UNESCO
coupons welcome.)*

☐ **BILL ME LATER:** ($5 service charge will be added)
(Bill-me option is good on US/Canada/Mexico orders only;
not good to jobbers, wholesalers, or subscription agencies.)

☐ Check here if billing address is different from
shipping address and attach purchase order and
billing address information.

Signature _____

☐ **PAYMENT ENCLOSED: $** _____

☐ **PLEASE CHARGE TO MY CREDIT CARD.**

☐ Visa   ☐ MasterCard   ☐ AmEx   ☐ Discover
☐ Diners Club
Account # _____

Exp. Date _____

Signature _____

Prices in US dollars and subject to change without notice.

NAME _____

INSTITUTION _____

ADDRESS _____

CITY _____

STATE/ZIP _____

COUNTRY _____ COUNTY (NY residents only) _____

TEL _____ FAX _____

E-MAIL_____
May we use your e-mail address for confirmations and other types of information? ☐ Yes   ☐ No

Order From Your Local Bookstore or Directly From
The Haworth Press, Inc.
10 Alice Street, Binghamton, New York 13904-1580 • USA
TELEPHONE: 1-800-HAWORTH (1-800-429-6784) / Outside US/Canada: (607) 722-5857
FAX: 1-800-895-0582 / Outside US/Canada: (607) 772-6362
E-mail: getinfo@haworth.com
PLEASE PHOTOCOPY THIS FORM FOR YOUR PERSONAL USE.

BOF96

OVERSEAS DISTRIBUTORS OF HAWORTH PUBLICATIONS

AUSTRALIA
Edumedia
Level 1, 575 Pacific Highway
St. Leonards, Australia 2065
(mail only) PO Box 1201
Crows Nest, Australia 2065
Tel: (61) 2 9901–4217 / Fax: (61) 2 9906-8465

CANADA
Haworth/Canada
450 Tapscott Road, Unit 1
Scarborough, Ontario M1B 5W1
Canada
(Mail correspondence and orders only. No returns or telephone inquiries. Canadian currency accepted.)

**DENMARK, FINLAND, ICELAND, NORWAY
& SWEDEN**
Knud Pilegaard
Knud Pilegaard Marketing
Mindevej 45
DK-2860 Soborg, Denmark
Tel: (45) 396 92100

ENGLAND & UNITED KINGDOM
Alan Goodworth
Roundhouse Publishing Group
62 Victoria Road
Oxford OX2 7QD, U.K.
Tel: 44–1865–521682 / Fax: 44–1865-559594
E-mail: 100637.3571@CompuServe.com

GERMANY, AUSTRIA & SWITZERLAND
Bernd Feldmann
Heinrich Roller Strasse 21
D–10405 Berlin, Germany
Tel: (49) 304–434–1621 / Fax: (49) 304–434–1623
E-mail: BFeldmann@t-online.de

JAPAN
Mrs. Masako Kitamura
MK International, Ltd.
1–50–7–203 Itabashi
Itabashi–ku
Tokyo 173, Japan

KOREA
Se–Yung Jun
Information & Culture Korea
Suite 1016, Life Combi Bldg.
61–4 Yoido–dong
Seoul, 150–010, Korea

MEXICO, CENTRAL AMERICA & THE CARIBBEAN
Mr. L.D. Clepper, Jr.
PMRA: Publishers Marketing & Research Association
P.O. Box 720489
Jackson Heights, NY 11372 USA
Tel/Fax: (718) 803–3465
E-mail: clepper@usa.pipeline.com

NEW ZEALAND
Brick Row Publishing Company, Ltd.
Attn: Ozwald Kraus
P.O. Box 100–057
Auckland 10, New Zealand
Tel/Fax: (64) 09–410–6993

PAKISTAN
Tahir M. Lodhi
Al-Rehman Bldg., 2nd Fl.
P.O. Box 2458
65–The Mall
Lahore 54000, Pakistan
Tel/Fax: (92) 42–724–5007

PEOPLE'S REPUBLIC OF CHINA & HONG KONG
Mr. Thomas V. Cassidy
Cassidy and Associates
470 West 24th Street
New York, NY 10011 USA
Tel: (212) 727–8943 / Fax: (212) 727–8539

**PHILIPPINES, GUAM & PACIFIC TRUST
TERRITORIES**
I.J. Sagun Enterprises, Inc.
Tony P. Sagun
2 Topaz Rd. Greenheights Village
Ortigas Ave. Extension Tatay, Rizal
Republic of the Philippines
P.O. Box 4322 (Mailing Address)
CPO Manila 1099
Tel/Fax: (63) 2–658–8466

SOUTH AMERICA
Mr. Julio Emöd
PMRA: Publishers Marketing & Research Assoc.
Rua Joauim Tavora 629
São Paulo, SP 04015001 Brazil
Tel: (55) 11 571–1122 / Fax: (55) 11 575-6876

**SOUTHEAST ASIA & THE SOUTH PACIFIC,
SOUTH ASIA, AFRICA & THE MIDDLE EAST**
The Haworth Press, Inc.
Margaret Tatich, Sales Manager
10 Alice Street
Binghamton, NY 13904–1580 USA
Tel: (607) 722–5857 ext. 321 / Fax: (607) 722–3487
E-mail: getinfo@haworth.com

RUSSIA & EASTERN EUROPE
International Publishing Associates
Michael Gladishev
International Publishing Associates
c/o Mazhdunarodnaya Kniga
Bolshaya Yakimanka 39
Moscow 117049 Russia
Fax: (095) 251–3338
E-mail: russbook@online. ru

LATVIA, LITHUANIA & ESTONIA
Andrea Hedgecock
c/o Iki Tareikalavimo
Kaunas 2042
Lithuania
Tel/Fax: (370) 777-0241 / E-mail: andrea@soften.ktu.lt

**SINGAPORE, TAIWAN, INDONESIA, THAILAND
& MALAYSIA**
Steven Goh
APAC Publishers
35 Tannery Rd.
#10–06, Tannery Block
Singapore, 1334
Tel: (65) 747–8662 / Fax: (65) 747–8916
E-mail: sgohapac@signet.com.sg